PRENTICE HALL LITERATURE

PENGUIN EDITION

Teaching Resources

Unit 4
Division, Reconciliation, and Expansion

The American Experience

PEARSON
Prentice Hall

Upper Saddle River, New Jersey
Boston, Massachusetts

PEARSON
Prentice Hall

ISBN 0-13-165222-2

1 2 3 4 5 6 7 8 9 10 09 08 07 06 05

Contents

UNIT 4

from *My Bondage and My Freedom* by Frederick Douglass

"An Occurrence at Owl Creek Bridge" by Ambrose Bierce

"The Gettysburg Address" and "Second Inaugural Address" by Abraham Lincoln

"Letter to His Son" by Robert E. Lee

"Heading West" by Miriam Davis Colt

"I Will Fight No More Forever" by Chief Joseph

"To Build a Fire" by Jack London

"The Story of an Hour" by Kate Chopin

Unit 4 Concept Map

The Big Picture: Division, Reconciliation, and Expansion (1850–1914)

Name: ____________________

Starting Date: ____________________

Ending Date: ____________________

Forms and Movements

which are demonstrated in these selections:

- Realism
- Naturalism
- Regionalism
- Autobiography

Characteristics of the Period and Its Literature

- The grim realities of the Civil War and of sprawling cities lead to new literary trends.
- The Civil War ends Romanticism; writers chart fateful forces at work in life.
- The nation expands rapidly, and writers record the local color of its many regions.
- As slavery divides the nation, African Americans testify to their experiences.
- A new African American literature emerges from song and oral traditions.
- War, including war against Native Americans, inspires charged persuasive works.
- Classic short stories reflect the nation's expansion into new territory.
- Writers use innovative techniques to explore war and daily life.
- Even as women agitate for their rights, new female voices emerge in literature.

Elements and Techniques

which are demonstrated in these selections:

- Refrain/Rhyme
- Diction/Tone
- Humor/Conflict
- Point of View/Speaker
- Irony/Characterization

Focus on Literary Forms:

- Distinguishing fact from opinion in—

Journals/Letters

are characterized by

- informal style
- a personal purpose
- limited audience
- an intended function as a historical narrative

and demonstrate the impact of

the Civil War:
- deep national divisions
- hope and suffering
- sacrifice and bravery

as is shown in these selections:

UNIT 4 STUDENT LOG

VOCABULARY				WRITING & EXTEND YOUR LEARNING	WORKSHOPS

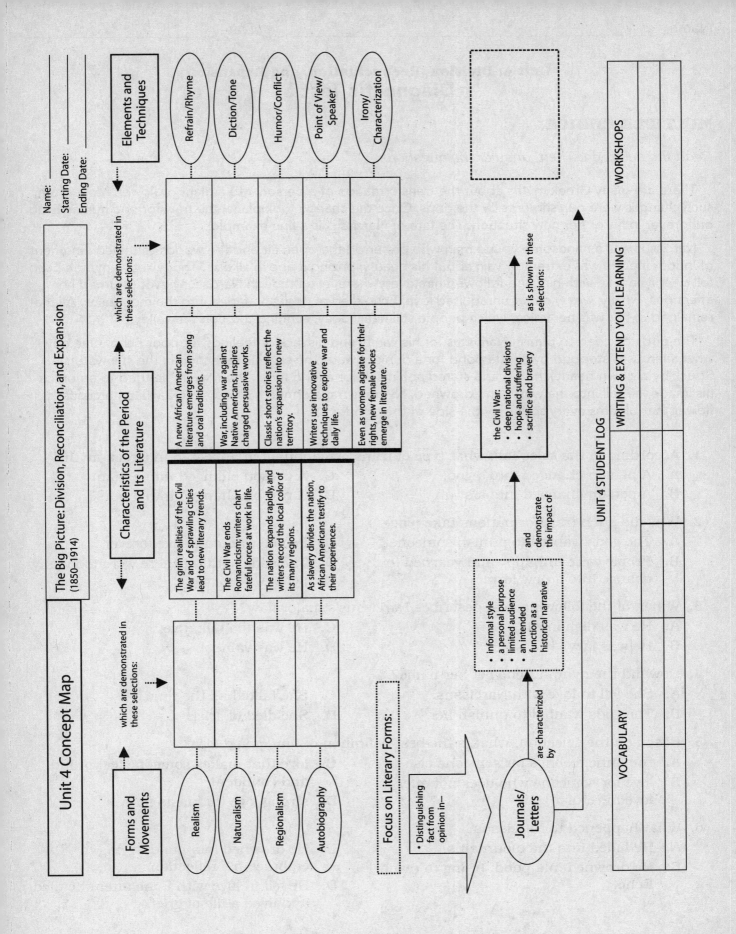

Name ______________________ Date ______________

Unit 4: Division, Reconciliation, and Expansion

Diagnostic Test 5

MULTIPLE CHOICE

Read the selection. Then, answer the questions.

There are many Greek myths about the transformation of a person into a plant or flower. Most often, such changes were punishments by the gods. Once the change took place, the transformed human lived on forever in his or her new situation. The fate of Narcissus is a fine example.

Narcissus was a handsome young man who preferred the open air and the woods to the confinement of indoor life. He was extremely vain about his beauty, prizing it above all else. The talkative nymph Echo fell deeply in love with him and followed him everywhere, even though Narcissus never returned her affections. Finally, weary of her unrequited love, Echo died of grief and faded into the mountains. All that remained of her was her voice, which people still hear today, echoing through the valleys.

The gods decided to punish Narcissus for his vanity and his lack of feelings for poor Echo. One day, when Narcissus stopped by a little pond for a drink of water, he saw his reflection in the still waters. Struck by his own beauty, he sat and stared at himself for a long time. Then, when he tried to embrace his image, he fell into the water and drowned. Nymphs transformed his body into a white narcissus flower that blooms every spring by the side of the pond.

1. According to the selection, what type of transformation often appeared in Greek myths?
   - **A.** A person changed into a god.
   - **B.** A person changed into a swan.
   - **C.** A person changed into a plant.
   - **D.** A person changed into a horse.

2. Why did such transformations take place?
   - **A.** The gods wanted to punish someone.
   - **B.** People were unhappy and yearned to change into a new form.
   - **C.** People wanted to live forever.
   - **D.** The gods felt that there were too many people.

3. Which of the following best describes Narcissus's major flaw?
   - **A.** He was dishonest.
   - **B.** He was lazy.
   - **C.** He was too talkative.
   - **D.** He was vain.

4. How did the nymph Echo get her name?
   - **A.** She fell in love with Narcissus.
   - **B.** The gods wanted to punish her.
   - **C.** She talked all the time.
   - **D.** She died of grief.

5. Based on the selection, what is the best definition of *unrequited love*?
   - **A.** romantic feelings for someone else
   - **B.** love for someone who does not offer love in return
   - **C.** love that makes someone feel proud and confident
   - **D.** strong love that lasts forever

6. What happened to Narcissus?
   - **A.** He faded into the mountains.
   - **B.** He drowned in a pond, trying to reach Echo.
   - **C.** He drowned in a pond, trying to embrace his reflection.
   - **D.** He fell in love with Echo after she died and lived a life of grief.

Name ______________________________ Date ______________

7. In his transformed state by the side of the pond, what can Narcissus do forever?
   - A. listen to echoes
   - B. see his reflection
   - C. float through the valleys
   - D. wander through the woods

Read the selection. Then, answer the questions.

Probably the most famous symbol of romance is the winged infant Cupid. Armed with a bow and a quiver of arrows, he inspires love in anyone whom he shoots with an arrow. Originally a character in the myths of ancient Greece and Rome, Cupid has remained popular for more than two thousand years, and is commonly seen on modern valentines and celebrated in love songs.

The ancient Greeks and Romans differed in their views of Cupid. The Romans usually depicted him as a mischievous baby boy. Often he appeared blindfolded, to indicate that love is blind. Sometimes he appeared as an infant angel, draped in a garland of flowers and cuddled by his mother Venus, the goddess of love and beauty. By contrast, the Greeks saw Cupid as a fickle teenaged boy, and they called him Eros. His mother was Aphrodite, the Greek goddess of love and beauty. Along with his arrows that made people fall in love, Eros had a special arrow that he used to make a person feel indifferent. Therefore, Eros could create unrequited love—the sad type that occurs when someone is in love with a person who does not feel or return the same strong affections.

8. What is the best description of Cupid, as he is portrayed in Roman myths?
   - A. a baby angel with a bow and arrow
   - B. a fickle teenaged boy with a bow and arrow
   - C. a fickle teenaged boy who is blindfolded
   - D. a young man suffering from unrequited love

9. Why did Cupid shoot people?
   - A. to punish them
   - B. to make them beautiful, like his mother
   - C. to make them fall in love
   - D. to drape them in garlands of flowers

10. Based on the selection, what is the best meaning of the saying *Love is blind*?
    - A. People often have no power over whom they fall in love with.
    - B. Love can be a difficult handicap.
    - C. Cupid often strikes people with his bow and arrow.
    - D. Unrequited love is very painful.

11. How is Cupid portrayed in Greek myth?
    - A. an infant angel draped with flowers
    - B. a baby sitting on the lap of his mother, Venus
    - C. a baby sitting on the lap of his mother, Aphrodite
    - D. a teenaged boy

12. How were Venus and Aphrodite alike?
    - A. Both had sons named Cupid.
    - B. Both were Roman goddesses.
    - C. Both were Greek goddesses.
    - D. Both were goddesses of love and beauty.

13. According to the selection, how are Cupid and Eros alike?
   A. Both are blindfolded.
   B. Both have bows and arrows.
   C. Both are celebrated in modern love songs.
   D. Both are the children of Venus.

14. According to the selection, how are Cupid and Eros different?
   A. Eros can make someone fall in love by shooting him or her with an arrow.
   B. Eros can make someone feel indifferent toward a person who loves him or her.
   C. Cupid does not shoot his arrows at young people.
   D. Cupid will not shoot someone if his mother advises him not to.

15. Which fact shows that many people still believe in the power of Cupid's bow and arrow?
   A. According to myths, he could make people fall in love.
   B. He appears on modern valentines.
   C. He often appears blindfolded.
   D. He is often portrayed as being full of mischief.

Name ______________________ Date ______________

Unit 4 Introduction

Names and Terms to Know

A. Directions: *Match each name or term on the left with its fact on the right. Write the letter of the fact on the line before the name or term it defines.*

Names and Terms

___ 1. Fugitive Slave Act (1850)

___ 2. Civil War

___ 3. Abraham Lincoln

___ 4. Transcontinental Railroad

___ 5. Second Industrial Revolution

___ 6. Frederick Douglass

___ 7. Gettysburg Address

___ 8. Mark Twain

___ 9. Realism

___10. Naturalism

Facts

A. person elected President of the United States in 1860; assassinated in April 1865

B. period of invention and industrialization marked by the appearance of electric lights, telephones, and automobiles

C. person who was born into slavery and later became an eloquent spokesperson against it; known for great oration

D. period of battles between the North and the South; lasted from 1861–1865

E. speech by Lincoln to honor soldiers who had died and inspire people to continue to fight for the Union

F. one of the best known American writers; conved the freshness of everyday speech

G. literary movement following the Civil War; focused lives of ordinary people

H. literary movement that focused on real situations but pitted individuals against larger forces; example of a writer in this movement is Jack London

I. law that required all citizens, whether they lived in free or slave states, to help catch and return runaway slaves

J. national train system that was completed in 1869; became the main means by which people traveled across the nation

B. Directions: *Write an additional fact about each of the following names and terms.*

1. Fugitive Slave Act: ______________________

2. Civil War: ______________________

____

3. Second Industrial Revolution: ______________________

____

4. Frederick Douglass: ______________________

____

Name ______________________ Date ______________

Unit 4 Introduction
Focus Questions

DIRECTIONS: *Use the hints below to help you answer the Focus Questions. You will find all of the information in the Unit Introduction in your textbook.*

1. What differences between the North and the South led to the Civil War?
   Hint: What was the difference in how the economy of each region was set up? ______

   Hint: What effect did the publication of works such as *Uncle Tom's Cabin* have on the public? ______

2. In the fifty years after the Civil War, what factors caused the most dramatic changes in American life?
   Hint: Where did most people live, and what technological changes occurred? ______

   Hint: What factors contributed to the change in the population of the United States? ______

3. How did the Civil War, westward expansion, and the Second Industrial Revolution help shape the literary movements known as Realism and Naturalism?
   Hint: Think about how idealistic Americans had been before the bitterness that led to the Civil War. ______

   Hint: What outside forces were at work that affected people's view of the places in which they lived? ______

"An Episode of War" by Stephen Crane
"Willie Has Gone to War" by George Cooper and Stephen Foster

Vocabulary Warm-up Word Lists

Study these words from the selections. Then, complete the activities.

Word List A

bugler [BYOOG luhr] *n.* person who plays a bugle or trumpet
The bugler played "Taps" slowly and beautifully, and the entire crowd was moved.

comrades [KAHM radz] *n.* members of the same group; friends
Because we all want the same freedoms in life, we should consider ourselves comrades.

infantry [IN fuhn tree] *n.* branch of an army trained to fight on foot
Troops in the infantry can't move as quickly as sailors or air force personnel.

lieutenant [loo TEN uhnt] *n.* commissioned military officer
After serving as a lieutenant for two years, Steve was promoted to the rank of captain.

roaming [ROHM ing] *v.* wandering; roving
Willa spent Saturday morning roaming around town, dropping in at various garage sales.

spectators [SPEK tay terz] *n.* onlookers; witnesses; observers
When the game went into overtime, the spectators became very excited.

stragglers [STRAG lerz] *n.* those who have strayed or fallen behind
Every marathon has a few stragglers who are happy just to finish the race.

sympathetically [sym puh THET ik uhl ee] *adv.* in a manner showing feeling and care
To show us that he understood, Larry nodded his head sympathetically.

Word List B

aggregation [ag ruh GAY shuhn] *n.* cluster; group of individuals or objects
The art dealer is interested in Betsy's aggregation of antique vases.

appropriated [uh PROH pree ayt uhd] *v.* took possession of
Before our exam, Professor Wright appropriated all the students' textbooks.

astoundingly [uh STOWN ding lee] *adv.* very surprisingly; astonishingly
Oscar is astoundingly tall for a boy his age.

berating [bee RAYT ing] *v.* scolding
We could hear the father berating his son for breaking the rules.

catastrophe [kuh TAS truh fee] *n.* complete failure; disaster
No one showed up, so the surprise party was a catastrophe.

endowed [en DOWD] *v.* equipped with
We were lucky because our team was endowed with new helmets and ice hockey sticks.

pine [PYN] *v.* to yearn; to long for
As Sam's days at summer camp lengthened, he started to pine for home.

singular [SING yoo ler] *adj.* unusual; remarkable
The critic was positive, asserting that Gladys gave a singular performance last night.

Name ______________________________ Date ______________

"An Episode of War" by Stephen Crane

"Willie Has Gone to War" by George Cooper and Stephen Foster

Vocabulary Warm-up Exercises

Exercise A *Fill in each blank in the paragraph below with the appropriate word from Word List A.*

Kyle was an exceptionally talented student. His grades were excellent, and he had impressive athletic ability, especially in football and baseball. Very popular among his [1] ________________, Kyle was the best [2] ________________ in the high school band. When he thought about what he'd do after graduation, he viewed the idea of enlisting in the armed forces [3] ________________. His grandfather had been a(n) [4] ________________ in the [5] ________________ during the Vietnam War. Kyle himself thought that military service would give him focus. He didn't want to be [6] ________________ aimlessly or be counted among the [7] ________________ in getting started with a career. His philosophy was that you had to be a doer in life and not sit back in the ranks of [8] ________________, passively looking on.

Exercise B *Revise each sentence so that the underlined vocabulary word is logical. Be sure to keep the vocabulary word in your revision.*

Example: Because the task was so fatiguing, we didn't feel any need to rest.
Because the task was so fatiguing, we had to stop often for a rest.

1. On the beach, we saw an aggregation of one or two seagulls.
____
2. Ollie appropriated Mike's bicycle, allowing Mike to ride it for the rest of the day.
____
3. We were not surprised at the astoundingly large number of concertgoers.
____
4. Berating me soundly, Dad warmly praised my report card.
____
5. The game was a catastrophe for our football team, which won by a score of 35-0.
____
6. That school was very well endowed, with barely adequate facilities for athletics.
____
7. Away at camp, Manuel felt satisfied and happy and would pine for home every day.
____
8. The art exhibit was singular, resembling lots of other shows.
____

Name ______________________________ Date ______________

"An Episode of War" by Stephen Crane
"Willie Has Gone to War" by George Cooper and Stephen Foster

Reading Warm-up A

Read the following passage. Pay special attention to the underlined words. Then, read it again, and complete the activities. Use a separate sheet of paper for your written answers.

Almost everyone knows "Taps," the haunting melody played by a military bugler at military and memorial services. This tune has twenty-four solemn notes, one for each hour of the day, and all the notes are part of a single chord.

"Taps" had its beginnings in Europe. It is a revision of a French bugle tune played in the evening. A lieutenant or another officer in charge of a regiment in the infantry—soldiers on foot—would order the tune played to notify everyone it was time to return to their barracks. "Taps" thus functioned as a kind of curfew call. It warned late stragglers that they had only a short time to return to base. Troops who were roaming at liberty needed to report to their officers, or they would be disciplined.

One evening during the Civil War, General Daniel Butterfield, a Union officer, fondly and sympathetically recalled the French tune. Somehow "Taps" had crossed the ocean. Butterfield made a speech to his comrades, asking those in the group that the melody be played each evening at sundown instead of a bugle call named "Extinguish the Lights." The tune soon spread to the Confederate army, and it was even played at the funeral of Confederate General Stonewall Jackson.

These days, "Taps" no longer symbolizes a curfew call. Instead, it functions as a solemn farewell. When its twenty-four notes ring out at a state occasion, mellow and true, they often bring tears to the eyes of the spectators in attendance.

1. Underline the words in this sentence that give a clue to bugler. Use the word *bugler* in a sentence.
2. Circle the words in this sentence that give a clue to the meaning of lieutenant. Use *lieutenant* in a sentence of your own.
3. Circle the phrase that means nearly the same as infantry. In an army, where does the *infantry* fight?
4. Underline the word in this sentence that gives a clue to the meaning of stragglers. Where would the *stragglers* be in a marathon?
5. Circle the words in this sentence that give a clue to the meaning of roaming. What is a synonym for *roaming*?
6. Circle the word that is a clue to the meaning of the word sympathetically. Name a noun, verb, and adjective related to *sympathetically*.
7. Underline the words that mean nearly the same as comrades. Write a sentence using *comrades*.
8. Underline the words that give a clue to the meaning of spectators. What is a synonym for *spectators*?

Name ______________________________ Date ______________

"An Episode of War" by Stephen Crane

"Willie Has Gone to War" by George Cooper and Stephen Foster

Reading Warm-up B

Read the following passage. Pay special attention to the underlined words. Then, read it again, and complete the activities. Use a separate sheet of paper for your written answers.

When Mason McClane played his first concert in high school, he was still a shy kid whose face could hardly be seen behind his long hair. The audience was an aggregation of high school students and local music fans, none of them expecting too much from a timid singer of acoustic ballads. Mason had no money for equipment, so he had appropriated a microphone and P.A. from his high school's theater department.

It took Mason almost five minutes to tune his guitar, and soon a group of boys started shouting criticisms, berating him for taking so much time. He appeared disastrously nervous, unable to begin singing, and everyone in the crowd expected a catastrophe. Then he began, strumming three simple chords, but with such vigor that the strings seemed in danger of breaking. He closed his eyes and then opened them, turning to the audience with an astoundingly fierce and surprisingly confident expression as if he had turned into another person.

It turned out that Mason was endowed with a powerful voice that was like a gift. It was so strong that he almost didn't need the microphone. His folk ballads were fascinating stories about people that everyone in the audience could understand. There were songs about parents and children, work and politics. They were sophisticated, especially for a teenager, but Mason used simple, everyday language in his lyrics. No one had ever heard anything like them—they were utterly singular. When he stopped singing, people sat in stunned silence before they applauded. Mason had been an outcast before the concert, but now he had become a kind of star. Already, some of the girls in the audience had started to pine for him, sighing and calling his name as he bowed and left the stage.

1. Underline the words in this sentence that give a clue to the meaning of the word aggregation. What is a synonym for *aggregation*?

2. Circle the phrase that gives a clue to the meaning of appropriated. Use *appropriated* in a sentence.

3. Underline the words in this sentence that give a clue to the meaning of berating. What is the opposite of *berating*?

4. Circle the word that gives a clue to the meaning of catastrophe. Why might a hurricane be considered a *catastrophe*?

5. Circle the word in this sentence that means nearly the same as astoundingly. What is an antonym for *astoundingly*?

6. Circle the word in this sentence that helps you undersrand endowed. Use *endowed* in a sentence.

7. Underline the phrase that is a clue to the meaning of singular. What are two synonyms for *singular*?

8. Underline the words that give a clue to the meaning of pine. For what might a person away from home *pine*?

Name ______________________ Date ______________

"An Episode of War" by Stephen Crane

"Willie Has Gone to the War" words by George Cooper, music by Stephen Foster

Literary Analysis: Realism and Naturalism

Realism is a type of literature that tries to show people and their lives as realistically as possible. Authors who write material within this literary movement focus on ordinary people rather than on exaggerated models of idealistic behavior. Often such writers emphasize the harsh realities of ordinary daily life, even though their characters are fictional.

Naturalism expands on the base begun by realism. Writers who create naturalistic literature follow the traits of realism, but they add the ideas that people and their lives are often deeply affected by natural forces such as heredity, environment, or even chance. People cannot control such forces, yet they must carry on the best way they can.

The main difference between the two movements is that naturalism emphasizes the lack of control its realistic characters have over the changes taking place in their lives. The influence of both literary movements can often be seen in the same piece of literature, such as "An Episode of War" by Stephen Crane.

DIRECTIONS: *Read the following passages from "An Episode of War." Tell whether you think each one reflects realism, naturalism, or both. Explain your answer.*

1. He was on the verge of a great triumph in mathematics, and the corporals were thronging forward, each to reap a little square [of coffee], when suddenly the lieutenant cried out and looked quickly at a man near him as if he suspected it was a case of personal assault. The others cried out also when they saw blood upon the lieutenant's sleeve.

   Realism, Naturalism, or both: ______________________

   Explain: ______________________

   ____

   ____

2. When he reached home, his sisters, his mother, his wife, sobbed for a long time at the sight of the flat sleeve. "Oh, well," he said, standing shamefaced amid these tears. "I don't suppose it matters so much as all that."

   Realism, Naturalism, or both: ______________________

   Explain: ______________________

   ____

Name ______________________ Date ______________

"An Episode of War" by Stephen Crane

"Willie Has Gone to the War" words by George Cooper, music by Stephen Foster

Reading Strategy: Recognize Historical Details

Your knowledge of the historical time period of a selection can help you make the most of a reading experience. Consider the historical, social, and political climate surrounding a piece of writing as part of its setting and context. For example, in "An Episode of War," the author writes, "His lips pursed as he drew with his sword various crevices in the heap . . ." The detail about the sword helps you to realize that the story did not happen recently—it happened in a time when swords were weapons of war.

Pay careful attention to **historical details** that make the story more vivid and meaningful.

Directions: *Record some of your historical knowledge about the following issues during the American Civil War. Then write how the details affect your reading of the selections.*

Issues	Historical Knowledge	Affect on Reading
1. War tactics		
2. Medicine		
3. Communication		
4. Transportation		

Name ______________________ Date ______________

"An Episode of War" by Stephen Crane
"Willie Has Gone to the War" words by George Cooper, music by Stephen Foster

Vocabulary Builder

Using the Root *-greg-*

A. DIRECTIONS: *The word root -greg- means "herd or flock." On the line, write a word from the list that is suggested by the bracketed word or phrase.*

gregarious	egregious	aggregate	congregation

1. Marc is so ___[sociable]___ that he always has a crowd of friends around him.
2. His mistake was so ___[conspiciously bad]___, Eli asked if he could begin his audition again.
3. Lourdes' family has belonged to the same ___[church group]___ for generations.
4. The students at Hoffman School are a(n) ___[collection]___ of the city's diverse population.

Using the Word List

glade	precipitate	disdainfully	inscrutable

B. DIRECTIONS: *On the line, write the letter of the word or phrase that has the same meaning as the word in CAPITAL letters.*

___ 1. GLADE:
A. jungle B. clearing in a wood C. alcove D. covered bridge

___ 2. PRECIPITATE:
A. prevent B. dissuade C. cause D. expect

___ 3. DISDAINFULLY:
A. loudly B. contemptuously C. gladly D. beautifully

___ 4. INSCRUTABLE:
A. visible B. immediate C. different D. obscure

C. DIRECTIONS: *Write the letter of the word or phrase that best completes each sentence.*

1. Laurel looked upon her brother disdainfully when he ______.
A. spilled syrup on her skirt
B. won the race
C. helped her fix her car
D. gave her the CD she'd wanted

2. Amelie was afraid that her grandmother's pneumonia might precipitate her ______.
A. recovery B. cough C. death D. lungs

3. The moving van was stuffed with an ______ of furniture, tools, and automobile parts.
A. extravaganza B. aggregation C. imbalance D. offload

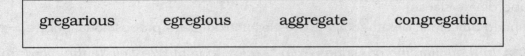

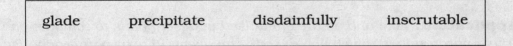

Name ______________________________ Date ______________

"An Episode of War" by Stephen Crane

"Willie Has Gone to the War" words by George Cooper, music by Stephen Foster

Grammar and Style: Correct Use of *Like* and *As*

Although they are often used interchangeably, the words *as, as if, as though,* and *like* serve different functions. *As, as if,* and *as though* are subordinate conjunctions that are used to introduce a subordinate clause. *Like* is a preposition that takes a noun or a pronoun as its object and is used to introduce a prepositional phrase, rather than a clause. Look at these examples:

> . . . this aggregation of wheels, levers, motors had a beautiful unity, *as if* it were a missile. [introduces subordinate clause]
>
> This wounded officer . . . breathed *like* a wrestler. [introduces a prepositional phrase]

A. Practice: *In the following passages from "An Episode of War," circle the word from the pair in* italics *that best fits.*

1. . . . contemplated the distant forest (*as if/like*) their minds were fixed upon the mystery. . . .
2. He looked at it in a kind of stupefaction, (*as if/like*) he had been endowed with a trident. . . .
3. . . . It is (*as if/like*) the wounded man's hand is upon the curtain. . . .
4. It was, for a wonder, precisely (*as/like*) a historical painting.
5. . . . where the shooting sometimes crackled (*as/like*) bush-fires. . . .

B. Writing Application: Like *and* as *are often used in descriptions to compare one thing to another. Write a paragraph in which you describe an event. In your paragraph, use the preposition* like *at least twice. Include at least two examples of the subordinating conjunctions* as, as if, *and* as though. *Be sure to distinguish correctly between the uses of* like *and* as.

____

____

____

____

____

____

____

____

____

____

____

____

____

Name ______________________ Date ______________

"An Episode of War" by Stephen Crane

"Willie Has Gone to the War" words by George Cooper, music by Stephen Foster

Support for Writing

Prepare to write your **field report** on the state of hospital care during the Civil War by entering information into the graphic organizer below.

Conditions in Civil Hospitals

Issues and Details from Background (page 476)	
Issues and Details from Photographs (pages 476 and 480)	
Issues and Details from "An Episode of War"	

On a separate page, write a draft of your field report to your Civil War colonel. When you revise your report, be sure to support each complaint you make with specific details related to your wound. Reread "An Episode of War" to check your work.

Name ______________________________ Date ______________

"An Episode of War" by Stephen Crane

"Willie Has Gone to the War" words by George Cooper, music by Stephen Foster

Support for Extend Your Learning

Listening and Speaking

As you prepare for your **musical presentation** of Civil War songs, do the following to introduce yourself to the history of this kind of music:

- Evaluate several songs before choosing one.
- Consider the musical qualities of the song, such as the tempo and the mood.
- Provide background on where the song came from.

You may wish to play a recording of the song for the class, or you may choose to perform it by singing it or playing it on a musical instrument.

Research and Technology

To write a **definition essay** about the literary form naturalism and compare it to "An Episode of War," do research on the Internet and enter your findings into the chart below.

Naturalism and "An Episode of War"

Naturalism: A Definition ______________________________

____

Example of a character who represents an ordinary person	Example of how the environment affects the character	Example of forces the character cannot control

Share your definition and examples with those of your classmates. Discuss where you agree with one another and how you may differ.

Name ______________________________ Date ______________

"An Episode of War" by Stephen Crane
"Willie Has Gone to the War" words by George Cooper, music by Stephen Foster

Enrichment: Photography

The Words a Picture Speaks

DIRECTIONS: *Look at the Civil War photographs of wounded soldiers that accompany the selections. Fill in the following chart with quotations from "An Episode of War" and "Willie Has Gone to the War" that you think fit the photographs.*

Selection	Quotation
1.	
2.	
3.	
4.	

5. Stephen Crane thought that "a wound gives strange dignity to him who bears it." How do these photographs support that idea? Or don't they? Explain your reasoning.

Name ______________________________ Date ______________

"An Episode of War" by Stephen Crane

"Willie Has Gone to the War" by George Cooper and Stephen Foster

Selection Test A

Critical Reading *Identify the letter of the choice that best answers the question.*

____ **1.** What is the setting of "An Episode of War," based on the use of horses?

A. the First World War

B. the Second World War

C. the Vietnam War

D. the Civil War

____ **2.** In "An Episode of War," which element shows that soldiers become friends during wartime?

A. how the lieutenant makes coffee

B. how the men treat the wounded lieutenant

C. how the doctors talk to the soldiers

D. how the hospital is set up

____ **3.** Which element of "An Episode of War" helps to identify the historical setting of the story?

A. the division of men into military ranks

B. the fear of the lieutenant over his wound

C. the grief of the lieutenant's family

D. the use of swords as a weapon of war

____ **4.** Which of these statements describes why "An Episode of War" is a naturalistic story?

A. The events take place outdoors.

B. The characters cannot control events.

C. The events romanticize war.

D. The characters act as symbols for ideas.

____ **5.** In "An Episode of War," which historical description helps you predict what will happen to the lieutenant's arm?

A. the description of the camp layout

B. the description of the medical facilities

C. the description of the battle

D. the description of the cavalry

Name ______________________ Date ______________

____ 6. Which element of "An Episode of War" shows it to be an example of naturalism?
A. It is set in the Civil War.
B. It shows lives controlled by outer forces.
C. It shows people who control their lives.
D. It uses formal language.

____ 7. What serves as a hospital in "An Episode of War"?
A. an old horse barn
B. a group of ambulances
C. an old schoolhouse
D. a former jailhouse

____ 8. In "An Episode of War," what happens before the lieutenant is reunited with his family?
A. He has been wounded several more times.
B. He has deserted the army and made his way home.
C. He has lost his wounded arm through amputation.
D. He has refused to let the doctor treat his wounded arm.

____ 9. In "Willie Has Gone to the War," why does the speaker spend so much time in the glade?
A. Willie picked lilies for her in the glade.
B. She last saw her Willie in the glade.
C. She expects Willie to come to the glade.
D. Willie is buried in the glade.

____ 10. In what way is "Willie Has Gone to the War" an example of realism?
A. It shows ordinary people affected by war.
B. It uses nature as a symbol of rebirth.
C. It uses the song form to show grief.
D. It repeats important words and ideas.

Vocabulary and Grammar

____ 11. In which sentence is the meaning of the word *disdainfully* suggested?
A. The men looked upon their wounded lieutenant with shock.
B. A surgeon speaks scornfully about the lieutenant's wound.
C. Some men helpfully showed the lieutenant to the hospital.
D. The lieutenant was embarrassed at his family's grief.

Name ______________________ Date ______________

____ 12. Which of the following sentences uses the preposition *like* correctly?
A. The medical personnel behaved like men with too much to do.
B. The surgeon said he would not amputate, like he promised.
C. The men looked at him like they had never seen someone wounded before.
D. The stray bullet acted like it had been fired directly at the lieutenant.

Essay

13. Naturalism is a literary movement that suggests that what happens to people is out of their control. Write a brief essay to show how "An Episode of War" illustrates naturalism. Use examples from the story to support your ideas.

14. Even though the song "Willie Has Gone to the War" is about a young man's death in war, the song itself is upbeat. Write a brief essay to compare the mood of the song with the content it reflects. Include your opinion about why you think the writer chose this mood.

Name ____ Date ____________________

"An Episode of War" by Stephen Crane

"Willie Has Gone to the War," words by George Cooper, music by Stephen Foster

Selection Test B

Critical Reading *Identify the letter of the choice that best completes the statement or answers the question.*

____ 1. "Willie Has Gone to War" is primarily about
- **A.** a brook.
- **B.** a young lieutenant who has been injured.
- **C.** a young woman who misses her beloved young man.
- **D.** a young soldier who has died.

____ 2. "An Episode of War" is the story of
- **A.** a young soldier named Willie.
- **B.** how a lieutenant lost his arm.
- **C.** the Battle at Gettysburg.
- **D.** the conflict between a soldier and a doctor.

____ 3. Which statement best explains why "An Episode of War" may be viewed as a naturalistic story?
- **A.** It takes place outdoors.
- **B.** In this tale an ordinary man's life is shaped by a force he cannot control, but he endures this life-changing event with strength and dignity.
- **C.** It shows the harsh realities of everyday life rather than an optimistic view of the world.
- **D.** It shows the sentimental side of war.

____ 4. In "An Episode of War," Crane seldom directly reveals the lieutenant's thoughts or feelings. He may have chosen to do this to show
- **A.** that a good soldier has no feelings.
- **B.** how fascinated the lieutenant has become with the war.
- **C.** that the lieutenant likes to observe events around him.
- **D.** how his injury has stunned or shocked the lieutenant.

____ 5. One way in which Cooper helps listeners identify with the woman in "Willie Has Gone to the War" is by
- **A.** revealing poignant feelings that listeners will have experienced as well.
- **B.** describing a beautiful place that is special to this woman.
- **C.** likening her to a bird pining for its mate.
- **D.** talking about war.

____ 6. As you read "An Episode of War," thinking about the grave injuries inflicted during the Civil War makes you
- **A.** better able to envision the setting.
- **B.** more likely to think the lieutenant is going to have complications with his wound.
- **C.** better able to laugh at the humorous parts.
- **D.** more likely to notice details about the lieutenant's wife, mother, and sisters.

Name ______________________________ Date ______________

____ 7. By describing a battery of men engaged in battle as an "aggregation of wheels, levers, motors," with "a beautiful unity," what does Crane emphasize about the wounded lieutenant?
A. He is alone.
B. He is an outsider now who has no place in the machinery of war.
C. He has become more observant.
D. He is witnessing something noble and patriotic.

____ 8. If you make predictions about the fate of the lieutenant's arm in "An Episode of War," you must
A. believe that the story will end happily.
B. recognize the story's witty tone.
C. consider the medical situation in its historical context.
D. assume the doctor is telling the truth.

____ 9. In "An Episode of War," details such as the rubber blanket, neat squares of coffee, breast-work, puffs of white smoke in the woods, and even an ashen looking man smoking a corncob pipe all serve to heighten the ________ of the story.
A. naturalism
B. sentimentalism
C. romanticism
D. realism

____ 10. *Realism* is the name given to a literary movement that
A. was the foundation for Romanticism.
B. focused on showing that people's lives are often shaped by forces they can't understand or control.
C. focused on ordinary people faced with the harsh realities of everyday life.
D. grew out of Naturalism.

____ 11. In "An Episode of War," why do you suppose Crane chose not to depict the amputation procedure?
A. It was too gruesome.
B. He couldn't find out what such an experience was like.
C. He didn't want to shock his readers.
D. He wanted to focus the story on the lieutenant's changing perspective on life.

____ 12. To better understand the lieutenant's battlefield experiences in "An Episode of War," you must consider your knowledge of
A. the 1990 Persian Gulf War.
B. the terrible conditions facing injured Civil War soldiers.
C. the lieutenant's military training.
D. the lieutenant's relationship with his soldiers.

Name ______________________________ Date ______________

Vocabulary and Grammar

____ **13.** "An Episode of War" focuses on a wounded ________, rather than on an *aggregation* of wounded soldiers.
A. individual
B. platoon
C. congregation
D. army

____ **14.** The lieutenant looks *disdainfully*, or ________ toward the woods.
A. scornfully
B. harshly
C. sympathetically
D. considerately

____ **15.** When the lieutenant leaves the front line, he sees a scene that looks just ________ a historical painting.
A. as if
B. like
C. as though
D. as

____ **16.** The officer who bandages the lieutenant's wound makes the lieutenant feel ________ he doesn't know how to be properly wounded.
A. like
B. as if
C. just like
D. as

____ **17.** The lieutenant stood looking at the distant forest, ________ contemplating how it was that a bullet could emerge from those woods and strike a man, forever changing his life.
A. like
B. kind of
C. as if
D. as

Essay

18. How do "An Episode of War" and "Willie Has Gone to the War" move readers to identify with their main characters? Choose either selection and answer the question in a short essay supported with examples from the text.

19. Do you think "Willie Has Gone to the War" is a song of hope, despair, or some other sentiment? In a short essay, state what you believe to be the main sentiment expressed by this song. Use lyrics from the song to support your opinion.

20. "An Episode of War" is characteristic of two literary movements that were popular at the time Crane was writing: Realism and Naturalism. In an essay, define Realism as a literary movement. Then use details from "An Episode of War" to show the ways in which the story can be seen as a product of this movement.

Vocabulary Warm-up Word Lists

Study these words from the selections. Then, complete the activities.

Word List A

band [BAND] *n.* group
In Charles Dickens's famous novel, Oliver Twist was forced to join a band of pickpockets.

banned [BAND] *v.* forbade; outlawed
In many restaurants and other public places, smoking has now been banned.

captivity [cap TIV uh tee] *n.* state of being imprisoned, enslaved, or held captive
Some slaves wrote interesting narratives describing their captivity.

deprived [dee PRYVD] *v.* took away from
When the plants were deprived of water, they wilted.

fugitives [FYOO ji tivz] *n.* runaways; exiles
The police successfully hunted down those fugitives from justice.

legal [LEE guhl] *adj.* lawful
Driving under the age of sixteen is not legal in this state.

rebellions [ree BEL i yuhnz] *n.* uprisings; revolts
Several rebellions against the king's rule signaled that his subjects were not happy.

spiritual [SPI ri choo uhl] *n.* folk song that originated among enslaved African Americans
"Swing Low, Sweet Chariot" is a famous spiritual that is still often sung.

Word List B

activists [AK tiv ists] *n.* energetic workers for a cause
Thousands of activists took part in the civil rights movement, fighting for social justice.

chariot [CHA ree uht] *n.* ornamental wagon-like carriage, usually drawn by horses
In the parade, the ancient Roman general rode at the head of his troops in a splendid chariot.

enacted [en AK tuhd] *v.* passed or put into effect
The legislature enacted a new law to restrict smoking in public places.

eventually [ee VEN choo uhl ee] *adv.* after the passage of some time
With practice, Sam eventually will become fluent in Spanish.

network [NET werk] *n.* group of connected or linked members
That news service has an extensive network of reporters spread across several continents.

oppressed [oh PRESD] *v.* treated harshly; put down
Oppressed by his misfortunes, Josh was in a constantly sullen, disagreeable mood.

pharaoh [FA roh] *n.* supreme ruler in ancient Egypt
Tutankhamen ruled as pharaoh in ancient Egypt in the late fourteenth century B.C.

smite [SMYT] *v.* to strike forcefully; to hit hard
Muscular and strong, the blacksmith prepared to smite the anvil with a gigantic hammer.

Name ______________________________ Date ______________

Spirituals

Vocabulary Warm-up Exercises

Exercise A *Fill in each blank in the paragraph below with the appropriate word from Word List A. Use each word only once.*

Everyone agreed that Althea had one of the most beautiful singing voices. Every time she sang gospel music or a(n) [1] ______________, her listeners were on the verge of tears. She was able to put such feeling in her music because she visualized the scenes behind the words. As she sang "Go Down, Moses," for example, Althea could see a(n) [2] ______________ of [3] ______________, released at last from [4] ______________ in ancient Egypt. They had suffered so much, just like enslaved African Americans in later times, when the [5] ______________ authorities [6] ______________ rights for them or put down their [7] ______________. Althea experienced the slaves' anguish when masters [8] ______________ them of their chance to learn to read and right. Such were the feelings that lay behind Althea's passionate singing.

Exercise B *Decide whether each statement below is true or false. Circle* T *or* F, *and explain your answer.*

1. Activists are generally reluctant to get involved in political issues or social causes.
   T / F ______________________________
2. In ancient times, a horse-drawn chariot was a luxurious form of transportation.
   T / F ______________________________
3. If a state legislature has enacted a law, it has considered the measure and rejected it.
   T / F ______________________________
4. Events that occur eventually are separated from the present by a significant time span.
   T / F ______________________________
5. A network of broadcasting stations is linked in an association.
   T / F ______________________________
6. When people are oppressed, they feel generally happy and content.
   T / F ______________________________
7. The ruler of modern Egypt is called the pharaoh.
   T / F ______________________________
8. When you smite an object, you give it a gentle nudge.
   T / F ______________________________

Name ______________________________ Date ______________

Spirituals

Reading Warm-up A

Read the following passage. Pay special attention to the underlined words. Then, read it again, and complete the activities. Use a separate sheet of paper for your written answers.

For two years, Mary had been making songs with a drum machine, two turntables, and a computer. Her friends were excited when she played a new piece that included a sample of a man's voice. When asked where she had gotten it, she explained that it was from an old spiritual, a song sung by African American slaves.

She decided to put together a songbook of the old spirituals, along with their history. It amazed her that such beautiful music had been made by people who had had so many rights taken away from them; they had been cruelly deprived of education or training. Held in captivity like hostages without freedom, they managed to rise above their situation through music. At a time when slaves had no rights, their songs were like little rebellions against the system that enchained them. Any song that spoke out too strongly against slavery would have been banned; no one could have sung about forbidden topics for fear of punishment. However, the singers found a way to talk about slavery by using Bible stories. It was perfectly legal and lawful to sing about the Israelites who were slaves in Egypt. In this way, slaves disguised their dangerous but empowering messages within spirituals.

Mary's songbook included many spirituals that deserved to be remembered. Her favorite one remained the first song she had sampled on her computer. It told the story of a band of escaped slaves—a group making their way north to freedom. Although Mary had never been a slave, she understood how it felt to be trapped, unhappy, and forced to do things she didn't want to do. When she listened to the song, she could imagine herself as one of the fugitives, running from the law, heading toward a better life.

1. Circle the word in this sentence that means nearly the same as spiritual. Use the word ***spiritual*** in an original sentence.

2. Underline the words in this sentence that give a clue to the meaning of deprived. What would happen to a tree that is ***deprived*** of sunlight?

3. Underline the words that give a clue to the meaning of captivity. What is an antonym for ***captivity***?

4. Circle the word that gives a clue to the meaning of rebellions. What is a synonym for ***rebellions***?

5. Circle the word in this sentence that means nearly the same as banned. What is the opposite of ***banned***?

6. Underline the word in this sentence that means nearly the same as legal. What are two antonyms for ***legal***?

7. Circle the word in this sentence that gives a clue to the meaning of band. Use the word ***band*** in an original sentence.

8. Underline the words in this sentence that give a clue to the meaning of fugitives. Use ***fugitives*** in a sentence of your own.

Name ______________________________ Date ______________

Spirituals

Reading Warm-up B

Read the following passage. Pay special attention to the underlined words. Then, read it again, and complete the activities. Use a separate sheet of paper for your written answers.

One of the great movie classics tells the story of Moses. Released in 1956, this film, *The Ten Commandments*, was directed by Cecil B. DeMille and starred Charlton Heston, Yul Brynner, and Anne Baxter. The film had a huge cast and won an Oscar for special effects.

Before he became a prophet, teacher, and leader of the Hebrew people, Moses was brought up as an Egyptian. The Egyptians had enacted a law ordering the death of all newborn Hebrew boys. Therefore, according to tradition, Moses's parents hid their baby for three months and then set him adrift in a reed basket on the river Nile. The child was found by the daughter of the pharaoh, and so Moses was brought up in the ruler's house as a prince at the royal court. He learned martial arts and, like other high-ranking Egyptian nobles, was privileged to ride in his own beautifully decorated chariot.

After some time, Moses eventually discovered his Hebrew origins. Shocked and saddened by the oppressed condition of his people, he gave his support to a network of activists—groups of like-minded Hebrews who were intent on the cause of throwing off the yoke of slavery and escaping from Egypt to freedom.

Moses's beliefs soon led to an open confrontation with the pharaoh. In some of the most dramatic scenes of the film, Moses warns the ruler to let the Hebrew people go. At first, the pharaoh firmly refuses. However, plagues of locusts and serpents smite the Egyptians, hitting hard and causing great suffering. Finally, the pharaoh's own son is stricken and dies. Reluctantly, the ruler allows Moses to lead the Hebrews out of Egypt to the Promised Land.

1. Underline the word in this sentence that gives a clue to the meaning of enacted. Use the word *enacted* in an original sentence.
2. Circle the words in this sentence that give a clue to the meaning of pharaoh. Where and when was the word *pharaoh* a term for "king" or "ruler"?
3. Underline the words that give a clue to the meaning of chariot. Give an example of a modern-day *chariot*.
4. Underline the words that give a clue to the meaning of eventually. What is the opposite of *eventually*?
5. Circle the words in this sentence that give a clue to the meaning of oppressed. What is an antonym for *oppressed*?
6. Underline the words in this sentence that mean nearly the same as network. Use *network* in an original sentence.
7. Underline the words that give a clue to the meaning of activists. What might pollution *activists* support?
8. Circle the words that give a clue to the meaning of smite. Use *smite* in a sentence.

Name ______________________________ Date ______________

"Swing Low, Sweet Chariot" and **"Go Down, Moses"** Spirituals

Literary Analysis: Refrain

A **refrain** is a word, phrase, line, or group of lines repeated at regular intervals. In spirituals, one of the main things a refrain does is emphasize the most important ideas. In "Go Down, Moses," for example, the refrain "Let my people go" is repeated seven times. The constant repetition serves to turn the cry for freedom into a demand for freedom.

DIRECTIONS: *Answering the following questions will help you understand how the refrains in "Go Down, Moses" and "Swing Low, Sweet Chariot" function to enrich the spirituals' meanings.*

1. Identify a refrain in "Swing Low, Sweet Chariot." ______________________________

2. In "Go Down, Moses," are the words "Tell old Pharaoh" a refrain? Why or why not?

3. In "Swing Low, Sweet Chariot," are the words "a band of angels coming after me" a refrain? Why or why not? ______________________________

4. In "Go Down, Moses" what emotional effect does the continual repetition of the refrains have? ______________________________

5. Compare the refrains of "Go Down, Moses" and "Swing Low, Sweet Chariot." How are they alike and different? In your answer, consider what the refrains ask for or hope for and how those desires are conveyed in the two spirituals. ______________________________

Name ______________________________ Date ______________

"**Swing Low, Sweet Chariot**" and "**Go Down, Moses**" Spirituals

Reading Strategy: Listen

DIRECTIONS: *Listen carefully to the sounds and rhythms of "Swing Low, Sweet Chariot" and "Go Down, Moses" as the two spirituals are read aloud. Pay particular attention to the rhymes and the sounds or phrases that are repeated. Often rhythm and repetition suggest a certain mood or attitude and contribute to the intensity of feeling generated by the song and its message. Fill in the two charts below to help you focus on your listening skills and identify the message presented in each spiritual.*

"Swing Low, Sweet Chariot"
Words that rhyme
Words or phrases that are repeated
Mood or attitude suggested by rhyme and repetition
Overall message of spiritual

"Go Down, Moses"
Words that rhyme
Words or phrases that are repeated
Mood or attitude suggested by rhyme and repetition
Overall message of spiritual

Name ______________________________ Date ______________

"Swing Low, Sweet Chariot" and **"Go Down, Moses"** Spirituals

Vocabulary Builder

Using the Root *-press-*

A. DIRECTIONS: *The root* -press- *means "push." In addition to being a complete word itself in English,* press *is also combined with many different prefixes and suffixes to form other words. Choose one of the words in the box to complete each sentence.*

express	suppress	pressurize
depression	press	impression

1. Barry tried hard to control himself, but he could not ______________ his laughter.
2. In order to communicate with others, you must ______________ your ideas clearly.
3. It is necessary to ______________ an airplane's cabin so people can breathe at higher altitudes.
4. The dry cleaners will ______________ the suit so it looks neat.
5. Anyone going on a job interview wants to make a good ______________.
6. A person who feels sad all the time may be suffering from ______________.

Using the Word List

oppressed	smite

B. DIRECTIONS: *Match each word in the left column with its definition in the right column. Write the letter of the definition on the line next to the word it defines.*

___ 1. oppressed

___ 2. smite

A. kill with a powerful blow

B. kept down by a cruel power or authority

C. DIRECTIONS: *On the line, write the letter of the pair of words that best expresses a relationship similar to that expressed in the pair in CAPITAL LETTERS.*

___ 1. SMITE: SLAP ::
A. language : French
B. seek : discover
C. costume : clothing
D. happy : miserable
E. laugh : smile

___ 2. OPPRESSED : FREE ::
A. myth : legend
B. waiter : restaurant
C. temporary : permanent
D. computer : monitor
E. scuff : scrape

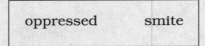

Name ______________________________ Date ______________

"**Swing Low, Sweet Chariot**" and "**Go Down, Moses**" Spirituals

Grammar and Style: Direct Address

Direct address is the addressing of something or someone by name. In written works, the name of the person or thing being addressed directly is set off by one or more commas, depending on the element's location in the sentence.

Anne, sing this spiritual. [comma follows]

Sing the words more clearly, **Anne.** [comma precedes]

One goal of a spiritual, **Anne,** is to arouse strong emotion. [commas precede and follow]

A. Practice: *In each sentence that contains an example of direct address, add one or more commas where necessary. If there is no direct address in a sentence, write* N *next to the number.*

___ 1. Boys you should sing only the refrain.

___ 2. Listen carefully Stephanie and you'll hear the rhythm.

___ 3. Hand in the sheet music to Mr. Taylor after class.

___ 4. Spirituals often referred to biblical people and places such as Moses and Jordan.

___ 5. You can be the next soloist Troy.

___ 6. Let Caitlin improvise new lyrics.

___ 7. My dear child you must not be nervous about singing.

___ 8. Once again Ms. Lipton you've done an excellent job of preparing the chorus.

B. Writing Application: *Direct address is often used in dialogue. Imagine a conversation among three or more characters on a subject of your own choosing. Write several lines of dialogue. Use three examples of direct address in your dialogue: one at the beginning of a sentence, one in the middle of a sentence, and one at the end of a sentence. Punctuate each example correctly.*

Name ______________________ Date ______________

"**Swing Low, Sweet Chariot**" and "**Go Down, Moses**" Spirituals

Support for Writing

To gather material for your **reflective essay** on spirituals, enter your ideas in the graphic organizer below.

Spirituals and Their Connection to Slavery

What I knew about slavery *before* I read/heard spirituals	Summary of each spiritual	What I learned about slavery *after* I read/heard spirituals	What spirituals mean to me now

On a separate page, write a draft of your **reflective essay,** based on the information you have collected. Summarize each spiritual. As you revise your work, be sure to include information about what each spiritual means to you.

Name ______________________________ Date ______________

"Swing Low, Sweet Chariot" and **"Go Down, Moses"** Spirituals

Support for Extend Your Learning

Listening and Speaking

As you prepare to conduct a **choral reading** of a spiritual you have chosen, use these tips:

- Determine who will say which lines.
- Learn your lines from memory.
- Emphasize the call-and-response format.
- Encourage one another to make up at least one new verse to perform as a solo.

When you have rehearsed your call-and-response verses and the new verses, perform your choral reading for the class.

Research and Technology

Use the Internet and library resources to put together an **anthology** of spirituals. Enter the information you find in the graphic organizer below to help you arrange your anthology. Print out copies of the spirituals you plan to use. If you need more room for your chart, use another sheet of paper.

Anthology of Spirituals

Title of Spiritual 1	Background for Introduction:
Title of Spiritual 2	Background for Introduction:
Title of Spiritual 3	Background for Introduction:

Put together your anthology, with copies of the music for the spirituals, and place it in your classroom library.

Name ______________________________ Date ______________

"**Swing Low, Sweet Chariot**" and "**Go Down, Moses**" Spirituals

Enrichment: Social Studies

The Message in Spirituals

Some spirituals contained disguised messages concerning escape from slavery. Spirituals such as "Follow the Drinking Gourd," for example, advised slaves to follow the north-pointing Big Dipper star constellation. Other verses were altered to give specific directions for slaves to locate Underground Railroad routes. "Go Down, Moses" also has a freedom-related message.

DIRECTIONS: *Answer the series of questions below to help you decode the message of the spiritual "Go Down, Moses."*

1. What is a pharaoh, and what kind of power does a pharaoh have?

 ____

 ____

2. In a southern plantation, who might hold a position similar to that of a pharaoh?

 ____

3. What was the condition of the people of Israel when they were in Egypt?

 ____

4. How was the situation of the slaves in the American South similar to that of the people of Israel?

 ____

5. What demand did Moses make of the pharaoh?

 ____

 ____

6. What demand does "Go Down, Moses" convey, and to whom is the demand directed?

 ____

 ____

Name ______________________________ Date ______________

"Swing Low, Sweet Chariot" and **"Go Down, Moses"** Spirituals

Selection Test A

Critical Reading *Identify the letter of the choice that best answers the question.*

____ 1. "Swing Low, Sweet Chariot" is a spiritual with a coded meaning related to slaves escaping the south. Given this fact, what is surprising about the mood of the refrain?

A. It is scary and suspenseful.

B. It is lyrical and relaxed.

C. It is demanding and rude.

D. It is fearful and timid.

____ 2. How does the chariot in "Swing Low, Sweet Chariot" represent an escape from slavery?

A. It is a wagon with very fast horses.

B. It is a wagon driven by slaveowners.

C. It is a chariot sent from heaven.

D. It is part of the Underground Railroad.

____ 3. In a spiritual such as "Swing Low, Sweet Chariot," what does the refrain establish for the reader?

A. a rhyme scheme

B. the setting of the song

C. the rhythm and mood

D. the singer's identify

____ 4. In "Swing Low, Sweet Chariot," what emotion is communicated as you listen to the refrain?

A. anger

B. boredom

C. longing

D. fear

____ 5. In "Swing Low, Sweet Chariot," to whom does the singer refer in the following: "If you get there before I do . . . Tell all my friends I'm coming too"?

A. relatives who have abandoned her

B. slaves who have already escaped

C. blacks who were born in the North

D. whites on the Underground Railroad

Name ______________________ Date ______________

___ 6. As you listen to the three stressed syllables at the beginning of the refrain of "Go down, Moses," what do you hear?
A. a command
B. a question
C. a statement
D. a plea

___ 7. Which element of "Go down, Moses" is characteristic of many spirituals?
A. references to biblical places
B. references to Moses
C. warnings of punishment
D. demands upon leaders

___ 8. In "Go down, Moses," what do Pharaoh and the people of Israel stand for?
A. Egypt and Moses
B. the U.S. and Egypt
C. the president and U.S. citizens
D. slaveowners and slaves

___ 9. Why were spirituals such as "Go down, Moses" a threat to slaveowners?
A. They made fun of slaveowners.
B. They carried coded messages.
C. They called for work strikes.
D. They ignored white culture.

___ 10. In "Go down, Moses," what effect does repeating "Let my people go" have on the listener?
A. It shows confusion.
B. It shows determination.
C. It shows disgust.
D. It shows secrecy.

Vocabulary and Grammar

___ 11. In which sentence is the meaning of the word *oppressed* suggested?
A. The company treated the workers badly.
B. The workers decided to strike.
C. Protesters supported workers' rights.
D. The company raised workers' pay.

Name ______________________ Date ______________

____ **12.** Which of these sentences contains an example of direct address?
  A. "Coming for to carry me home."
  B. "Go down, Moses"
  C. "When Israel was in Egypt land"
  D. "A band of angels coming after me"

Essay

13. "Swing Low, Sweet Chariot" refers to a chariot "Coming for to carry me home." However, "Go down, Moses" announces: "Tell old Pharaoh," / "Let my people go!" Both refrains express the wish for freedom, but they have different moods. Write a brief essay to compare the two refrains in terms of their mood and message.

14. Spirituals were often coded messages among slaves, as well as being spiritually uplifting. Select at least two of these words or phrases from "Swing Low, Sweet Chariot": *chariot, home, Jordan, band of angels, get there,* and *tell my friends*. Write a brief essay to discuss the messages they contain about freedom or how to get to freedom.

Name ______________________ Date ______________

"Swing Low, Sweet Chariot" and **"Go Down, Moses"** Spirituals

Selection Test B

Critical Reading *Identify the letter of the choice that best completes the statement or answers the question.*

____ 1. "Swing Low, Sweet Chariot" is about the
- A. importance of community.
- B. need for equality.
- C. desire for freedom.
- D. uncertainty of religious faith.

____ 2. In what literary element of a spiritual will you most likely find its key ideas?
- A. refrain
- B. opening line
- C. solo lyrics
- D. title

____ 3. How does the sound of the repetition of the word *home* in "Swing Low, Sweet Chariot" convey the mood of the spiritual?
- A. It lulls the listener into a sense of contentment.
- B. It reminds the listener that the singer is at home.
- C. It tells the listener of the hominess of plantation life.
- D. It builds on the listener's feelings about home to emphasize the message of longing.

____ 4. In "Swing Low, Sweet Chariot," what is home a metaphor for?
- A. the South
- B. Africa
- C. Heaven
- D. Jordan

____ 5. Which of the following phrases is part of the refrain of "Swing Low, Sweet Chariot"?
- A. "If you get there before I do"
- B. "A band of angels coming after me"
- C. "Tell all my friends I'm coming too"
- D. "Coming for to carry me home"

____ 6. What is the most important function of the refrain in "Swing Low, Sweet Chariot"?
- A. The refrain introduces a biblical context for the spiritual.
- B. The refrain separates the soloist and chorus.
- C. The refrain reinforces the idea of deliverance.
- D. The refrain ends the spiritual on a happy tone.

____ 7. What mood is suggested by listening to the rhythm and repetition of "Swing Low, Sweet Chariot"?
- A. longing, patience, and hope
- B. rebellion
- C. secrecy
- D. fear and resignation

Name ______________________________ Date ______________

____ 8. What makes "Go Down, Moses" typical of spirituals?
A. quotations from Moses
B. lack of a refrain or chorus
C. warnings of rebellion
D. references to biblical figures

____ 9. Moses is an appropriate figure for a spiritual because he
A. received the Ten Commandments.
B. owned slaves in Egypt.
C. brought plagues to Egypt.
D. led his people to freedom.

____ 10. The spiritual is most closely related to which of the following literary traditions?
A. call-and-response
B. narrative poetry
C. autobiography
D. sermon

____ 11. Enslaved African Americans experienced which of the following circumstances described in "Go Down, Moses"?
I. oppression
II. having lived in Egypt
III. captivity
IV. resisting an unjust authority with force
A. I and II
B. III and IV
C. I and III
D. I and IV

____ 12. From the point of view of the slaveholder, what made spirituals most dangerous?
A. They were insulting to white people.
B. They carried hidden messages.
C. They rejected organized Christianity.
D. They kept alive African musical traditions.

____ 13. How does listening to a repeated phrase such as "Let my people go" in "Go Down, Moses" help convey the spiritual's mood and message?
A. The repetition dulls listeners' ears to key messages of the spiritual.
B. The phrase reminds listeners that the slaves' plight is similar to that of the Israelites.
C. The phrase is a demand and helps convey a mood of determination.
D. The repetition of such phrases could be decoded to reveal hidden messages.

____ 14. In a spiritual, the part sung by the chorus seldom changed because the chorus
A. was an African tradition.
B. sang the refrain.
C. played the role of the Lord.
D. let everyone take part.

Name ______________________________ Date ______________

Vocabulary and Grammar

___ 15. In "Swing Low, Sweet Chariot," the singer uses direct address. What effect does directly addressing the "sweet chariot" have?
- **A.** It intensifies the urgency of the singer's plea.
- **B.** It makes the chariot seem unattainable.
- **C.** It indicates that the chariot must come down from Heaven.
- **D.** It lets listeners know that the chariot isn't real.

___ 16. Which of the following phrases includes an example of direct address?
- **A.** "Thus saith the Lord,"
- **B.** "Go down, Moses,"
- **C.** "bold Moses said"
- **D.** "Tell old Pharaoh"

___ 17. Choose the word that could best substitute for the underlined word in the following line from "Go Down, Moses".

<u>Oppressed</u> so hard they could not stand.

- **A.** starved
- **B.** rewarded
- **C.** exhausted
- **D.** abused

Essay

18. Which of the two spirituals, "Swing Low, Sweet Chariot" or "Go Down, Moses," do you think would have been considered more "dangerous" by a slave owner who paid careful attention to the words of the spirituals? Use examples from each of the spirituals to support your ideas.

19. "Swing Low, Sweet Chariot" and "Go Down, Moses" are both about the hope for release from hardship. However, the spirituals express very different views in regard to *when* release might come about. In an essay, identify for each spiritual when release is expected and how this affects the overall mood of each spiritual.

20. Make a case for the Moses of "Go Down, Moses" as a symbol for the activities of the abolitionist Harriet Tubman. Use what you have learned about her to interpret the spiritual in this light.

from **My Bondage and My Freedom** by Frederick Douglass

Vocabulary Warm-up Word Lists

Study these words from the selection. Then, complete the activities.

Word List A

apt [APT] *adj.* capable; quick to learn or understand
An apt student will usually do well on exams.

congenial [kuhn JEE nee uhl] *adj.* agreeable
Sue is congenial, so it is very easy to get along with her.

consternation [kahn ster NAY shuhn] *n.* shock or fear causing bewilderment
When Gary saw how steeply the mountain descends, he was struck with consternation.

domestic [doh MES tik] *adj.* typical of home life
I enjoy domestic activities, such as cooking, gardening, and knitting.

incompatible [in kuhm PAT uh buhl] *adj.* incapable of blending with one another
They were incompatible roommates because their interests were so different.

overthrow [oh ver THROH] *v.* to overturn or throw over
The angry crowd at the rock concert threatened to overthrow the stage.

variable [VAY ree uh buhl] *adj.* likely to change or vary
The interest Janice earns from her savings account is variable, so she can't depend on it.

victorious [vik TOR ee uhs] *adj.* winning a contest or struggle
The victorious team celebrated their win in the championship game.

Word List B

chafed [CHAYFD] *v.* wore away; annoyed
The tight dress chafed Nancy's skin, and she felt extremely uncomfortable.

consenting [kuhn SENT ing] *adj.* agreeing
Consenting to drive us into town, Lori went to fetch her car keys.

depravity [dee PRAV it ee] *n.* corruption; wickedness
The violence and depravity depicted in the movie caused people to stay away.

destitute [DES ti toot] *adj.* utterly lacking; very poor
These destitute orphans live in appalling conditions.

mirth [MERTH] *n.* gladness; amusement; merriment
The audience's mirth rewarded the actors' efforts at comedy.

opposition [op uh ZISH uhn] *n.* resistance
Despite opposition from his boss, Fred went ahead and ordered more office supplies.

prudence [PROOD uhns] *n.* caution; careful management
A wise and cautious person exhibits prudence at all times.

riveted [RIV uh tuhd] *v.* fastened; fixed firmly
The movie was intriguing, and Jack was riveted to the screen.

Name ______________________________ Date ______________

***from* My Bondage and My Freedom** by Frederick Douglass

Vocabulary Warm-up Exercises

Exercise A *Fill in each blank in the paragraph below with the appropriate word from Word List A. Use each word only one.*

Twelve-year-old Kelsey badly wanted a dog. She had set her sights on a golden retriever puppy she'd seen in a pet store window. To her [1] ________________, though, her parents thought a large dog would be [2] ________________ with their crowded living conditions in a small apartment. Kelsey, though, who sometimes felt lonely, thought a dog would be a[n] [3] ________________ companion. She didn't want to provoke a(n) [4] ________________ crisis, and she wondered how to convince her parents that she would be a(n) [5] ________________ pet owner. Finally, she had the idea of drawing up a formal contract. She included all the promises she would make, such as walking the dog, supervising its food and water, and grooming it. She had to persuade her parents that her attention to the dog would be constant, rather than [6] ________________. When her parents saw the contract, they knew it was time to [7] ________________ their misgivings. The whole family signed the agreement, and Kelsey was [8] ________________ in her campaign.

Exercise B *Revise each sentence so that the underlined vocabulary word is logical. Be sure to keep the vocabulary word in your revision.*

Example: The horror movie's plot included scenes of depravity and wickedness, so it earned a "G" rating.

The horror movie's plot included a scene of <u>depravity</u> and wickedness, so only adults went to see it.

1. The T-shirt label <u>chafed</u> the back of my neck and made my skin feel comfortable.

   ____

2. <u>Consenting</u> to our proposal, Rose denied us permission to begin the plan's first phase.

   ____

3. Ken was so <u>destitute</u> that he had to make do with a large suburban house and two cars.

   ____

4. When she heard that comment, Yolanda expressed her <u>mirth</u> with a stern frown.

   ____

Name ______________________________ Date ______________

from **My Bondage and My Freedom** by Frederick Douglass

Reading Warm-up A

Read the following passage. Pay special attention to the underlined words. Then, read it again, and complete the activities. Use a separate sheet of paper for your written answers.

One afternoon, Debbie discovered her new foster brother, Nate, struggling to read a comic book that he'd found in a chest. Since his arrival at their house the week before, Nate's shyness had kept them from talking very much. When Debbie came into the room, Nate looked up at her and tried to hide the comic book in consternation, as if she might be angry. Everything about domestic life—the family meals, the after-dinner TV sessions—made him anxious.

"Don't get upset," said Debbie in a congenial voice, trying to make friends. "Why don't you show me what you're reading?"

Unfortunately, it turned out that Nate didn't know how to read; he was simply looking at the pictures. This startled Debbie, because at the age of nine, Nate was surely old enough to know how to read. The fact that he couldn't seemed incompatible with the intelligence she could see in his eyes.

Although Debbie had never taught anyone how to read, Nate wanted so desperately to learn that she couldn't refuse. She taught him the alphabet, how to sound out words, and how to guess a word's meaning from the other words surrounding it in the sentence. At first, his success was variable—sometimes he understood, sometimes he didn't. However, he turned out to be an apt student, eventually grasping everything she explained to him. They worked their way gradually through the comic book and Nate improved immensely. The comic book concerned a gang of villains who tried to overthrow the government and rule the country. Debbie found the story tedious, but Nate's progress fascinated her. When he got to the end—the moment when the superhero defeats the villains—Nate turned to her with a victorious smile, having conquered his first book.

1. Underline the words in this sentence that give a clue to the meaning of consternation. Use this word in a sentence.
2. Circle the words in this sentence that hint at the meaning of domestic.
3. Underline the words in this sentence that give a clue to the meaning of congenial. Use a word meaning the opposite of *congenial* in a sentence of your own.
4. Underline the words in this and the previous sentence that hint at the meaning of incompatible. What is an antonym for *incompatible*?
5. Circle the words that offer a clue to the meaning of variable. What is a synonym for *variable*?
6. Underline the words that hint at the meaning of apt. Use an antonym of *apt* in a sentence.
7. Circle the words that hint at the meaning of overthrow. What is a synonym for this word?
8. Underline the word in this sentence that hints at the meaning of victorious. What are two synonyms for *victorious*?

Name ______________________ Date ______________

from **My Bondage and My Freedom** by Frederick Doulass

Reading Warm-up B

Read the following passage. Pay special attention to the underlined words. Then, read it again, and complete the activities. Use a separate sheet of paper for your written answers.

Frederick Douglass once predicted that, if an African American were allowed to serve in the U.S. Army, "there is no power on earth which can deny that he has earned the right to citizenship in the United States."

During the first year of the Civil War, many people supported military service by African Americans in the Union army. There was some <u>opposition</u> to the idea, however. Such a plan <u>chafed</u> against the preconceived notions of some white soldiers and officers, who believed that African Americans lacked the courage to fight well. Some critics of the plan reacted with disbelief, even with amusement or <u>mirth</u>, at what they considered a ridiculous risk for the army to take.

In July 1862, Congress passed two acts <u>consenting</u> to the enlistment of African Americans. Official <u>prudence</u> prevailed, however, and actual enrollment of black soldiers was cautiously delayed until the issuance of the Emancipation Proclamation in September. Frederick Douglass's two sons, in fact, were among the first to serve in the Union forces. Both free Americans and runaways from the moral <u>depravity</u> of slavery joined the fight.

It was soon clear that the critics were drastically mistaken. Far from being <u>destitute</u> of courage and skill, black regiments <u>riveted</u> the attention of all Americans with their heroic deeds. At engagements in Missouri, Louisiana, and the Indian Territory (now Oklahoma), African American soldiers distinguished themselves for courage and fighting ability. General James Blunt said of them, "I never saw such fighting . . . they make better soldiers in every respect than any troops I have ever had under my command."

In all, some 180,000 African Americans served in the Union army during the Civil War. Of these, about 38,000 gave their lives for the cause of freedom.

1. Underline the words in this and the previous sentence that hint at the meaning of <u>opposition</u>. What is a synonym for *opposition*?

2. Circle the words in this sentence that hint at the meaning of the word <u>chafed</u>. What is a synonym for this word?

3. Underline the words that hint at the meaning of <u>mirth</u>. Use *mirth* in a sentence.

4. Underline the words that hint at the meaning of <u>consenting</u>. What is an antonym for *consenting*?

5. Circle the words that hint at the meaning of <u>prudence</u>. Use *prudence* in a sentence.

6. Circle the words that are clues to the meaning of <u>depravity</u>. What is a synonym for *depravity*?

7. Underline the words that hint at the meaning of <u>destitute</u>. Use an antonym of *destitute* in a sentence.

8. Underline the words that hint at the meaning of <u>riveted</u>. What is a synonym for *riveted*?

Name ______________________________ Date ______________

***from* My Bondage and My Freedom** by Frederick Douglass

Literary Analysis: Autobiography

In his autobiography, Frederick Douglass provides his readers with a unique view of what it was like to be a slave. Douglass could have chosen to write a fictional work instead of an autobiography, but using an autobiographical form adds the power of real experiences to Douglass's story.

DIRECTIONS: *Read the following passages from the selection. Describe the effect of each passage and suggest how the use of autobiography strengthens that effect.*

It was no easy matter to induce her to think and to feel that the curly-headed boy, . . . who was loved by little Tommy, and who loved little Tommy in turn; sustained to her only the relation of a chattel. I was *more* than that, and she felt me to be more than that. I could talk and sing; I could laugh and weep; I could reason and remember; I could love and hate.

____

____

____

I was no longer the light-hearted, gleesome boy, full of mirth and play, as when I landed first at Baltimore. Knowledge had come . . . This knowledge opened my eyes to the horrible pit, and revealed the teeth of the frightful dragon that was ready to pounce upon me, but it opened no way for my escape.

____

____

____

It was slavery—not its mere *incidents*—that I hated. I had been cheated. I saw through the attempt to keep me in ignorance . . . The feeding and clothing me well, could not atone for taking my liberty from me. The smiles of my mistress could not remove the deep sorrow that dwelt in my young bosom. Indeed, these, in time, came only to deepen my sorrow. She had changed; and the reader will see that I had changed, too. We were both victims to the same overshadowing evil—*she* as mistress, *I* as slave.

____

____

____

Name ______________________________ Date ______________

from **My Bondage and My Freedom** by Frederick Douglass

Reading Strategy: Establish a Purpose

Establishing a purpose for reading helps you get more out of what you read. In reading the excerpt from *My Bondage and My Freedom,* one possible purpose is to find out what slavery was like from the point of view of an enslaved person. As you read the selection, use this chart to list things that Frederick's intimate view of that experience can tell you.

Thoughts	
Feelings	
Events	

Name ______________________________ Date ______________

from **My Bondage and My Freedom** by Frederick Douglass

Vocabulary Builder

Using the Root *-bene-*

A. Directions: *The root* -bene- *means "well" or "good" and is part of many words relating to goodness. Complete each sentence with one of these words:* beneficent, beneficial, beneficiary, benign.

1. As a ____________________, my mother received some money and jewelry after her aunt's death.
2. The petitioners were fortunate to have a judge with a ____________________ temperament.
3. Her work with the sick in Calcutta made Mother Teresa one of the most ____________________ people of our time.
4. The labor reforms of the nineteenth century were ____________________ to factory workers struggling for better working conditions.

Using the Word List

congenial	benevolent	stringency
depravity	consternation	redolent

B. Directions: *Match each word in the left column with its definition in the right column. Write the letter of the definition on the line next to the word it defines.*

___ 1. benevolent	A. agreeable
___ 2. congenial	B. strictness; severity
___ 3. consternation	C. kindly; charitable
___ 4. depravity	D. dismay; alarm
___ 5. redolent	E. corruption; wickedness
___ 6. stringency	F. suggestive

Name ______________________________ Date ____________________

from **My Bondage and My Freedom** by Frederick Douglass

Grammar and Style: Correlative Conjunctions

Correlative conjunctions are pairs of connectors that link words and phrases that are grammatically similar. Common correlative conjunctions include *either . . . or; neither . . . nor; whether . . . or; not only . . . but also;* and *just as . . . so.* The following sentence from *My Bondage and My Freedom* illustrates the use of the correlative conjunctions *either . . . or.*

She **either** thought it unnecessary, **or** she lacked the depravity indispensable to shutting me up in mental darkness.

A. PRACTICE: *In the following sentences, underline the correlative conjunctions. Write* N *next to the number if the sentence has none.*

____ **1.** Not only was he speeding, but he also ran a stop sign.

____ **2.** The superintendent was concerned with whether the board would pass or vote down the resolution for a new gymnasium.

____ **3.** Neither the ice cream parlor nor the supermarket had butter pecan ice cream.

____ **4.** She collected money for the coaches' gifts just as she said she would.

____ **5.** Did you read either of the books I gave you?

B. Writing Application: *Complete each sentence so that the final version contains a pair of correlative conjunctions.*

1. Just as soldiers must obey their superiors, ______________________________

____

2. Neither the general ______________________________

____

3. We didn't know whether we should visit the battlefield ______________________________

____

4. Not only did soldiers fight each other, ______________________________

____

5. The armies must either march through the forest ______________________________

____

Name ______________________________ Date ______________

from **My Bondage and My Freedom** by Frederick Douglass

Support for Writing

As you prepare to write a **college application,** think about one experience that has shaped your life, just as Douglass describes how knowledge led to his freedom. Think about events that have made a difference in how you think or act today. Use the graphic organizer below to collect your information.

An Experience that Has Shaped My Life

My Experience (title): ______________________________		
What happened first **How I felt or what kind of action I took**	**What happened next** **How I felt or what kind of action I took**	**What happened finally** **How I felt or what kind of action I took**

On a separate page, write a first draft of the experience that helped shaped who you are today. Put your events in chronological order. When you revise your work, be sure to make it clear to readers how this experience affected you.

Name ______________________ Date ______________

from **My Bondage and My Freedom** by Frederick Douglass

Support for Extend Your Learning

Listening and Speaking

As you prepare to deliver an **oral presentation** of a passage from Douglass's selection, think about your audience, which is made up of abolitionists. Add a statement of your own, based on what you have learned from Douglass. Use these tips:

- Add strong emotion to convey Douglass's tone.
- Use persuasive language to convince your audience.

Deliver your oral presentation to the class and ask for feedback.

Research and Technology

As you work with a group to collect words, pictures, and sounds for a **multi-media presentation** about the value of literacy, keep track of your materials in the graphic organizer below. If you need more room, use another sheet of paper.

List of Examples from Magazines/Newspapers	List of Pictures/Graphics/Charts	List of Recorded Speeches

Put together your multi-media presentation. Present it to the class and add the collection to your classroom library.

Name ______________________________ Date ____________________

from **My Bondage and My Freedom** by Frederick Douglass

Enrichment: Career as a Teacher

Teacher Training

Frederick Douglass wrote about both teaching and learning in his autobiography. In addition to teaching basic skills, successful teachers motivate students and inspire them to learn.

DIRECTIONS *Find passages in which Frederick Douglass describes the process and the excitement of learning to read. Identify each passage and make a note of the lesson you think a teacher could learn from it. In particular, describe how a teacher could use Douglass's experiences to teach and encourage others to read.*

Lessons for Teachers From Frederick Douglass	
Passage	**Lesson**
1.	
2.	
3.	

Name ______________________________ Date ______________

from **My Bondage and My Freedom** by Frederick Douglass

Selection Test A

Critical Reading *Identify the letter of the choice that best answers the question.*

____ 1. What does Douglass like most about Baltimore life in *My Bondage and My Freedom*?

A. changes in the weather
B. learning to read and write
C. playing with the boys in the street
D. working for Mr. and Mrs. Auld

____ 2. Based on *My Bondage and My Freedom,* which statements express Douglass's beliefs?

I. People should be trained to be both slaves and slaveowners.
II. Slavery can be endured as long as the slaveowner is kind.
III. Slavery destroys both the slave and the slaveowners.
IV. Slavery makes enemies out of people who should be friends.

A. I, II, III
B. II, III, IV
C. I, III, IV
D. I, II, IV

____ 3. What made *My Bondage and My Freedom* an important work in 1855, years before the Civil War?

A. It led the North eventually to declare war on the South.
B. It presented a scathing portrait of a slaveowning family.
C. It was one of few books written from a former slave's viewpoint.
D. It revealed the forbidden practice of teaching slaves to read.

____ 4. What common attitudes did *My Bondage and My Freedom* challenge?

I. Slaves were incapable of reading and writing.
II. Slaves were not the equal of their whites.
III. Slaves wished to escape their enslavement.
IV. Slaves were comfortable with their position in life.

A. I, II, III
B. I, II, IV
C. I, III, IV
D. II, III, IV

Name ______________________________ Date ______________

___ 5. If your purpose for reading is to understand slavery's effect on people, what conclusion can you draw about Mrs. Auld's opposition to Douglass's learning to read in *My Bondage and My Freedom*?
- **A.** Mrs. Auld should have fought to resist slavery.
- **B.** Mrs. Auld did not possess a strong conscience.
- **C.** Mrs. Auld's conscience was destroyed by slavery.
- **D.** Mrs. Auld should have fed and clothed more slaves.

___ 6. Given what Douglass endures as a slave, what element of *My Bondage and My Freedom* surprises you?
- **A.** He trades reading lessons for biscuits.
- **B.** He feels real affection for Mrs. Auld.
- **C.** His learning makes him unhappier.
- **D.** The Aulds try to keep him ignorant.

___ 7. In *My Bondage and My Freedom*, what does Douglass suggest will probably happen to the white boys in the future, when they are older and dealing with "the cares of life"?
- **A.** They will one day help him escape from his slaveowners.
- **B.** They will likely accept slavery when they become adults.
- **C.** They will grow up to be abolitionists and resist slavery.
- **D.** They will be overwhelmed by business concerns.

___ 8. If your purpose in reading *My Bondage and My Freedom* was to find out how a former slave wrote world-famous books, which question might you ask before reading?
- **A.** How did Douglass escape slavery?
- **B.** How did Douglass end up in Baltimore?
- **C.** How did Douglass learn to write?
- **D.** How did Douglass meet Mrs. Auld?

___ 9. What is Douglass's final judgment of Mrs. Auld in *My Bondage and My Freedom*?
- **A.** She should not have taught him to read.
- **B.** She should have helped him to escape.
- **C.** She was not well-suited to slavery.
- **D.** She could not run a household well.

Name ______________________________ Date ______________

____ 10. What is an important message in *My Bondage and My Freedom*?

A. Slaveowners and slaves should be friends.

B. The wish for freedom can be rooted out of one's soul.

C. Slaves have a generally good life in Baltimore.

D. A kind owner cannot relieve the injustice of slavery.

Vocabulary and Grammar

____ 11. In which of these sentences is the meaning of the word *congenial* suggested?

A. Douglass had friendly relations with the white boys on his block.

B. Mrs. Auld took offense at Douglass's growing unhappiness.

C. Mr. Auld persuaded his wife to stop teaching Douglass.

D. Douglass paid his friends in bread and biscuits for teaching him.

____ 12. Which of these sentences uses a pair of correlative conjunctions?

A. At first, Mrs. Auld was committed to teaching Douglass to read and write.

B. Then Mr. Auld told her that slavery could not work if slaves were educated.

C. Mrs. Auld not only stopped teaching Douglass but also kept him from reading on his own.

D. He hoped to find quiet times to read but was usually discovered and stopped.

Essay

13. How do you think you might have handled the changes Douglass discusses in *My Bondage and My Freedom*? In a brief essay, offer a response that describes how you might have reacted to events if you had been in Douglass's position.

14. How does *My Bondage and My Freedom* make a case for the education of all people? How does it relate to education in today's world? In a brief essay, describe why you think education is important. Use examples from Douglass's writing to support your viewpoint.

Name ______________________________ Date ______________

***from* My Bondage and My Freedom** by Frederick Douglass

Selection Test B

Critical Reading *Identify the letter of the choice that best completes the statement or answers the question.*

____ 1. Which of the following statements best expresses Douglass's attitude toward slavery?
A. Under the care of a decent master, slavery can be a tolerable situation.
B. What makes slavery evil is how comfortable it becomes.
C. Slavery is only possible for children to endure.
D. Slavery goes against the nature of both slaves and slaveholders.

____ 2. One of the most successful strategies Douglass used for learning to read was
A. having Mrs. Auld teach him.
B. memorizing books read by Mrs. Auld.
C. buying books from Mr. Knight on Thames street.
D. getting his young white playmates to teach him in exchange for biscuits.

____ 3. In what way are Douglass's efforts to educate himself paradoxical?
A. The more he learns, the more unhappy he becomes.
B. Even as he accumulates more facts, he is more uncertain of his principles.
C. The faster he reads, the more books he enjoys.
D. Forbidden to read as a child, he grows up to be an important writer.

____ 4. *My Bondage and My Freedom* reveals that in the South of its time slaves and women were both
A. enemies of slavery.
B. against Christian teaching.
C. emotional rather than reasonable.
D. subject to white male authority.

____ 5. What additional information would be most appropriate to Douglass's autobiography?
A. Mrs. Auld's feelings about her husband
B. a description of Douglass's views about Baltimore during the 1830s
C. the bookseller's rationale for allowing Douglass to purchase a schoolbook
D. what Mrs. Auld would have done if she had known of Douglass's unhappiness

____ 6. If your reading purpose is to learn from a slave about his life, what overall conclusion can you draw about Frederick Douglass from this excerpt?

> My feelings were not the result of any marked cruelty in the treatment I received; they sprung from the consideration of my being a slave at all. It was *slavery*—not its mere *incidents*—that I hated.

A. Douglass was not treated badly by his owners.
B. Douglass did not object to the day-to-day aspects of his life as a slave.
C. Douglass thought slavery often inspired slaveholders to commit acts of cruelty.
D. Douglass was a proud man who believed himself entitled to freedom.

Name ______________________ Date ______________

____ 7. What does Douglass mean by saying "Conscience cannot stand much violence"?
A. Conscience and violence often work together.
B. Most people have no conscience.
C. Compromise one belief and the conscience is easily broken down.
D. Anyone with a strong conscience hates violence.

____ 8. What is the most important message of *My Bondage and My Freedom*?
A. Slavery harms both master and slave.
B. A little learning is a dangerous thing.
C. Human nature cannot be changed.
D. Knowledge makes slaves better workers.

____ 9. Why is it helpful to set a purpose for reading?
A. It helps you understand concepts such as slavery.
B. You can debate the author's purpose for writing.
C. It helps you focus on ideas and information as you read.
D. You can learn about the writer's personal experiences and attitudes.

____ 10. What might you have learned had this account been written by Master Hugh?
A. Douglass's thoughts and feelings about Mrs. Auld
B. why Master Hugh believed that educating slaves was a bad thing to do
C. how Douglass learned to read and write
D. what caused Mrs. Auld to realize that she should stop trying to educate Douglass

____ 11. How do you know that Douglass is writing about his childhood from the point of view of an adult?
A. He cannot imagine any view other than his own.
B. He uses a very simple vocabulary.
C. He idealizes his memories of his childhood with the Aulds.
D. He interprets his childhood experiences with an adult's insight.

____ 12. Which of the following details would help you achieve your reading purpose of understanding slavery from a slave's point of view?
A. Mrs. Auld often gave bread to the hungry.
B. Little Tommy loved Mrs. Auld.
C. Frederick had to sneak reading lessons from his white friends.
D. Frederick's friends studied from the *Columbian Orator*.

Vocabulary and Grammar

____ 13. The word most opposite in meaning to *congenial* is ________.
A. friendly
B. hostile
C. thickened
D. thinned

____ 14. The word most nearly opposite in meaning to *stringency* is ________.
A. strictness
B. leniency
C. harshness
D. charity

Name ______________________ Date ______________

___ 15. __________ had slavery made a victim of Douglass, __________ of Mrs. Auld.
A. Not only, but also
B. Just as, so
C. Whether, or
D. Neither, nor

___ 16. Because she was so __________ when he first arrived there, Douglass says that Mrs. Auld was a model of affection and tenderness.
A. depraved
B. benevolent
C. stringent
D. affected

___ 17. Correlative conjunctions are used to connect __________.
A. words and word groups that are grammatically different
B. nouns and adjectives
C. similar kinds of words and word groups that are grammatically alike
D. items in a series

Essay

18. Mrs. Auld's character changed dramatically after her husband persuaded her not to teach young Frederick to read and write. Write a comparison-contrast essay in which you describe the character of Mrs. Auld before and after this turning point. Use incidents and examples from the text to show the changes in her.

19. Douglass says that

> Nature has done almost nothing to prepare men and women to be either slaves or slaveholders. Nothing but rigid training, long persisted in, can perfect the character of the one or the other. One cannot easily forget to love freedom; and it is as hard to cease to respect that natural love in our fellow creatures.

Write an essay in which you argue for or against this statement. Use examples from Douglass's autobiography to support your position.

20. To explain Mrs. Auld's change in behavior towards him, Douglass says

> Conscience cannot stand much violence. Once thoroughly broken down, who is he that can repair the damage? . . . It must stand entire, or it does not stand at all.

Write an essay in which you support this explanation for Mrs. Auld's behavior or present an alternative explanation.

"**An Occurrence at Owl Creek Bridge**" by Ambrose Bierce

Vocabulary Warm-up Word Lists

Study these words from the selection. Then, complete the activities.

Word List A

assassin [uh SAS in] *n.* murderer, usually of a prominent person
John Wilkes Booth was the assassin who killed President Abraham Lincoln.

assented [ih SENT uhd] *v.* agreed
When Clara asked her father for permission to visit Tulsa, he readily assented.

audibly [AW duh blee] *adv.* in a manner that can be heard
Tom spoke audibly so the person in the next row heard every word.

convulsively [kahn VUL siv lee] *adv.* in a manner marked by spasms and twitches
The dog's tail twitched convulsively, and we immediately called the vet.

intervals [IN ter vuhlz] *n.* spaces between objects or points in time
Gina will record the behavior of her lab mice at 10-minute intervals.

keen [KEEN] *adj.* sharp; vivid; strong
Evelyn's memory is so keen that she can recall what our teacher wore last Tuesday.

matchless [MACH les] *adj.* unequaled; unsurpassed
Matchless musical talent makes Vivian our town's greatest pianist.

rustic [RUS tik] *adj.* of or relating to country life or country people; unrefined
In a rustic cottage, there are few decorations.

Word List B

congestion [kuhn JES chuhn] *n.* crowded condition; excessive build-up
Alice is suffering from lung congestion due to her recent bout of pneumonia.

etiquette [ET i ket] *n.* appropriate behavior; code or system of good manners
Since proper etiquette is important to Lola, she never interrupts when others are talking.

ineffable [in EF uh buhl] *adj.* too overwhelming to be spoken or expressed
After being caught stealing his sister's money, Ian blushed with ineffable shame.

luminous [LOOM in uhs] *adj.* full of light; illuminated
Glowing candlelight makes Jane's face seem luminous.

perilous [PER il uhs] *adj.* dangerous
Traveling through the vast desert can be perilous for children.

sentinel [SEN ti nel] *n.* watchman; guard
Each gate at the military post was guarded day and night by a sentinel.

summarily [sum AYR uh lee] *adv.* promptly and without formality
Kevin was summarily called to the principal's office after being late again.

velocity [vel AHS uh tee] *n.* speed; swiftness
The velocity of that high-speed train amazes me.

Name ______________________________ Date ______________

"An Occurrence at Owl Creek Bridge" by Ambrose Bierce

Vocabulary Warm-up Exercises

Exercise A *Fill in each blank in the paragraph below with the appropriate word from Word List A.*

When Matthew asked me to go bird watching with him last Saturday, I readily [1] ______________. Sunrise is a lovely time of day, and the [2] ______________ surroundings outside of town were beautiful. Walking along the nature trail, we could hear a bird calling [3] ______________ and at regular [4] ______________. Knowing what a(n) [5] ______________ bird watcher Matthew is, I asked him if he could identify the call. "Sure," he said, "that's a Northern Shrike. What an elegant little [6] ______________! Shrikes feed on insects, worms, little snakes, and field mice. You can often see the prey wriggling [7] ______________ in a shrike's beak." Matthew continued, "Shrikes have a(n) [8] ______________ ability to plan for the future. No other birds are quite like them. They store up their food, much the same as we keep groceries in a fridge or on a kitchen shelf."

Exercise B *Decide whether each statement below is true or false. Circle* T *or* F*, and explain your answer.*

1. With *congestion* on the highway, you may not arrive on time at your destination.
   T / F ______________________________
2. People respecting *etiquette* can be expected to behave impolitely.
   T / F ______________________________
3. If an emotion is *ineffable,* it is impossible to put into words.
   T / F ______________________________
4. A *luminous* theory fails to shed light on a scientific issue or problem.
   T / F ______________________________
5. If you undertake a *perilous* mission, you should be prepared for danger.
   T / F ______________________________
6. A person acting as a *sentinel* at night must take good care not to fall asleep.
   T / F ______________________________
7. An action performed *summarily* is carried out slowly and deliberately.
   T / F ______________________________
8. The *velocity* of a vehicle is its total weight.
   T / F ______________________________

Name ______________________________ Date ______________

"An Occurrence at Owl Creek Bridge" by Ambrose Bierce

Reading Warm-up A

Read the following passage. Pay special attention to the underlined words. Then, read it again, and complete the activities. Use a separate sheet of paper for your written answers.

Because of his pessimistic and sour views of human nature, Ambrose Bierce is often labeled a cynic. Indeed, Bierce's belief that death is meaningless is just as ruthless as the attitude of an assassin.

Today's cynics audibly—sometimes even loudly—raise doubts about the motives of others. Cynics believe that people are selfish and insincere. According to cynics, people strongly pursue personal goals, driven mostly by a keen desire for their own success. There is no such thing as unselfish concern for others. Try to convince a cynic that some people possess the potential for doing good without being rewarded. He or she might laugh convulsively and then gasp spasmodically for breath. Cynics have never assented to the notion that people may act out of a desire to help others. True cynics would vigorously disagree with that idea.

Cynicism can be traced back to the Greek philosopher Diogenes who lived during the fourth century B.C. The most famous story about Diogenes is that he would roam the streets with a lighted lantern in the daytime, as though he was searching. At intervals—each day at dawn and midday—passersby would stop him to ask what he was doing. "I am looking for an honest man," Diogenes would answer, implying that his unending search really meant that he had little or no hope of finding one. Instead, Diogenes believed that matchless dishonesty is a human trait that overcomes all others.

The Cynics—the philosophical group Diogenes led—stressed self-sufficiency and rejection of luxury. The group led a simple, almost rustic life, even when they did not live in the country. The word *cynic* itself comes from the Greek word for "dog," and one legend has it that because the cynics lived so plainly, they were regarded as dogs, not humans. If you think about it, that is a rather cynical view of Cynics!

1. Underline the phrase in this sentence that gives a clue to the meaning of assassin. What is a synonym for ***assassin***?
2. Circle the words in this sentence that add to the meaning of audibly. What are two antonyms for ***audibly***?
3. Circle the adverb in this sentence that offers a clue to the meaning of keen. What is a synonym for ***keen***?
4. Underline the phrase in this sentence that helps define convulsively. What is a synonym for ***convulsively***?
5. Underline the words in the next sentence that are the opposite of assented. Then, rewrite that sentence using a synonym of ***assented***.
6. Circle the words in this sentence that give a clue to the meaning of intervals.
7. Circle the words in this sentence that give a clue to the meaning of matchless. What are two synonyms for ***matchless***?
8. What clue can you find in this sentence to the meaning of rustic?

Name ______________________ Date ______________

"An Occurrence at Owl Creek Bridge" by Ambrose Bierce

Reading Warm-up B

Read the following passage. Pay special attention to the underlined words. Then, read it again, and complete the activities. Use a separate sheet of paper for your written answers.

In his story, Ambrose Bierce uses all three types of irony: verbal, dramatic, and situational. In verbal irony, a word or phrase is used to suggest the opposite of its usual meaning. Consider, for example, Bierce's statement that death is a "dignitary" who must be greeted politely according to a formal code of etiquette. Bierce describes Peyton Farquhar as "the man who was engaged in being hanged," as if Farquhar was leisurely indulging in a favorite pastime rather than being summarily executed. Both these examples illustrate verbal irony.

The story's unusual structure allows Bierce to create dramatic irony in the flashback in Part II. In this type of irony, there is a striking conflict between what a character thinks and what the reader knows. When Farquhar sets out on his perilous mission to destroy the Owl Creek bridge, we know he has been tricked by a Federal scout.

In Part III, Bierce slows down the velocity of his fast-paced plot so that the story moves at a crawl. Through vivid, luminous images, he sheds light on Farquhar's inner state of consciousness. Slowly, the overcrowding and congestion of thoughts in Farquhar's mind give way to a single goal: to get home to his wife. At length he glimpses her, standing watchfully like a sentinel near the veranda of their home. The joy that seizes Farquhar is ineffable, and he cannot translate his emotions into words. Then, in an almost unbearable stroke of situational irony, Bierce reveals the climax of the story, a surprise ending that violently contradicts our expectations.

1. Underline the words that hint at to the meaning of etiquette. Write a sentence using this word.
2. Circle the words that help define summarily through contrast. What is a synonym for *summarily*?
3. Underline the words that hint at the meaning of perilous. What are two antonyms for *perilous*?
4. Underline the words that hint at the meaning of velocity. What is a synonym for *velocity*?
5. Circle the words in this sentence that give a clue to the meaning of luminous. Use a word meaning the opposite of *luminous* in a sentence.
6. Underline the words in this sentence that help define congestion. What is a synonym for *congestion*?
7. Circle the words in this sentence that hint at the meaning of sentinel. Use the word *sentinel* in an original sentence.
8. Underline the words that give a clear definition of ineffable. What is an antonym for *ineffable*?

Name ______________________________ Date ______________

"An Occurrence at Owl Creek Bridge" by Ambrose Bierce

Literary Analysis: Point of View

A writer's purpose helps to determine the **point of view** from which a story is told. In "An Occurrence at Owl Creek Bridge," for example, Ambrose Bierce reveals the tragically ironic nature of war through the events surrounding one person—Peyton Farquhar. Limited third-person narration allows Bierce to explore Farquhar's thoughts and feelings while preserving the objective distance needed for the story's ironic ending.

DIRECTIONS: *Rewrite the following passages of "An Occurrence at Owl Creek Bridge" from the point of view indicated. Be prepared to explain how each point of view changes the story.*

1. The man who was engaged in being hanged was apparently about thirty-five years of age. He was a civilian, if one might judge from his habit, which was that of a planter. His features were good—straight nose, firm mouth, broad forehead, from which his long, dark hair was combed straight back, falling behind his ears to the collar of his well-fitting frock coat.
   First-person point of view ______________________________

2. As Peyton Farquhar fell straight downward through the bridge he lost consciousness and was as one already dead. From this state he was awakened—ages later, it seemed to him—by the pain of a sharp pressure upon his throat, followed by a sense of suffocation.
   Third-person omniscient point of view ______________________________

Name ______________________________ Date ______________

"An Occurrence at Owl Creek Bridge" by Ambrose Bierce

Reading Strategy: Identify Chronological Order

To make their stories interesting, writers often begin with an especially dramatic event and then flash backward in time to supply the reader with necessary information. In "An Occurrence at Owl Creek Bridge," the author begins with Peyton Farquhar standing on the railroad bridge about to be hanged. Then he follows with a flashback to tell how Peyton Farquhar got into that situation. In addition, Bierce flashes forward to show events leaping forward in time.

As you read stories like this one, it is a good strategy to keep the **chronological order** clear in your mind.

DIRECTIONS: *In the "mental" flashforward, Ambrose Bierce gives the reader many clues that the events are taking place in an imaginary future rather than in an actual present. Below are excerpts from the story. In the space provided, explain how each excerpt provides a clue to the nature of the flashforward.*

1. He was now in full possession of his physical senses. They were, indeed, preternaturally keen and alert. Something in the awful disturbance of his organic system had so exalted and refined them that they made record of things never before perceived. He felt the ripples upon his face and heard their separate sounds as they struck.

____

____

____

____

2. Suddenly he felt himself whirled around and round—spinning like a top. The water, the banks, the forests, the now distant bridge, fort and men—all were commingled and blurred.

____

____

____

____

3. At last he found a road which led him in what he knew to be the right direction. It was as wide and straight as a city street, yet it seemed untraveled. No fields bordered it, no dwelling anywhere. Not so much as the barking of a dog suggested human habitation.

____

____

____

____

Name ______________________________ Date ______________

"An Occurrence at Owl Creek Bridge" by Ambrose Bierce

Vocabulary Builder

Using the Root *-sum-*

A. DIRECTIONS: *The word root -sum- is Latin in origin and means "the highest." Some Latin phrases including this root are common in English. Given the meaning of the other words in these phrases, write a probable definition for each one.*

1. *summum bonum; bonum* means "good" ______________________
2. *summa cum laude; cum laude* means "with praise" ______________________

Using the Word List

etiquette	deference	imperious	summarily
effaced	oscillation	apprised	malign

B. DIRECTIONS: *Replace the underlined word or phrase with a synonym from the Word List.*

1. Any citizen caught . . . will be <u>immediately</u> hanged.
____
2. The intellectual part of his nature was already <u>erased</u>.
____
3. circumstances of an <u>urgent</u> nature
____
4. in the code of military <u>behavior</u>
____
5. which had a secret and <u>very harmful</u> significance
____
6. He swung through unthinkable arcs of <u>regular back-and-forth movement</u>.
____
7. silence and fixity are forms of <u>courtesy</u>
____
8. A sharp pain in his wrist <u>informed</u> him
____

Name ______________________________ Date ______________

"**An Occurrence at Owl Creek Bridge**" by Ambrose Bierce

Grammar and Style: Semicolons in Compound Sentences

Compound sentences can be formed by linking independent clauses with a **semicolon** instead of a conjunction. A semicolon emphasizes a very close connection between the ideas in the clauses; it can be a powerful stylistic writing tool.

No; I will not be shot; that is not fair.

A. Practice: *Use a semicolon to combine each pair of sentences into a compound sentence.*

1. It did not appear to be the duty of these two men to know what was occurring at the center of the bridge. They merely blockaded the two ends of the foot planking that traversed it.

 ____

 ____

2. He wore a mustache and pointed beard, but no whiskers. His eyes were large and dark gray, and had a kindly expression which one would hardly have expected in one whose neck was in the hemp.

 ____

 ____

3. The intervals of silence grew progressively longer. The delays became maddening.

 ____

 ____

B. Writing Application: *Write a pair of compound sentences about what Peyton Farquhar thinks is happening and what is actually happening. In the first version, link the two clauses with a conjunction. In the second pair, link the two clauses with a semicolon. Both versions should contain the same information.*

1. compound sentence with conjunctions:

 ____

 ____

 ____

2. compound sentence with semicolon:

 ____

 ____

 ____

Name ______________________ Date ______________

"An Occurrence at Owl Creek Bridge" by Ambrose Bierce

Support for Writing

To organize your information to write a **critical essay** about the story you have just read, enter examples of Bierce's stream of consciousness into the chart below.

Stream of Consciousness in "An Occurrence at Owl Creek Bridge"

Example 1 of stream of consciousness from story	How it reveals character's thoughts
Example 2 of stream of consciousness from story	**How it reveals character's thoughts**
Example 3 of stream of consciousness from story	**How it reveals character's thoughts**

On a separate page, write your first draft, showing how each example of stream of consciousness contributes to the dramatic impact of the story. As you revise, add direct quotes from the story to support your opinions.

Name ______________________________ Date ______________

"An Occurrence at Owl Creek Bridge" by Ambrose Bierce

Support for Extend Your Learning

Listening and Speaking

After you find reports about the effects stress has on people's perceptions of time, follow these tips to compile your **summary:**

- Summarize the reports you have reviewed.
- Summarize the distortions of time that Farquhar experiences.
- Note the ways in which Bierce's use of time supports or does not support the research.

Share your summary with the class. Compare it with the summaries written by your classmates.

Research and Technology

Use the graphic organizer below to organize the facts you need to create a **visual model** of Farquhar's journey. Enter information based on the map on page 513 and your own mathematical processes.

Distance from Farquhar's place to the bridge	Rate of speed if Farquhar rode horse/how long journey took	Rate of speed if Farquhar walked/how long journey took

Use the information to create your model of Farquhar's journey. Use art materials or slide show software.

Name ______________________ Date ______________

"An Occurrence at Owl Creek Bridge" by Ambrose Bierce

Enrichment: The Legal System

Defending Peyton Farquhar

The reader infers from the selection that the hanging of Peyton Farquhar was done without benefit of a formal trial. Would the outcome have been different in a court of law?

DIRECTIONS: *Prepare a legal defense for Peyton Farquhar. You may use anything from the selection, including the map and photographs, to make your case. In the following chart, list at least four issues or facts you will address in Farquhar's defense. You may focus on facts and issues that will help your client, or those the prosecution will probably raise. Conclude with the plea you will enter (innocent or guilty) and the sentence, if any, you will ask for your client. A defense lawyer often considers the following points when preparing a case:*

A. motive of the client
B. past offenses of the client
C. amount and quality of prosecution evidence against the client
D. extenuating or unusual circumstances affecting the crime
E. any remorse shown by the client
F. likelihood of the client's repeating the crime

Fact/Issue	How will you handle this in the trial?

Plea: ______________________

Sentence: ______________________

Name ______________________________ Date ______________

"An Occurrence at Owl Creek Bridge" by Ambrose Bierce

Selection Test A

Critical Reading *Identify the letter of the choice that best answers the question.*

___ 1. What activity opens the story "An Occurrence at Owl Creek Bridge"?
A. A Southern spy is put on trial.
B. A man is about to be hanged.
C. Union soldiers are fixing a bridge.
D. Troops are laying railroad tracks.

___ 2. What must readers figure out in order to understand "An Occurrence at Owl Creek Bridge"?
A. how the characters act
B. the setting and the mood
C. the order of the events
D. the reason for the hanging

___ 3. Which of the following contributes most to the mystery of "An Occurrence at Owl Creek Bridge"?
A. the breaking of the hangman's noose
B. the shooting by the Union sentries
C. Farquhar's underwater struggle
D. the order in which events occur

___ 4. In "Occurrence at Owl Creek Bridge," why does Farquhar hear his watch ticking as he dies?
A. He hopes the watch will start to work.
B. He wants to know his time of death.
C. His senses are extra strong before death.
D. Everything else around him is quiet.

___ 5. In "An Occurrence at Owl Creek Bridge," which is in third-person limited point of view?
A. "Peyton Farquhar was a well-to-do planter . . ."
B. "A man stood upon a railroad bridge in northern Alabama . . ."
C. "He wore a mustache and a pointed beard . . ."
D. "He was awakened - ages later, it seemed to him - by. . . a sharp pressure."

Name ________________________ Date ____________

___ **6.** In "Occurrence at Owl Creek Bridge," why does the Federal scout want to burn the bridge?

A. He wants to help the South win.

B. He wants to set Farquhar up.

C. He wants a job building a new bridge.

D. He wants to disrespect his commandant.

___ **7.** In "Occurrence at Owl Creek Bridge," Farquhar is a gentleman. Why might he be hanged?

A. for being from the Confederacy

B. for spying on Union activities

C. for planning against the enemy

D. for refusing to feed Union soldiers

___ **8.** Which of these passages from "An Occurrence at Owl Creek Bridge" is written from an omniscient point of view?

A. "If I could free my hands," he thought, "I might throw off the noose. . ."

B. "The man who was engaged in being hanged was . . . about thirty-five . . ."

C. "The thought of his wife and children urged him on."

D. "To be hanged and drowned . . . that is not so bad; but I do not wish to be shot."

___ **9.** In "Occurrence at Owl Creek Bridge," in which order do the following events occur?

A. Farquhar imagines reuniting with his wife.

B. Farquhar is approached by a Federal scout.

C. Farquhar's board is released and he falls.

D. Farquhar dies of hanging.

A. A, B, C, D **B.** C, A, B, D **C.** A, D, B, C **D.** B, C, A, D

___ **10.** Which of these events happens last in the real-time sequence of events in "Occurrence at Owl Creek Bridge"?

A. Farquhar falls through the bridge.

B. Farquhar's neck snaps and he dies.

C. Farquhar imagines greeting his wife.

D. Farquhar imagines dodging bullets.

Name ____________________ Date ____________________

Vocabulary and Grammar

____ 11. In which sentence is the meaning of the word *apprised* suggested?

A. Farquhar was not a soldier but hoped to contribute to the Southern cause.

B. Mrs. Farquhar was informed of her husband's death.

C. The federal scout encouraged Farquhar to commit sabotage.

D. The authorities went through the proper formalities.

____ 12. In which of the following sentences is the semicolon used correctly?

A. Bierce's world view was pessimistic; and he wrote with the same view.

B. Although he was seriously wounded in the Civil War; he returned to fight again.

C. Bierce enjoyed fame as a newsman; he wrote a column for the *Examiner.*

D. Bierce disappeared in Mexico in 1914; and it is believed he died there.

Essay

13. How is Bierce's dark view reflected in "An Occurrence at Owl Creek Bridge"? Write a brief essay that gives examples of events that reflect a negative view of human experience.

14. What do you think Bierce's view of war is, based on "An Occurrence at Owl Creek Bridge"? Does he find it uplifting or hopeless? Write a brief essay to give your opinion about Bierce's viewpoint. Use at least two examples from the story to support your opinion.

Name ______________________________ Date ______________

"An Occurrence at Owl Creek Bridge" by Ambrose Bierce

Selection Test B

Critical Reading *Identify the letter of the choice that best completes the statement or answers the question.*

____ 1. Which of the following quotations from this story reveals an objective point of view?
- A. "He was a captain."
- B. "He closed his eyes in order to fix his last thoughts upon his wife and children."
- C. "His whole body was racked and wrenched with an insupportable anguish!"
- D. "He had not known that he lived in so wild a region."

____ 2. Why does the author describe how Peyton Farquhar reacts to the sound of his watch?
- A. to show that Farquhar's sense perceptions had become very distorted
- B. to illustrate the cruelty of the Union soldiers
- C. to explain why Farquhar had come to the bridge
- D. to draw a parallel between Farquhar and his executioners

____ 3. In order to understand the relationship between the three distinct parts of the story, the reader must clarify
- A. how a civilian like Farquhar became a military prisoner.
- B. shifts in the geographical setting.
- C. the sequence of events.
- D. the story's several conflicting attitudes about the Civil War.

____ 4. Which of the following contributes most to the feeling of suspense in "An Occurrence at Owl Creek Bridge"?
- A. the vivid descriptions of the physical setting
- B. the unexpected sequence in which the events are related
- C. the emotionless description of the procedures used to prepare for the hanging
- D. the sympathetic depiction of Peyton Farquhar's personality

____ 5. When Peyton Farquhar suggests sabotage, the Federal scout suggests that the bridge can be burned down. What does this say about the scout's character?
- A. He is an honest and straightforward man.
- B. He is an arsonist at heart.
- C. He is not above setting up Farquhar.
- D. He dislikes his commandant.

____ 6. What points of view does Bierce use in this story?
- A. objective as well as first person
- B. objective and third-person limited
- C. first person and third person
- D. only third-person limited

____ 7. What is the main function of the flashback in this story?
- A. to describe the effects of the war on women and children
- B. to provide insight into the treacherous nature of the Union soldiers
- C. to generate sympathy for the Southern cause
- D. to explain why Peyton Farquhar is being hanged

Name ______________________ Date ______________

____ 8. Which message is Bierce trying to convey in this story?
A. People often get themselves into trouble by taking foolish risks.
B. Whatever can go wrong, probably will.
C. Soldiers must follow orders regardless of their personal feelings.
D. War makes men cruel and indifferent to human life.

____ 9. Which event happens first in the true sequence of events?
A. Farquhar stands on the Oak Creek bridge with his neck "in the hemp."
B. Farquhar's wife brings the soldier water.
C. The rope breaks, causing Farquhar to fall into the water.
D. Farquhar runs to greet his wife with open arms.

____ 10. Which of the following excerpts provides a clue that certain events occur in Peyton Farquhar's imagination rather than in reality?
A. ". . . he had frequented camps enough to know the dread significance of that deliberate, drawing, aspirated chant . . ."
B. "The trees upon the bank were giant garden plants; he noted a definite order in their arrangement, inhaled the fragrance of their blooms."
C. "Suddenly he heard a sharp report and something struck the water smartly within a few inches of his head, spattering his face with spray."
D. "At last he found a road which led him in what he knew to be the right direction."

____ 11. Why is the narrator surprised to find Peyton Farquhar about to hanged?
A. Farquhar looks kindly and is a gentleman.
B. Hanging has been outlawed in Alabama.
C. Farquhar is already dead.
D. Only gentleman are hanged in Alabama.

____ 12. Which of the following excerpts shows a limited third-person point of view?
A. "Peyton Farquhar was a well-to-do planter, of an old and highly respected Alabama family."
B. "The company faced the bridge, staring stonily, motionless."
C. "The power of thought was restored; he knew that the rope had broken and he had fallen into the stream."
D. "The man's hands were behind his back, the wrists bound with a cord."

Vocabulary and Grammar

____ 13. What are the meanings of the italicized words in the following sentence? "In the code of military *etiquette*, silence and fixity are forms of *deference*."
A. training, soldiering
B. manners, disrespect
C. hangings, bravery
D. behavior, courtesy

____ 14. When Peyton Farquhar swings through "unthinkable arcs of *oscillation*," he swings
A. through thick fog.
B. like a pendulum.
C. with a vertical motion.
D. with wrenching pain.

Name ______________________ Date ______________

____ 15. Which word is closest in meaning to the italicized word in the phrase ". . . will be *summarily* hanged"?

A. quietly
B. promptly
C. justifiably
D. brutally

____ 16. Compound sentences can be formed by joining two closely related independent clauses with a __________.

A. colon
B. comma
C. semicolon
D. slash

____ 17. What is the main reason for connecting independent clauses with a semicolon?

A. to emphasize the close connection between the clauses
B. to eliminate descriptions
C. to show that the clauses are separate
D. to indicate a pause in the action

Essay

18. Do you think Bierce agreed that "all is fair in love and war"? Answer this question in a short essay, using examples from "An Occurrence at Owl Creek Bridge" to support your position.

19. In "An Occurrence at Owl Creek Bridge," the reader is surprised to learn that the man with whom Farquhar discusses Owl Creek bridge is not a Confederate soldier but a Federal, or Union, scout. What is the true significance of their brief conversation, and how does the incident set the tone for the rest of the story? In an essay, relate this flash back to the events of the story and explore how this initial deception might be said to foreshadow the story's ending.

20. Ambrose Bierce uses both a flashback and different points of view to tell "An Occurrence at Owl Creek Bridge." Imagine that Bierce had written the story in the true sequence of events and from an objective point of view. Do you think the story would have been as effective? State your opinion in a brief essay, supporting your opinion with examples from the story.

Selections by Abraham Lincoln and Robert E. Lee

Vocabulary Warm-up Word Lists

Study these words from the selections. Then, complete the activities.

Word List A

arrayed [UH rayd] *v.* arranged in order, specifically troops in battle
Both sides were arrayed against the other, desperately looking for a way out.

duration [der AY shuhn] *n.* the amount of time in which something lasts or exists
The two girls had a friendship of long duration.

establishment [eh STA blish mint] *n.* the act or condition of being established; set up
His establishment here as a doctor has helped the town.

prosperity [prah SPER uh tee] *n.* the condition of having good fortune or financial success
The family is experiencing a happy time of peace and prosperity.

pursued [per SOOD] *v.* to seek to accomplish
The hounds pursued the fox through the forest.

restrict [ree STRIKT] *v.* confine within bounds
The police chief said he would restrict his comments to a few words.

strive [STRYV] *v.* make effort
Barbara said she would strive to be successful for the entire school year.

virtuous [VER choo us] *adj.* leading a good life; obeying rules of right and wrong
Mr. Green always led a virtuous life.

Word List B

anticipate [an TIS uh payt] *v.* expect or realize beforehand
People anticipate stormy weather when they see dark clouds approach.

attributes [A tri byoot] *n.* characteristics belonging to a person or thing
Intelligence is one of Sara's attributes.

avert [uh VERT] *v.* to turn away
Sometimes the dog will avert his eyes from his owner in order to hide his guilt.

calamity [khuh LAM i tee] *n.* a disaster
The earthquake was a calamity when it destroyed the small town.

contend [khuhn TEND] *v.* to fight or strive for something, particularly in battle
Susan had to contend with difficulties all her life.

localized [loh khu LYZD] *v.* confined to a particular area or source
The boxer's toothache was localized to the right side of his mouth.

restraint [ri STRAYNT] *n.* the act of holding back
When the family came to America, they were free to live without restraint.

strife [STRYF] *n.* bitter conflict
The strife between them went on for years.

Name ________________________________ Date ________________

Selections by Abraham Lincoln and Robert E. Lee

Vocabulary Warm-up Exercises

Exercise A *Fill in each blank in the paragraph below with the appropriate word from Word List A.*

The battle troops were [1] ________________ on the field in their colorful uniforms. The night before, they had been [2] ________________ by enemy troops and were forced to retreat. Backing them into the wilderness in order to [3] ________________ mobility was part of the offensive strategy. Despite the setback of being poorly situated, the assembled troops would [4] ________________ to win the next round. They planned on charging the offensive troops for the [5] ________________ of the day. Their [6] ________________ leader inspired great courage among the men as he informed them of the long battle ahead. Once the [7] ________________ of priorities was explained, each troop prepared himself accordingly. The goal was to achieve victory so that peace and [8] ________________ could be returned to the town that they were defending.

Exercise B *Decide whether each statement is true or false. Circle* T *or* F, *and explain your answers.*

1. While telling the truth, it is common for people to <u>avert</u> their eyes.
   T / F ____
2. To <u>anticipate</u> the arrival of a long, lost friend could be exciting.
   T / F ____
3. If young children were left alone all day, a <u>calamity</u> would be expected upon return.
   T / F ____
4. Showing <u>restraint</u> is necessary when trying to remain objective about a situation.
   T / F ____
5. Heat waves are common in the U.S., but are generally <u>localized</u> to northern states.
   T / F ____
6. <u>Strife</u> is a desirable feeling amongst friends and family.
   T / F ____
7. Personality <u>attributes</u> can consist of a variety of unique traits and behaviors.
   T / F ____
8. If a cause is worthy, one might expect to <u>contend</u> in its defense.
   T / F ____

Name ______________________________ Date ______________

Selections by Abraham Lincoln and Robert E. Lee

Reading Warm-up A

Read the following passage. Pay special attention to the underlined words. Then, read it again, and complete the activities. Use a separate sheet of paper for your written answers.

The so-called "Rebel Yell" began on the battlefields of the Civil War. A now-famous battle cry began as a method for the southern soldiers to release their stress before a fight. Hoping for a victory, the nervous Rebels yelled as they pursued the Yankees. Because it seemed to scare the northern forces, intimidation became another function of the yell. Often the Rebels hollered for the duration of their charge, minutes at a time. Sometimes the Yankees thought that they were outnumbered based on the amount of noise coming from their enemy.

The reputation of such shouting earned the "Rebel Yell" its establishment into our vocabulary because it is still referred to today. It was used a lot when fighting occurred under the cover of trees or the night sky. Out of nowhere, the northern soldiers would hear the eerie and frightening "Rebel Yell." However, this tactic was not just used when visual conditions were poor. On fields set for a large-scale battles with cannons arrayed in long, neat lines, troops standing shoulder to shoulder, and generals, whom soldiers admired and thought of as virtuous leaders, even the mounted generals heard the yelling.

While the "Rebel Yell" became famous during the Civil War, its origins began prior to it. Some people believe that the shout was used for hunting or sporting. For example, some hunters would shout in order to scare deer into an area where they could be cornered or trapped, that way the hunter could restrict their movement. Other research discusses the Southern Appalachian region, where there used to be quite some distance between neighbors, therefore people climbed the hilltops and shouted in order to talk with one another; they would strive to be as loud as possible, therefore they yelled. Good fortune and prosperity were thought to belong to people who didn't have to go to such extreme measures to communicate.

1. Why is pursued an accurate verb to describe the action of the sentence? Used ***pursued*** in a sentence.
2. How might charging an enemy affect the duration of the run itself? Quantify the ***duration*** of your English class.
3. Underline the phrase that provides more information about the establishment of "Rebel Yell" into our vocabulary. Use ***establishment*** in a sentence.
4. Describe three aspects of how the battle scene was arrayed. Name something in the classroom that is ***arrayed*** alphabetically.
5. Who thought of the generals as virtuous men? Name a famous American who is considered by many to be ***virtuous***. Explain.
6. Why would it be difficult to restrict a deer? Name a sport or activity in which it would be good to ***restrict*** something. Why?
7. How did the Appalachian dwellers strive to be heard by their neighbors? Use ***strive*** in a sentence.
8. As a resident of Appalachia, why was it considered advantageous to have prosperity? Why do people want ***prosperity***?

Name ______________________________ Date ______________

Selections by Abraham Lincoln and Robert E. Lee

Reading Warm-up B

Read the following passage. Pay special attention to the underlined words. Then, read it again, and complete the activities. Use a separate sheet of paper for your written answers.

Once the union fell apart and the calamity of the Civil War began, men became soldiers and left the security of their homes for makeshift and temporary campsites. Such drastic changes to their lifestyles added to the amount of strife that both northern and southern soldiers felt throughout the war. Despite the hardships, soldiers had to persevere and make themselves, and their campsites as comfortable as possible.

Contrary to what some people think, many Civil War soldiers spent weeks, sometimes months, without firing one shot. There are many reports from both sides of the fighting that boredom was a common hardship. Soldiers were better off if they showed restraint by not giving in to the waiting game. Instead they stopped trying to predict when battle would happen and they focused more on making the campsite comfortable and livable.

The attributes of these campsites vary depending on many factors, but most were undesirable regardless of their unique characteristics. Frequently, soldiers had to contend with poor weather as they fought to stay adequately sheltered. It was difficult for them to anticipate how bad camp conditions would be, as this was a new experience for each of them. Most soldiers attempted to avert their attention from such things and focus on more positive and entertaining aspects of "tenting" with fellow soldiers. These social areas within the camps were localized, each having their specific place depending upon the activity. Most entertainment consisted of playing cards, reading newspapers, and simply talking about family and home. These types of activities were popular on both sides of the Mason Dixon line and brought relief to the soldiers when camp conditions were bad. While they filled their days and nights with things to pass the time, the campsite was still a far cry from the comfort and security of their houses at home.

1. Why is calamity appropriate to describe the Civil War? List another ***calamity*** in our nation's history.
2. How can drastic changes cause strife in someone's life? Use ***strife*** in a sentence.
3. Underline the words in the sentence that help define restraint. Why is ***restraint*** beneficial in this situation?
4. Explain how the attributes of camp life contributed to the overall atmosphere. Name two ***attributes*** of the camp that made life there tough.
5. What was the major factor that the soldiers had to contend with during the Civil War? Use ***contend*** in a sentence.
6. Why was it difficult for soldiers to anticipate camp conditions? In modern times, how do people best ***anticipate*** the weather?
7. If soldiers could avert their attention from bad camp situations, where did they refocus it? Use ***avert*** in a sentence.
8. Underline the words that help define localized. Why might particular areas be ***localized*** in group settings?

Name ______________________________ Date ______________

"The Gettysburg Address" and **"Second Inaugural Address"** by Abraham Lincoln
"Letter to His Son" by Robert E. Lee

Literary Analysis: Diction

Diction, or word choice, gives the writer's voice its unique quality. The writer's diction reflects the audience and purpose of the work.

DIRECTIONS: *Read each question and pair of phrases or sentences below. Circle the letter of the phrase or sentence in which the diction suits the indicated writing purpose.*

1. Which phrase is better suited for a letter?
   A. Four score and seven years ago . . .
   B. Eighty-seven years ago . . .
2. Which phrase is better suited for a letter?
   A. . . . that this awful war will end soon.
   B. . . . that this mighty scourge of war may speedily pass away.
3. Which phrase is better suited for a public speech?
   A. As a citizen of these United States, . . .
   B. As someone who lives in America, . . .
4. Which phrase is better suited for a letter?
   A. . . . we are stuck between chaos and war.
   B. . . . we find ourselves entrapped between anarchy and civil war.
5. Which phrase is better suited for a letter?
   A. No one will remember or pay attention to today's speeches, . . .
   B. The world will little note, nor long remember what we say here, . . .
6. Which sentence is better suited for a public speech?
   A. These slaves constituted a peculiar and powerful interest.
   B. These slaves were very valuable to some.
7. Which sentence is better suited for a public speech?
   A. We are met on a great battlefield of that war.
   B. Here we are at this great battlefield.
8. Which phrase is better suited for a public speech?
   A. Neither side expected it would be so bad or so long . . .
   B. Neither party expected . . . the magnitude, or the duration . . .

Name ________________________________ Date ____________________

"The Gettysburg Address" and **"Second Inaugural Address"** by Abraham Lincoln
"Letter to His Son" by Robert E. Lee

Reading Strategy: Use Background Knowledge

Background knowledge may include information about the author, about the characters or subjects of the selection, or about the times and events discussed in the selection. Background knowledge can often include personal experience of people and experiences similar to those in the selection. You learned that Robert E. Lee believed in the Union but opposed both slavery and secession. In this activity, you will learn more about Robert E. Lee to understand further the personal conflict he felt.

DIRECTIONS: *Read the information below. Then use the facts to explain your understanding of each excerpt from Lee's letter to his son.*

- Lee attended the United States Military Academy at West Point in 1825, graduating in 1829.
- In the late 1840s, Lee served in the Mexican War, where he was recognized for his skill and courage.
- Lee's family was a well-established, important family of Virginia. His father was a cavalry commander in the Revolutionary War and a friend of George Washington. Lee admired the first president and named one of his sons George Washington Custis Lee.
- Lee was an honorable and respected man who displayed kindness and humor, and who did not smoke, drink alcohol, or swear.
- Lee did not believe in slavery. Long before the Civil War broke out, he freed the slaves he had inherited.
- Lee felt that Virginia stood for George Washington's principles. He considered the Civil War as a second "Revolutionary War" for independence.

1. How [Washington's] spirit would be grieved could he see the wreck of his mighty labors!

   ____

   ____

2. I feel the aggression [of acts of the North] and am willing to take every proper step for redress. It is the principle I contend for, not individual or private benefit.

   ____

   ____

3. As an American citizen, I take great pride in my country, her prosperity and institutions, and would defend any state if her rights were invaded.

   ____

   ____

Name ____ Date ______________________

"The Gettysburg Address" and **"Second Inaugural Address"** by Abraham Lincoln
"Letter to His Son" by Robert E. Lee

Vocabulary Builder

Using the Root *-archy-*

A. DIRECTIONS: *The following words each contain the word root* -archy, *meaning "rule" or "government." Combine your knowledge of this root with the meaning of each prefix provided to match the words with their definitions.*

___ 1. oligarchy—*oligo-* "few"
___ 2. matriarchy—*matri-* "mother"
___ 3. monarchy—*mono-* "one", "alone", or "single"
___ 4. patriarchy—*patri-* "father"

A. rule by women
B. rule by only one person
C. rule by a faction or small group
D. rule by men

Using the Word List

consecrate	hallow	deprecated	insurgents	discern
scourge	malice	anarchy	redress	

B. DIRECTIONS: *Circle the synonym for the underlined word in each sectence or phrase.*

1. . . . we cannot consecrate (bless, profane)
2. . . . we cannot hallow (honor, haunt)
3. Both parties deprecated war (awaited, condemned)
4. . . . shall we discern therein any departure from those divine attributes (demand, recognize)
5. . . . that this mighty scourge of war may speedily pass away. (affliction, miracle)
6. With malice toward none; (spite, spirit)
7. As far as I can judge by the papers, we are between a state of anarchy and civil war. (progress, chaos)
8. I feel the aggression and am willing to take every proper step for redress. (armament, atonement)

Name ____________________ Date ____________________

"The Gettysburg Address" and **"Second Inaugural Address"** by Abraham Lincoln
"Letter to His Son" by Robert E. Lee

Grammar and Style: Parallel Structure

The use of **parallel structure,** or the expression of similar ideas in similar form, helps to emphasize important concepts. Often, the most memorable excerpts from literature are those that contain examples of parallel structure. Look at this example from "The Gettysburg Address."

But, in a larger sense, **we cannot** dedicate—**we cannot** consecrate—**we cannot** hallow this ground.

By repeating the phrase "we cannot," Lincoln creates a strong feeling of humility.

A. Practice: *Underline each element of parallel structure in the excerpts below.*

1. . . . testing whether that nation, or any nation so conceived and so dedicated, can long endure.
2. . . . —that from these honored dead we take increased devotion to that cause for which they gave the last full measure of devotion—that we here highly resolve that these dead shall not have died in vain—that this nation, under God, shall have a new birth of freedom. . . .
3. . . . —and that government of the people, by the people, for the people, shall not perish from the earth.

B. Writing Application: *Rewrite the paragraph below as a short speech introducing the subject of the Civil War. Use at least two instances of parallel structure in your speech.*

The Civil War was a unique and terrible time in American history. Although slavery was probably the catalyst that started the war, many other regional factors, including economics, climate, and land, also divided the nation. The land in the North could not support large farms, therefore the northern states turned to trade and industry. This economic trend led to the growth of large cities and a fast-paced urban lifestyle. The southern states relied on agriculture, which resulted in a demand for cheap labor, small communities, and a generally slower pace of life. Friends and families were often divided in their loyalties, and sometimes faced each other on opposite sides of the battlefield. One state, Virginia, even divided itself, with Virginia remaining a Confederate state and West Virginia becoming a Union state.

____

____

____

____

____

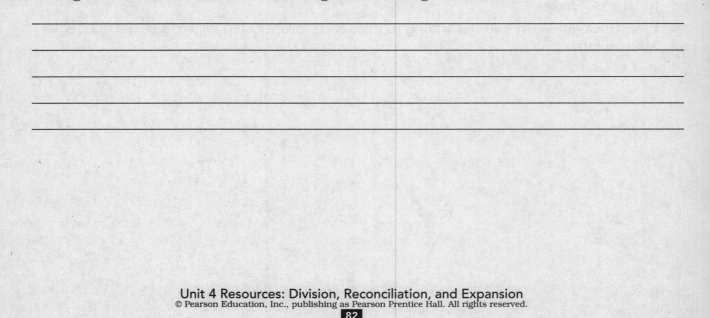

Name ______________________________ Date ______________

"The Gettysburg Address" and **"Second Inaugural Address"** by Abraham Lincoln
"Letter to His Son" by Robert E. Lee

Support for Writing

As you prepare to write your **diary entry,** reread the "Gettysburg Address" and enter information into the chart below.

"Gettysburg Address" and Lincoln's Feelings about Speech

Main Points	Lincoln's Feelings/Attitudes about each Point
First main point in Address	
Second main point in Address	
Third main point in Address	
Fourth main point in Address	

On a separate page, write a diary entry from Lincoln's point of view on the eve of the "Gettysburg Address." As you revise your work, be sure to show how Lincoln felt about the address he would give the next day.

Name ______________________ Date ______________

"The Gettysburg Address" and **"Second Inaugural Address"** by Abraham Lincoln
"Letter to His Son" by Robert E. Lee

Support for Extend Your Learning

Listening and Speaking

As you work with a group to plan for a **mock Supreme Court hearing** about whether a state has a right to secede from the Union, choose lawyers to present both sides and a judge to give an opinion. Remember the following:

- Lawyers should present their strongest arguments.
- Judges should explain why they believe certain arguments are best before they offer their decisions.

Stage your hearing for your classmates. Ask for feedback and listen to other presentations.

Research and Technology

As you plan your **Internet Web site** on the Civil War, make notes of the links you will use. Enter your information in the flow chart below.

Links to Primary Source Sites ▶	Links to Secondary Source Sites ▶	Links to Photo or Maps Sites ▶	Links to Music/ Art/Plays Sites

Work with other classmates to set up your website, using HTML software if possible.

Name ______________________________ Date ______________

"The Gettysburg Address" and **"Second Inaugural Address"** by Abraham Lincoln
"Letter to His Son" by Robert E. Lee

Enrichment: Music

Songs of Peace

The desire for peace, similar to the ideas in Lincoln's "Second Inaugural Address" and Lee's "Letter to His Son," have often been portrayed as a theme in music.

DIRECTIONS: *Find a song that you think portrays the desire for peace. Write the name of the song, the author or performer (if you know it), and the lyrics that display the desire for peace. Tell why you think it compares with the desire for peace expressed in either Lincoln's "Gettysburg Address" or Lee's "Letter to His Son."*

Song (and author or performer): ______________________________

Lyrics that display the desire for peace: ______________________________

How the song compares to either Lincoln's or Lee's desire: ______________________________

Name ______________________________ Date ______________

"The Gettysburg Address" and **"Second Inaugural Address"** by Abraham Lincoln
"Letter to His Son" by Robert E. Lee

Selection Test A

Critical Reading *Identify the letter of the choice that best answers the question.*

____ 1. Why does Lincoln deliver "The Gettysburg Address"?

A. to make a formal declaration of war
B. to dedicate ground for a cemetery
C. to end the Civil War
D. to make plans for the Civil War

____ 2. In "The Gettysburg Address," what kind of diction does Lincoln use in the phrase "Four score and seven years ago"?

A. abstract
B. informal
C. private
D. formal

____ 3. What event does Lincoln refer to when he says that "our fathers brought forth on this continent a new nation, conceived in Liberty" in "The Gettysburg Address"?

A. the end of the Civil War
B. the beginning of the Civil War in 1861
C. the signing of the Declaration of Independence in 1776
D. the exploration of the New World by Columbus

____ 4. What is another way to state the following from "The Gettysburg Address":

"The brave men, living and dead, who struggled here, have consecrated it [made it holy], far above our poor power to add or detract"?

A. Those who forget history are doomed to repeat it.
B. Actions speak louder than words.
C. Keep your friends close and your enemies closer.
D. The pen is mightier than the sword.

____ 5. Lincoln's "Second Inaugural Address" took place on March 4, 1865. Based on the content of this speech, when did it occur historically?

A. before the start of the Civil War
B. before the end of the Civil War
C. when he was a senator
D. during his presidential campaign

Name ______________________________ Date ______________

____ 6. What does Lincoln use his "Second Inaugural Address" to do?
A. condemn the South for the Civil War
B. look forward to a world after war ends
C. call on God to end the Civil War
D. talk about his successes as president

____ 7. What does Lincoln means by the words "With malice toward none; with charity for all" in his "Second Inaugural Address"?
A. with ill will to those who started the war, and with kindness to those who died
B. with ill will to those who lost the war and with kindness to those who won
C. without ill will toward anyone and with kindness toward everyone
D. with ill will toward everyone and with kindness toward no one

____ 8. Which of these elements in Lee's "Letter to His Son" gives historical background?
A. his reference to receiving a book as a gift from his son
B. his reference to his pride as a citizen of his country
C. his reference to the four states that have left the union
D. his reference to feeling helpless in the face of events

____ 9. What element in "Letter to His Son" makes it surprising that Lee became the military leader of the Confederate armies?
A. He says he will fight only to defend his or some other state.
B. He says the South has been badly treated by the North.
C. He says that George Washington would be unhappy with a civil war.
D. He hopes God will keep the nation from falling apart.

____ 10. In "Letter to His Son," Lee says he would be willing to sacrifice everything—except one—in order to avoid the separation of the Union. What is the one thing?
A. his sword
B. honor
C. evil
D. progress

Vocabulary and Grammar

____ 11. In which sentence is the meaning of the word *deprecated* expressed?
A. The dead made the ground holy.
B. Lincoln spoke of the nation in his speech.
C. Lee disapproved of a civil war.
D. Lincoln advised that wrongs be forgiven.

Name ______________________ Date ______________

___ 12. Which of these phrases displays parallel construction?

A. "I take great pride in my country, her prosperity and institutions"

B. "the government of the people, by the people, for the people"

C. "I received Everett's *Life of Washington* which you sent me"

D. "If the Union is dissolved . . . I shall return to my native state"

Essay

13. In "The Gettysburg Address," Lincoln states that the soldiers who died at Gettysburg died so that the nation might live. What was Lincoln encouraging his listeners to do? In a brief essay, express your thoughts about what Lincoln was trying to accomplish in this speech.

14. In his "Letter to His Son," Lee refers to the founders of the nation and its constitution. He hates the possibility of secession and civil war. Yet, he finally led the armies of the Confederacy. Write a brief essay to explain his decision. Include how his letter to his son might explain why he led the Southern armies against the Union.

Name ______________________________ Date ______________

"The Gettysburg Address" and **"Second Inaugural Address"** by Abraham Lincoln
"Letter to His Son" by Robert E. Lee

Selection Test B

Critical Reading *Identify the letter of the choice that best completes the statement or answers the question.*

____ 1. In "The Gettysburg Address" Lincoln explains that the stated purpose for meeting on this battlefield is to __________.
A. dedicate the nation to the Southern cause
B. dedicate themselves to revenging the Gettysburg dead
C. dedicate a portion of the field as a final resting place for fallen soldiers
D. dedicate themselves to God

____ 2. Lincoln's main purpose in "The Gettysburg Address" is to __________.
A. argue why the Union will win the war
B. explain the importance of the war and inspire people to support the Union
C. seek money for the families of those who died
D. identify the soldiers who died in battle

____ 3. Considering the diction of "The Gettysburg Address," describe Lincoln's view of himself and his audience.
A. powerless and defeated
B. humble and dedicated
C. cowardly and fearful
D. noble and proud

____ 4. The main idea of Lee's "Letter to His Son" could be expressed best as
A. belief that the integrity of the Union must be preserved at all costs.
B. determination that the South will not be subdued.
C. despair over a Union that can only be maintained by force.
D. an argument in favor of secession.

____ 5. In his letter, Lee reflects an attitude toward impending events that is
A. fatalistic about the prospects of war.
B. confident in the South's military strength.
C. hateful toward the North.
D. opposed to the principles of the Constitution.

____ 6. One of Lee's main reasons for opposing secession is his
A. pride as a Virginian.
B. belief in the importance of the Union.
C. commitment to states' rights.
D. position as an officer in the army.

____ 7. Lee's letter seeks to persuade by
A. appealing to emotion.
B. invoking the authority of great writers.
C. making an irrational argument.
D. analyzing events within historical context.

Name ______________________________ Date ______________

____ 8. Prior knowledge in which of the following areas would best help you understand the ideas Lee expresses in his letter?
A. the principles of the United States Constitution
B. Lee's military experience
C. the economy of the pre-Civil War South
D. the relationship between Lee and his son

____ 9. Lincoln's diction in "Second Inaugural Address" suggests which purpose?
A. to give comfort to the widows and orphans
B. to share his personal sorrow with a friend
C. to explore his thoughts in a private journal
D. to impress a national audience with the importance of his message

____ 10. Lee's diction in "A Letter to His Son" is somewhat informal because he is
A. delivering a public speech.
B. writing to his son.
C. discussing a trivial subject.
D. speaking in code to avoid suspicion.

____ 11. From what you know of the causes of the Civil War, by what "acts of the North" might southerners, including Lee, have been aggrieved?
A. the Union's policy regarding which states shall be slaveholding states
B. the Union's policy regulating how much slaves should cost
C. Lincoln's Emancipation Proclamation
D. the Union's granting to African Americans the right to vote

____ 12. From what you know of United States history, which document was Lincoln quoting when he said in "The Gettysburg Address" that the nation was dedicated to the proposition "that all men are created equal"?
A. the Emancipation Proclamation
B. the Declaration of Independence
C. the Equal Rights Amendment
D. the Missouri Compromise

____ 13. In "Second Inaugural Address," how does Lincoln explain the Civil War?
A. Insurgents sought to destroy the Union.
B. One party wanted to make war, and the other did not.
C. The North was aggrieved by the acts of the South.
D. God is punishing the United States for allowing slavery.

Vocabulary and Grammar

____ 14. The word or phrase closest in meaning to *malice* is ________.
A. good will
B. cup
C. spite
D. hurt feelings

Name ______________________________ Date ______________

____ 15. When Lincoln referred to war as a *scourge* he ________ war.
A. deprecated
B. consecrated
C. redressed
D. hallowed

____ 16. When Lincoln suggests that the living ought to dedicate themselves to the task of seeing "that government of the people, by the people, for the people, shall not perish from the earth," he is using which grammatical device to emphasize his ideas?
A. loaded language
B. sensory details
C. parallel structure
D. modifiers

____ 17. The word most opposite in meaning to *insurgents* is ________.
A. rebels
B. spies
C. patriots
D. soldiers

Essay

18. Both Lincoln and Lee placed a great deal of importance on preserving the Union. Write an essay in which you discuss either Lincoln or Lee's ideas about the Union. Use examples from the text of Lincoln's speeches or Lee's letter to support your points.

19. Lincoln chooses details and language in "The Second Inaugural Address" to accomplish a specific purpose. Write an essay explaining what you believe that purpose to be. Support your conclusion with details and diction from speech.

20. Lincoln's speeches convey a great deal about his beliefs and his character in general. Likewise, Lee's letter reveals a good deal about the nature of its author. Choose either Lincoln or Lee as your subject. Then write an essay in which you describe the man's character, using details from his writing to support your impressions.

Name ______________________________ Date ______________

From the Scholar's Desk

Nell Irvin Painter Introduces "An Account of an Experience with Discrimination" by Sojourner Truth

DIRECTIONS: *Use the space provided to answer the questions.*

1. According to Nell Irvin Painter, what kind of volunteer work did Sojourner Truth carry out in Washington, D.C. during the Civil War?

2. What were the events that Sojourner Truth dictated for publication in the antislavery press?

3. According to Painter, what are the "two American histories" to which Truth's experience of discrimination belongs?

4. Why was the war between black people and American railroads "national in scope"?

5. Identify three of the well-known African Americans named by Painter, and briefly describe how they suffered discrimination on railroad trains.

6. If you had a chance to interview Nell Irvin Painter, what are two questions you might ask her about how she performs historical research?

Name ______________________ Date ______________

Nell Irvin Painter

Listening and Viewing

Segment 1: Meet Nell Irvin Painter

- How did Nell Irvin Painter first become interested in studying history?
- Why do you think historical writing is so important to society?

____

____

____

____

Segment 2: Nell Irvin Painter Introduces Sojourner Truth

- Who was Sojourner Truth, and why was she an important historical figure during the Civil War?
- What two facts, that are often unknown, does Nell Irvin Painter want students to know?

____

____

____

____

Segment 3: The Writing Process

- What is a primary source, and why are primary sources important to Nell Irvin Painter's historical narratives?

____

____

____

____

Segment 4: The Rewards of Writing

- According to Nell Irvin Painter, why is it important that students view history critically?
- What do you think you can learn by reading historical narratives about people like Sojourner Truth?

____

____

____

____

Vocabulary Warm-up Word Lists

Study these words from the selections. Then, complete the activities.

Word List A

demonstration [dem uhn STRAY shuhn] *n.* an exhibition of feeling or emotion
The demonstration was smaller than most people originally thought.

discrimination [dis krim uh NAY shuhn] *n.* prejudiced treatment of a person, group, etc.
Discrimination on the job is a terrible thing because it is unfair and illegal.

extinguished [ek STING gwishd] *v.* to have put out; quenched
It took seven fire engines all night before the fire was completely extinguished.

proclamation [prahk luh MAY shuhn] *n.* an official announcement
The wedding proclamation was made at noon on Sunday.

recruits [ri KROOTS] *n.* new members to an activity or group
Five recruits walked into the meeting and went to the booth for new trainees.

suffrage [SUHF rij] *n.* the state of being oppressed or denied rights
The ongoing suffrage at work was unfair to females.

tatters [TAT uhrz] *n.* torn or shredded pieces of cloth
After running through the forest, his shirt was in tatters.

witty [WIT ee] *adj.* cleverly amusing in writing and speech capabilities
Mike was witty and full of interesting things to say.

Word List B

adjourned [uh JERND] *v.* suspended until a specific time
Court is adjourned until 8:00 A.M. Monday, when it will pick back up at that point.

communicative [kuh MYOO nuh cah tiv] *adj.* talkative
At today's assembly, the candidates were very communicative about their ideas.

consequence [KAHN suh kwins] *n.* an effect or result of something
Think twice before leaving too late because there could be a negative consequence.

intercepted [IN tuhr sep tid] *v.* interrupted or to have stopped the course of something
Anticipating his opponents move, he intercepted the pass and got control of the ball.

multitude [MUHL ti tood] *n.* a great number of
A multitude of parents crowded the event, causing traffic jams.

solace [SAHL is] *n.* comfort
I should take solace in having passed the test, as most of my friends did not.

strenuous [STREN yoo uhs] *adj.* requiring energetic effort
After the strenuous five-mile hike, the backpackers wanted to stop for lunch and rest.

valor [VAL uhr] *n.* courage or boldness, as in the face of battle
The soldier's valor in the field of combat earned him a medal of honor.

Name ________________________________ Date ________________

Civil War Diaries, Journals, and Letters

Vocabulary Warm-up Exercises

Exercise A *Fill in each blank in the paragraph below with the appropriate word from Word List A.*

Her brand new dishtowel was in [1] ______________, shredded and ruined. Despite her embarrassment, Ann didn't seem to mind because she [2] ______________ the fire on the stove without getting hurt. The audience attending her cooking show felt sorry for her but tried not show it; it would have been an unfair [3] ______________ against her because usually the show ran smoothly. Ann began putting on a [4] ______________ of flipping pancakes. While she tossed them in the air, she talked with the audience and made jokes. Ann was very [5] ______________ and clever, in fact, several [6] ______________ backstage thought she was hysterical. Suddenly she made a [7] ______________ about feeding pancakes to everyone in the audience. Ann wanted to pay tribute to all [8] ______________ movements and honor people who had been denied their rights; pancakes would be her gift! Unfortunately as she turned toward the stove, her dishtowel caught fire.

Exercise B *Decide whether each statement is true or false. Circle* T *or* F, *and explain your answers.*

1. Activity in the courtroom winds down once the session is adjourned.
T / F ________________________________

2. A communicative person is not likely to share ideas.
T / F ________________________________

3. Consequence follows action.
T / F ________________________________

4. An intercepted message is one that does not reach the intended person.
T / F ________________________________

5. A multitude of stars is visible in a clear, night sky.
T / F ________________________________

6. One should take solace in surviving a car accident with minor injuries.
T / F ________________________________

7. A person's heart rate decreases during strenuous exercise.
T / F ________________________________

8. Valor is uncommon among heroes.
T / F ________________________________

Name ______________________ Date ______________

Civil War Diaries, Journals, and Letters

Reading Warm-up A

Read the following passage. Pay special attention to the underlined words. Then, read it again, and complete the activities. Use a separate sheet of paper for your written answers.

At the town square, crowds of excited people gathered and they talked nervously. They knew that a proclamation was going to be made today because it had been reported in all of the newspapers the night before. Although they didn't know exactly what to expect, there were rumors that the announcement would address the recent issues about women's suffrage. The hope was that because of all of the years of discrimination against women, particularly with voting rights, the laws would change and take women's views into account as well.

Several recruits of the newly elected political party walked into the middle of the crowd toward the stage. From the platform, they looked around at the growing number of people and were amazed at the size of the demonstration that had assembled. They never expected so many people to come out in support of this issue. While making final preparations for the announcement, the speech writers were busy adding witty comments to the speeches in order to entertain, as well as inform the people; just because the information was important did not mean that it had to be boring.

The proclamation was made and the speeches were read with passion and commitment. Afterwards, the official notice was posted on the courthouse door for display. Unfortunately, not everyone was pleased with the news. Immediately after the crowd left, an angry man lit the posted document on fire and ran away. A woman who was close to the burning paper extinguished it and the fire was put out as quickly as it had started. She knew that not everyone was happy about the change, but she refused to let it get her down. Even though the new law appeared in tatters on the courthouse door, its message was still valid and hopes were still high about the future.

1. Why would a proclamation bring people together? What is a synonym for *proclamation*?
2. Explain why suffrage is not a good thing. Use *suffrage* in a sentence.
3. Name another group who experienced discrimination during the Civil War. Can *discrimination* ever be a good thing?
4. Why do the recruits probably not have much experience on the job? Have you ever been a *recruit*?
5. Underline the words in the passage that describe the demonstration. Use *demonstration* in a sentence.
6. What types of people are likely to be witty? Is being *witty* a good quality?
7. Circle the words in the sentence that define extinguished. Aside from fire, what else can be *extinguished*?
8. Explain why wearing clothing in tatters to a job interview would be bad. What is a synonym for *tatters*?

Name ______________________________ Date ______________

Civil War Diaries, Journals, and Letters

Reading Warm-up B

Read the following passage. Pay special attention to the underlined words. Then, read it again, and complete the activities. Use a separate sheet of paper for your written answers.

During the Civil War, the art of letter writing was very important. The telephone and the Internet had not been invented yet, therefore, the mail was heavily relied upon. At the time, most people had family members or friends fighting in the war, so receiving a letter from them often brought solace. Sharing news from the letters, neighbors were especially communicative during these times. In order to inform their neighbors of the latest happenings, as well as to try and learn new information from them, people relayed their letters openly in most cases.

Another significance of written correspondence during wartime was that sometimes the letters contained confidential information about upcoming battle plans or other strategic information. If mail could be intercepted from the enemy, it was then taken to the commanders for immediate inspection. The officers would have to decide whether or not they could rely on the information contained in the correspondence. They knew that the letter might have been falsified; acting upon such information could carry a big consequence if the leaders were wrong.

An additional, important function of letter writing was simply for personal reasons. A multitude of letters was written that provides valuable information about the life and times of that era. It is clear from the evidence that letter writing was a priority, perhaps even a strenuous task, as it could become exhausting after hours of printing and scripting.

From reports of war heroes and their valor on the field, to the announcements of a birth or death at home, this information sharing was a valuable and necessary tool. Countless hours were spent writing in order to keep everyone connected to family news and history in the making. Until the war was adjourned forever in the spring of 1865, the art of letter writing was perhaps at its greatest point in our nation's history.

1. Why would receiving a letter bring solace? Name something that typically gives people ***solace***.
2. Why were the neighbors communicative during wartime? Generally speaking, are humans ***communicative*** by nature? Explain.
3. Circle the word in the sentence that helps define intercepted. Aside from mail, what else could be ***intercepted***?
4. What type of consequence might acting upon bad information cause? Can a ***consequence*** ever be a good thing? Why?
5. What type of quantity is a multitude of letters? Use ***multitude*** in a sentence.
6. Why was letter writing such a strenuous task at the time? What other types of activities can be ***strenuous***?
7. Circle the word in the sentence that provides a clue to the meaning of valor. Write a synonym for ***valor***.
8. Why was it a positive thing when the Civil War was adjourned? Use ***adjourned*** in a sentence.

Name ______________________ Date ______________

from **Civil War Diaries, Journals, and Letters**

Literary Analysis: Diaries, Journals, and Letters

Diaries and **journals** are private, personal records of events, communications, and observations, and often reveal a writer's innermost thoughts and feelings. Personal **letters** are also often written in an informal style, since there is usually no intent of publication.

DIRECTIONS: *Complete each item using information from the selection and what you know about diaries, journals, and letters.*

1. Mary Chesnut writes "In addition to our usual quartet (Judge Withers, Langdon Cheves, and Trescot) our two governors dined with us, Means and Manning. These men all talked so delightfully. For once in my life I listened." What information of a personal nature indicates that this excerpt is from a diary or journal? ______________________

2. How is Mary Chesnut's description of sitting on the roof to watch the firing on Fort Sumter typical of information found in a diary or journal? ______________________

3. Much of the first paragraph of "Recollections of a Private" discusses Warren Lee Goss's shaving on the morning he went to enlist. What might you learn about Goss from such a description? ______________________

4. Warren Lee Goss writes "[w]ith a nervous tremor convulsing my system, and my heart thumping like muffled drumbeats, I stood before the door of the recruiting office. . . ." Use a short sentence to describe how Goss felt about enlisting. ______________________

5. Read Warren Lee Goss's description of his first day of drilling in company. What kind of personality do you think Goss had in civilian life? ______________________

6. Randolph McKim's account of the Battle of Gettysburg tells of only one small part of the battle. How is this indicative of a diary or journal? ______________________

7. Stonewall Jackson's letter to his wife tells of a coat. Why doesn't Jackson describe the coat in detail for his wife? ______________________

Name ______________________ Date ______________

from Civil War Diaries, Journals, and Letters

Reading Strategy: Distinguish Fact From Opinion

When reading a diary, journal, or letter, it is important to **distinguish fact from opinion.** You can do this by reading carefully and periodically determining which statements can be verified and which statements reflect the writer's personal views.

DIRECTIONS: *Read the following excerpts from the selection. Each statement contains both fact and opinion. Identify the elements of fact and opinion in each one.*

1. John Manning was pleased as a boy to be on Beauregard's staff while the row goes on.

   Fact: ______________________

   Opinion: ______________________

2. Why did that green goose Anderson go into Fort Sumter?

   Fact: ______________________

   Opinion: ______________________

3. "Get up, you foolish woman—your dress is on fire," cried a man.

   Fact: ______________________

   Opinion: ______________________

4. . . . the flannel shirt was coarse and unpleasant, too large at the neck and too short elsewhere.

   Fact: ______________________

   Opinion: ______________________

5. On swept the gallant little brigade . . .

   Fact: ______________________

   Opinion: ______________________

6. By the strenuous efforts of the officers of the line and of the staff, order was restored . . .

   Fact: ______________________

   Opinion: ______________________

Name ______________________________ Date ______________

from **Civil War Diaries, Journals, and Letters**

Vocabulary Builder

Using the Prefix *ob-*

A. DIRECTIONS: *The prefix* ob- *means "against" or "toward." Each word that follows contains the prefix* ob-. *Given the meaning of the other word part, match the words with their definitions.*

___ **1.** obliterate = *ob* + *littera* "letter"

___ **2.** oblong = *ob* + *longus* "long"

___ **3.** obnoxious = *ob* + *noxa* "harm"

___ **4.** obsequious = *ob* + *sequi* "to follow"

___ **5.** obtain = *ob* + *tenere* "to hold"

A. to get possession of

B. showing a great willingness to serve or obey

C. exposed to injury or evil

D. to blot out or leave no trace

E. longer in one direction than in the other

Using the Word List

capitulate	audaciously	foreboding
obstinate	imprecations	serenity

B. DIRECTIONS: *Circle the synonym for the underlined word in each sentence or phrase.*

1. Anderson will not capitulate. (argue, surrender)
2. Men were more audaciously wise and witty. (noisily, daringly)
3. We had a foreboding that it was to be our last pleasant meeting. (presentiment, pact)
4. If Anderson was **obstinate**—he was to order the forts on our side to open fire. (stupid, stubborn)
5. . . . if anything, more unruffled than usual in his serenity. . . . (calmness, dress)

C. DIRECTIONS: *For each item, choose the word pair that best expresses a relationship similar to that expressed in the numbered pair. Circle the letter of your choice.*

1. FOREBODING : EMOTION ::

   A. buyer : consumer

   B. headache : pain

   C. style : manner

   D. prologue : epilogue

2. FLEXIBLE : OBSTINATE::

   A. table : chair

   B. serene : quiet

   C. ecstatic : depressed

   D. invisible: fog

Name ______________________ Date ______________

from Civil War Diaries, Journals, and Letters

Grammar and Style: Capitalization of Proper Nouns

The capitalization of proper nouns helps the reader easily identify particular persons, places, things, or ideas. When a proper noun consists of more than one word, capitalize each word except articles, coordinating conjunctions, and prepositions with fewer than four letters.

Examples:

General Ewell's order [specific person]
the crest of Culp's Hill [specific place]
remnant of the Third North Carolina [specific thing]

A. Practice: *Rewrite each proper noun with correct capitalization. If there is no proper noun, write* none.

1. People rejoiced when they heard the emancipation proclamation. ______________
2. Many soldiers died in the battle of gettysburg. ______________
3. The general's troops camped along a river. ______________
4. Shells burst over fort sumter. ______________
5. General ulysses s. grant gave the order. ______________

B. Writing Application: *Rewrite each sentence to replace each underlined common noun with a proper noun. Your proper nouns can be real or imaginary people, places, or things. Be sure to capitalize the proper nouns correctly.*

1. The war caused great suffering to the civilian population.

   ____

2. Inhabitants of the city lacked food and other supplies.

   ____

3. Each morning, the newspaper announced the most recent casualties.

   ____

4. The president struggled to make the right decision.

   ____

5. The book is a fictionalized account of a spy's activities.

   ____

Name ______________________________ Date ______________

from **Civil War Diaries, Journals, and Letters**

Support for Writing

To prepare for writing an **essay** on the value of keeping a journal or writing letters today, enter information in the graphic organizer below.

Value of Journals/Letters

Personal Benefits: Journals can be passed down through family.	**My ideas:** ______________
Historical value: History is documented for society at large.	**My ideas:** ______________
Loss from No Journals/Letters: Valuable information can be lost forever.	**My ideas:** ______________

On a separate page, write a draft of your essay, beginning with an introduction. Write a paragraph about each of your ideas related to the value of journals and letters. As you revise, be sure your personal reflections are connected with the main ideas you have expressed.

Name ______________________________ Date ______________

from **Civil War Diaries, Journals, and Letters**

Support for Extend Your Learning

Listening and Speaking

Reread the "Emancipation Proclamation" in preparation for a **dramatic reading** of the document. Find music to accompany your reading that provides the mood you want. Follow these tips:

- Read main points with emotion for emphasis.
- Make eye contact or use hand gestures that convey power or determination.

Present your reading to your classmates and ask for feedback.

Research and Technology

Do Internet research on the Battle of Gettysburg in preparation for creating a **model or map** of the battlefield. Use the space below to mark the locations of key events, identify military leaders, and enter captions that describe what took place. If you need more room, use another sheet of paper.

The Battle of Gettysburg

Name ______________________ Date ______________

from **Civil War Diaries, Journals, and Letters**

Enrichment: Journals

Journals and other personal accounts often recount events or details omitted from more formal accounts. For example, "Recollections of a Private" tells you something about Civil War soldiers and the uniforms they wore. Other photographs show officers and enlisted men in battle. You can gain insight from both the photographs and the journal, but the journal tells you more about the enlisted man as a person.

DIRECTIONS: *Consider what you have learned about the Civil War through reading materials in history classes. Then think of what you have just read in these examples of diaries, journals, and letters. List in the following chart at least eight things you learned from them that you could not get from more formal histories.*

Source	Insight About Civil War
1.	
2.	
3.	
4.	
5.	
6.	
7.	
8.	

Name ______________________ Date ______________

from Civil War Diaries, Journals, and Letters

Selection Test A

Critical Reading *Identify the letter of the choice that best answers the question.*

____ **1.** Which historical event is the context for the selection from *Mary Chesnut's Civil War?*

A. the promotion of her husband to Beauregard's aide-de-camp

B. the attack on Fort Sumter that started the Civil War

C. the election of Davis as president of the Confederacy

D. the demand that Fort Sumter's commander surrender

____ **2.** Which of the following passages from *Mary Chesnut's Civil War* is an opinion?

A. "My husband has been made an aide-de-camp of General Beauregard."

B. "Now he tells me the attack upon Fort Sumter may begin tonight."

C. "Lincoln or Seward have made such silly advances. . ."

D. "Today Miles and Manning, colonels now . . . dine with us."

____ **3.** How does this quotation from *Mary Chesnut's Civil War* reflect the style of a journal:

"Had telegraphed to President Davis for instructions. What answer to give Anderson, etc., etc."?

A. It has information about her husband.

B. It uses people's titles.

C. It gives military information.

D. It uses incomplete sentences.

____ **4.** According to "Recollections of a Private," what do the recruitment posters promise soldiers?

A. the opportunity to fight for one's country

B. travel and promotion

C. a fine, new uniform

D. training in the use of weapons

____ **5.** In "Recollections of a Private," what part of being a soldier does Private Goss find difficult?

A. taking care of his uniform

B. drilling in formation

C. learning how to shoot

D. living with danger

Name ______________________________ Date ______________

____ **6.** Which words in this passage from "A Confederate Account of the Battle of Gettysburg" identify it as an opinion:

"On they pressed . . . a small but gallant band of heroes daring to attempt what could not be done by flesh and blood. The end came soon. We were beaten."?

A. flesh and blood

B. We were beaten.

C. The end came soon.

D. gallant band of heroes

____ **7.** Which part of "An Account of the Battle of Bull Run" helps identify it as a personal letter?

A. Jackson's description of his wound

B. Jackson's use of his wife's nickname

C. Jackson's praise of God

D. Jackson's description of the battle

____ **8.** In "An Account of the Battle of Bull Run," why doesn't Jackson want his acts made public?

A. He is ashamed.

B. He is proud.

C. He is humble.

D. He wants peace.

____ **9.** Which statement from "Reaction to the Emancipation Proclamation" can be proved as a fact?

A. The cheering as Turner ran down the street was very loud.

B. The Proclamation was printed in the *Evening Star* newspaper.

C. Mr. Hinton read the Proclamation with great force and clearness.

D. Nothing like it would ever be seen again in Turner's lifetime.

____ **10.** What does "An Account of an Experience with Discrimination" reveal about Sojourner Truth?

A. She was easily made afraid of whites.

B. She was capable of defending herself.

C. She disliked streetcar conductors.

D. She avoided standing up for her rights.

Name ______________________ Date ______________

Vocabulary and Grammar

____ 11. In which sentence is the meaning of the word *capitulate* suggested?
A. Mary Chesnut watched the battle of Fort Sumter from her home.
B. The fort's commander Anderson refused to surrender at first.
C. Mary Chesnut continued to entertain guests during the battle.
D. Chesnut was relieved that no one was injured in the battle.

____ 12. Which sentence contains correct capitalization?
A. "Wigfall was with them on morris island."
B. "Today Miles and Manning dined with us."
C. "They congratulated president lincoln."
D. "i had him arrested."

Essay

13. In Warren Lee Goss's "Recollections of a Private," how does the writer compare civilian life with military life? Write a brief essay about Goss's recollections. Use at least one example of civilian life and one example of military life from Private Goss's statements.

14. In "A Confederate Account of the Battle of Gettysburg," Randolph McKim says: "It remains only to say that . . . this single brigade was hurled unsupported against the enemy's works . . . Of course it is to be presumed that General Daniel acted in obedience to orders." What do you think McKim is trying to say? Write a brief statement that says, in a more direct way, what you think McKim is implying in this passage.

Name ______________________________ Date ______________

***from* Civil War Diaries, Journals, and Letters**

Selection Test B

Critical Reading *Identify the letter of the choice that best completes the statement or answers the question.*

____ **1.** Which is the main impression created by the passage from *Mary Chesnut's Civil War*?
A. Life must go on, even during war.
B. War is frightening but exciting.
C. All good men must defend the North.
D. The South should not have seceded.

____ **2.** Which excerpt from "Recollections of a Private" presents a fact?
A. "I was taught my facings . . ."
B. "I thought the drillmaster needlessly fussy . . ."
C. "The musket . . . seemed heavier . . . than it had looked to be . . ."
D. "no wisdom was equal to a drillmaster's . . ."

____ **3.** In "Reaction to the Emancipation Proclamation," how did the people of Washington, D.C., react to the news of the Proclamation?
A. with fear
B. with suspense
C. with excitement
D. with disgust

____ **4.** A fact is different from an opinion because a fact ________.
A. is a statement
B. can be false
C. can be proved
D. is a personal judgment

____ **5.** Sojourner Truth experienced difficulty in riding streetcars because she was ________.
A. African American
B. female
C. elderly
D. stubborn

____ **6.** Which of the following excerpts most clearly reflects the style of a journal?
A. "The convention has adjourned."
B. "Why did that green goose Anderson go into Fort Sumter?"
C. "Fort Sumter had surrendered."
D. "The Herald says that this show of war outside of the bar is intended for Texas."

____ **7.** What might be assumed about a letter that is not assumed about a journal?
A. that the intended reader knows background information about the writer
B. that no one except the writer will read the work
C. that the writer intends the work to be published eventually
D. that the work contains only opinions

Name ______________________ Date ______________

____ 8. Which statement is an opinion?
A. Then came General Ewell's order to assume the offensive.
B. We were exposed to enfilading fire.
C. Its nerve and spirit were undiminished.
D. The enemy did not make a countercharge.

____ 9. What in her journal tells you that Chesnut dislikes war?
A. her subjective descriptions of events and people
B. her direct statements of opinion
C. her excitement about watching the firing on Fort Sumter
D. her use of quotations

____ 10. Which phrase in the following statement expresses an opinion?
Mr. Hinton, to whom I handed the paper, read it with great force and clearness.
A. Mr. Hinton
B. to whom I handed the paper
C. read it
D. read it with great force and clearness

____ 11. In "Recollections of a Private," enlisted man Goss probably first looked upon enlisting in the war as
A. a serious and terrifying endeavor.
B. an opportunity to take part in military drills.
C. a patriotic adventure with opportunities for travel and promotion.
D. a chance to see Washington, D.C.

____ 12. In "Reaction to the Emancipation Proclamation," Reverend Henry M. Turner believes the issuance of President Lincoln's Emancipation Proclamation is
A. a high point of the nation's history.
B. a political move to increase Lincoln's popularity.
C. important only to African Americans.
D. important only to people in the Union.

____ 13. A journal is most like what other literary form?
A. novel
B. diary
C. short story
D. biography

Name ______________________________ Date ______________

Vocabulary and Grammar

____ 14. Which of the following actions might a soldier perform if the soldier behaved *audaciously*?
A. drill procedures over and over again
B. rush shooting into an enemy line
C. refuse to wear a poorly tailored uniform
D. get wounded during heavy fire

____ 15. Which of the following actions is characteristic of an *obstinate* person?
A. reacts calmly
B. refuses to surrender
C. curses aloud
D. fights boldly

____ 16. In discussing the case tried before Justice Thompson, why is "Justice Thompson" capitalized?
A. It contains a first and last name.
B. It contains a title used before a last name.
C. It is a particular place (building).
D. It is a particular court.

____ 17. Colonel Chesnut is described as a man who is characterized by *serenity*. This type of man would be most likely to ________.
A. speak softly and calmly
B. speak audaciously
C. partake in foreboding silence
D. shout imprecations

Essay

18. Each of these Civil War diaries, journals, or letters recounts at least one conflict related to the Civil War. These include external conflicts, such as military battles, as well as internal conflicts that take place within those who may not actually be engaged in battle but are still "at war." Describe the internal and external conflicts revealed in at least two of the selections you have read.

19. The styles of personal writing in "Recollections of a Private" by Warren Lee Goss and in "A Confederate Account of the Battle of Gettysburg" by Randolph McKim are very different. Describe the similarities and differences in the writing styles, supporting your explanation with details from the two works.

20. Compare and contrast two of the characters you learned about in the selections. For example, you may choose to compare a Union soldier with a Confederate soldier or a white northerner with an African American northerner. Explain the characteristics and concerns they share, and explain how their lives are different. Use details from the selection to support your explanation.

Name ______________________________ Date ______________

Unit 4: Division, Reconciliation, and Expansion

Benchmark Test 5

MULTIPLE CHOICE

Literary Analysis and Reading Skills

1. Imagine you are handed a magazine article called "Uncovering Hidden Biographical Treasures in the Poems of Emily Dickinson." What would be your purpose in reading the article?

A. to understand more about Dickinson's life in relationship to the content of her poetry
B. to find out why Emily Dickinson used odd punctuation
C. to test a theory about why Dickinson's poems are usually short in length
D. to determine whether Dickinson really existed

2. What would you expect "Uncovering Hidden Biographical Treasures in the Poems of Emily Dickinson" to express?

A. mostly facts
B. mostly opinions
C. equal number of facts and opinions
D. either facts or opinions

Read the selection. Then, answer the questions that follow.

A Letter to John Adams, 1796

Dear Sir—The public and the public papers have been much occupied lately in placing us in a point of opposition to each other. I trust with confidence that less of it has been felt by ourselves personally . . . I knew it impossible you should lose a vote North of the Delaware, and even if that of Pennsylvania should be against you in the mass, yet that you would get enough South of that to place your succession out of danger . . .

Thomas Jefferson

3. How might recognizing historical details help the reader's comprehension of this selection?

A. The reader might learn personal information about the life of the writer.
B. The reader might learn outmoded vocabulary.
C. The reader might learn about the selection's social and political context.
D. The reader might learn about contemporary ideas and beliefs.

4. What would be the best purpose for reading this selection?

A. to learn what historians think of Jefferson and Adams
B. to decide which man was a better writer
C. to decide which man contributed more to the founding of the country
D. to compare the political beliefs of Jefferson and Adams

Name ______________________________ Date ______________

5. Which is the best definition of diction?
   A. the dictionary definitions of the words an author uses
   B. the writer's choice of sentence structure and length
   C. the sound and pattern of the words
   D. a writer's choice and arrangement of words

6. What background knowledge would best help you understand the following sentences?

   The Northern soldiers ached for home. They were restless and angry. Was this Union really worth it?
   A. the reason the soldiers were in a war
   B. the type of family members they had left behind
   C. each soldier's rank
   D. the geography of the region

7. Why is listening a particularly important skill in appreciating song lyrics and poetry?
   A. They are particularly difficult to understand.
   B. They are intended to be heard.
   C. They are filled with interesting words.
   D. They have various types of rhyme and rhythm.

8. Which part of a song or poem is most likely to express its theme?
   A. introduction
   B. middle verses
   C. coda
   D. refrain

9. Chronological order is associated with which of the following?
   A. space
   B. distance
   C. position
   D. time

10. Which of the following would you expect to be organized in chronological order?
   A. directions for assembling a chair
   B. trip itinerary
   C. journal entry
   D. character sketch

11. How are the nineteenth-century literary movements Realism and Naturalism similar?
   A. They both have a great deal in common with Romanticism.
   B. They both portray the lives of ordinary people.
   C. They both had little influence on the literary movements that followed.
   D. They both have more interest in characters' motivations than in outward appearances.

Name ______________________________ Date ______________

12. How do Realism and Naturalism differ?
   A. Realism is more accurate than Naturalism.
   B. Realism generally depicts ordinary people and Naturalism is more concerned with extraordinary people.
   C. Realism is less optimistic than Naturalism.
   D. Realism depicts everyday reality and Naturalism focuses on helplessness in the face of chance.

Read the selection. Then, answer the questions that follow.

I was born in Tuckahow, near Hillsborough, and about twelve miles from Easton, in Talbot county, Maryland. I have no accurate knowledge of my age, never having seen any authentic record containing it. By far the larger part of the slaves know as little of their ages as horses know of theirs, and it is the wish of most masters within my knowledge to keep their slaves thus ignorant.

from *Narrative of the Life of Frederick Douglass: An American Slave, written by Himself*

13. What genre is the selection?
   A. biography
   B. autobiography
   C. science fiction
   D. historical fiction

14. Which of the following best describes the author's diction?
   A. quite abstract
   B. very casual
   C. rather formal
   D. extremely emotional

15. Which of the following statements most accurately characterizes the selection?
   A. The selection contains both facts and opinions.
   B. The selection contains factual material only.
   C. The selection contains opinions only.
   D. The selection is mostly made up.

16. Which of the following items is the most objective?
   A. score on a multiple choice exam
   B. response to a marketing survey
   C. book review
   D. polling data

17. Which type of beliefs are generally the most difficult to identify?
   A. stated
   B. implicit
   C. explicit
   D. objective

18. Of what point of view is this sentence an example?

While Janis dreamed of nothing more than fame and Marla was obsessed by her looks, Kayley wanted more than anything merely to blend in.

A. limited first person
B. limited third person
C. omniscient first person
D. omniscient third person

19. In which point of view is the narrator an objective observer?

A. omniscient
B. limited third person
C. first person
D. omniscient third person

Vocabulary

20. Based on your knowledge of the root *-greg-*, what is the meaning of *congregation*?

A. an injured farm animal
B. a group of children crowding around a painting
C. a couple taking a stroll around the lake
D. a man watching a large fire on the mountains

21. What is the meaning of the word root shared by the words *compress* and *impress*?

A. decrease
B. embellish
C. push
D. show

22. What is the meaning of the word *summation* in the following sentence?

The attorney wrapped up her argument with a summation of the case in favor of her client.

A. specific details
B. overview
C. mathematical equation
D. professional concern

23. Based on your knowledge of the root *-bene-*, what is the meaning of *beneficial*?

A. knowledgeable
B. confident
C. merciful
D. advantageous

Name ______________________________ Date ______________

24. Based on the meaning of the Latin prefix *-ob-*, what is the meaning of *objectionable*?
   A. hard to move
   B. squeamish
   C. unbiased
   D. offensive

Grammar *Choose the correct word to fill in the blank.*

25. Ray ran quickly, __________ a man being chased.
   A. like
   B. as though
   C. as if
   D. as

26. Do __________ I tell you!
   A. like
   B. as though
   C. as if
   D. as

27. Moving through the woods rapidly __________ found the others in the group in an hour.
   A. Nicole
   B. Nicole,
   C. , Nicole,
   D. , Nicole

28. __________ Dana __________ her sister had yet taken the driving course.
   A. Either . . . or
   B. Neither . . . nor
   C. Not only . . . but
   D. Just as . . . so

29. __________ the band __________ the orchestra will be playing at the graduation, we haven't yet decided which would be best.
   A. either . . . or
   B. neither . . . nor
   C. not only . . . but
   D. whether . . . or

30. The students asked to have the prom date changed __________ were several conflicts on that day.
   A. : there
   B. ; there
   C. , there
   D. - there

Name ______________________ Date ______________

31. The cat slid over the floor, climbed on the coach and _________ onto the window sill.
   A. is jumping
   B. had jumped
   C. jumps
   D. jumped

32. Which of the following statements is true of correlative conjunctions?
   A. They are not really conjunctions.
   B. They are always used in pairs.
   C. They join elements of unlike classes.
   D. They join like conjunctions.

33. Which of the following is a proper noun?
   A. a person's name
   B. a direction
   C. weather
   D. branch of service

ESSAY

34. Write a field report. To prepare, take notes as you observe an aspect of nature directly. Be as detailed and accurate as possible. Then, write up your notes. Present your observations in a logical, well-organized manner, and leave out your opinions.

35. Think of a life-altering experience. What was it? How did it change you? Write a reflective essay in which you think deeply about a significant experience and help readers understand why it was so important to you.

36. Respond to the following question from a college application:

    You have been approached to write your autobiography. Explain at what point you would begin your autobiography and at what point you would end it. Discuss the reasons that you would choose these points.

37. Critique a short story or a poem. Explain clearly what you do and do not like about the piece you select, and use copious examples and quotations to back up your opinions.

38. Step back in time and participate in a momentous event. Invent a diary entry that describes both the event and its importance, as well as your feelings about it. Make sure readers understand which event you are writing about it and why it is important.

Name ______________________________ Date ______________

Unit 4: Division, Reconciliation, and Expansion

Diagnostic Test 6

MULTIPLE CHOICE

Read the selection. Then, answer the questions that follow.

Poetry existed long before the written word. In the earliest civilizations, verse was used to immortalize heroism and to pay tribute to historical leaders and events. Additionally, many of the ancient world's religious writings consist of poetry rather than prose.

Some scholars believe that poetry had its beginnings in song. Rhythm, rhyme, and repetition may have been introduced as a way to fit words into musical forms to inspire and delight listeners with sounds, patterns, and choruses. Certainly, rhyme and repetition also helped the reciter reconstruct poems from memory.

Originally, poetry was composed for, and even during, performances before an audience. That meant that the exact wording of poems could change from one presenter to another, and from one performance to another. After written language was introduced, poems were deemed finished in whatever version was written down.

Once poets began to compose their works on paper, for an absent reader, poems became more personal. Instead of writing narrative poems about heroes, gods, and important events, poets began to write about feelings, personal experiences, and the sights and sounds of nature. Through sensory images that appealed to readers' senses of sight, sound, and touch, poets enabled readers to picture the described scenes, hear specific sounds, and share the poets' emotions and experiences.

1. According to the selection, which of the following would have been a likely topic for an ancient poem?
   A. the love between a mother and her child
   B. the story of a great warrior
   C. the beauty of a spring morning
   D. a frisky or mischievous dog

2. According to the selection, how are poems and songs alike?
   A. Both were used to express ancient religious doctrines.
   B. Both forms never changed when presented.
   C. Both contain rhythm and rhyme.
   D. Both contain narratives about heroes and gods.

3. Which of the following helps reciters reconstruct poems from memory?
   A. theme
   B. sensory images
   C. prose
   D. repetition

4. Why did the exact wording of an early poem often change, from presenter to presenter or from performance to performance?
   A. Without a written poem, each person tried to improve and refine the poem.
   B. Many poems contained sounds, patterns, and choruses.
   C. The presenter often composed the poem during the performance.
   D. Most poems paid tribute to historical leaders.

Name ______________________ Date ______________

5. How did the introduction of written language affect early poems?
   A. The poems began to contain more repetition.
   B. A poem was less likely to change once it was written down.
   C. A poem was more likely to resemble a song once it was written down.
   D. A poem usually became longer once it was written down.

6. How did the topics and themes of poems change, once poets began to compose them on paper?
   A. The poems began to tell about heroes and gods.
   B. The poems became shorter, with fewer rhymes.
   C. The poems became more personal, about feelings and nature.
   D. The poems became more musical, with patterns and choruses.

7. What did the use of sensory images help poets to do?
   A. create patterns and choruses
   B. share specific sights and sounds with readers
   C. entertain the reader with noble stories
   D. change the exact wording of groups of poems

Read the selection. Then, answer the questions that follow.

Although William Shakespeare based his famous tragedy *Macbeth* on a real Scottish king by that name, he included details, such as witches, and attributed actions and character traits to Macbeth that are not historically accurate. Shakespeare's Macbeth and his queen are ruthless murderers driven by ambition. They kill their first victim, King Duncan, while he sleeps, and proceed to kill all others who stand in their path to the throne.

Records kept by eleventh-century monks indicate that the real King Duncan died after an invasion, from a wound that he received during a battle. Macbeth may or may not have delivered the fatal blow, but he certainly was not a traitor who murdered his sleeping king. In addition, the real Lady Macbeth was innocent of any wrongdoing.

Naturally, there are no reports of the real Macbeth associating with witches. Neither are there indications that he killed anyone challenging his right to the throne. By all accounts, he ruled a united Scotland for seventeen prosperous years.

Macbeth was hailed as a great king at the time of his death, but his reputation for peace and harmony has almost completely vanished. Thanks to the vivid character created by Shakespeare, Macbeth is remembered erroneously as a warrior corrupted by his desire for power.

8. On what did Shakespeare base his famous tragedy *Macbeth*?
   A. the murder of a Scottish king
   B. events that witches envisioned, long before they actually took place
   C. an ancient myth about a king's desire for absolute power
   D. a real Scottish king named Macbeth

9. Which words most accurately describe Shakespeare's characters Macbeth and Lady Macbeth?
   A. peaceful rulers
   B. benevolent spirits
   C. ruthless murderers
   D. dishonest cowards

Name ______________________________ Date ______________

10. What force drove the actions of Shakespeare's Macbeth?

A. ambition
B. patriotism
C. romantic love
D. loyalty

11. Which statement is true about the real King Duncan and Shakespeare's King Duncan?

A. Both were murdered while they slept.
B. Both were wounded in battle.
C. Both came to power illegitimately.
D. Both ruled before Macbeth came to power.

12. From what source can scholars gather information on the real King Duncan and Macbeth?

A. Shakespeare's play
B. the diaries of Lady Macbeth
C. the journals of Scottish witches
D. the records of early monks

13. Why does the author state that "Naturally, there are no reports of the real Macbeth associating with witches"?

A. Witches are fictitious characters.
B. Shakespeare was famous for writing about witches and ghosts.
C. Witches live in England, but not in Scotland.
D. Macbeth was known to avoid witches whenever possible.

14. What statement is true about the real Macbeth?

A. Records indicate that he killed King Duncan, but it was an accident.
B. Records indicate that he killed competitors in order to become king.
C. Records indicate that he was at one time a monk.
D. Records indicate that he ruled Scotland for seventeen years.

15. How has Shakespeare's play led to misconceptions about the real Macbeth?

A. People believe that Macbeth ruled in Scotland.
B. People believe that Macbeth killed King Duncan.
C. People believe that Macbeth was a good person.
D. People believe that Macbeth was corrupted by a desire for power.

Selections by Mark Twain

Vocabulary Warm-up Word Lists

Study these words from the selections. Then, complete the activities.

Word List A

compliance [kum PLY ans] *n.* the act of following another's commands or wishes
Asking nicely often leads to more willing compliance than making demands.

contribution [kahn tri BYOO shun] *n.* something that is given
The charity mailed us a letter asking for a contribution of twenty dollars.

deliberate [de LIB er uht] *adj.* careful and slow
The old dog moves in a more deliberate way than she did as a puppy.

humbly [HUM blee] *adv.* in a meek and modest way
"Could you possibly give me your autograph?" the boy asked humbly.

monotonous [muh NAH tuh nus] *adj.* boring; dull; too much the same
That show is getting monotonous; let's change the channel.

narrative [NAR uh tiv] *n.* story
We looked at the snapshots as we listened to the narrative of their vacation.

sociable [SOH shuh bul] *adj.* pleasant and friendly in company
Lou is sociable, so she's always a hit at parties.

withstand [with STAND] *v.* successfully resist
Few people can withstand the aroma of freshly baked bread.

Word List B

conspicuous [kun SPIK yoo us] *adj.* easy to notice; standing out
Joe felt conspicuous walking down the street in a gorilla suit.

grandeur [GRAN jur] *n.* magnificence or splendor
The grandeur of the enormous palace took her breath away.

impressive [im PRES iv] *adj.* making a strong effect
Most tourists find the Grand Canyon a very impressive sight.

indifferent [in DIF er int] *adj.* having no strong feeling for or against
I love ice cream, but I feel indifferent about rice pudding.

loathe [LOHTH] *v.* hate intensely
Our cats loathe going to the veterinarian for their shots.

ruthless [ROOTH les] *adj.* having no compassion or pity
The gods of Greek mythology could be ruthless toward humans.

tranquil [TRAYN kwil] *adj.* calm or peaceful
We enjoyed a quiet picnic on the shore of the tranquil lake.

transient [TRAN zee int] *adj.* not permanent
Her interest in stamps was transient; now she collects dolls instead.

Name ______________________ Date ______________

Selections by Mark Twain

Vocabulary Warm-up Exercises

Exercise A *Fill in each blank in the paragraph below with the appropriate word from Word List A.*

Last night, my best friend called me and told me this [1] ______________ about a school dance. "I didn't really want to go," my friend said. "You know me—I'm not that [2] ______________, and I feel awkward in big groups. My sister was on the committee, though, and she asked so [3] ______________ that I could not [4] ______________ her. You'd think it was enough that she had won my [5] ______________ about showing up, but no! She insisted that I had to dance, too. Well, I have to admit it was a little [6] ______________ just standing around, so I agreed. I thought I was doing pretty well, concentrating hard on getting all the steps right, but my sister laughed at me and said it looked silly to dance in such a [7] ______________ way. Can you believe that? Next time she asks me to make a [8] ______________ by participating in something she plans, I am definitely saying no!"

Exercise B *Answer the following questions with complete explanations.*

1. What sort of person would most dislike being <u>conspicuous</u>?

____

2. If you were buying a house, would you look for comfort or <u>grandeur</u>? Why?

____

3. What makes a big thunderstorm <u>impressive</u>?

____

4. If you felt <u>indifferent</u> about sports, would you watch the whole Super Bowl?

____

5. Why do you think so many children <u>loathe</u> bedtime?

____

6. Would someone who is <u>ruthless</u> be likely to work in a soup kitchen?

____

7. Does carrying a cell phone make a person's life more <u>tranquil</u>?

____

8. Which is usually more <u>transient</u>, a regular student or an exchange student?

____

Name ______________________________ Date ______________

Selections by Mark Twain

Reading Warm-up A

Read the following passage. Pay special attention to the underlined words. Then, read it again, and complete the activities. Use a separate sheet of paper for your written answers.

"An American loves his family," the inventor Thomas Edison once wrote. "If he has any love left over for some other person, he generally selects Mark Twain."

Mark Twain—the pen name of Samuel Langhorne Clemens—was a huge celebrity during his life. People loved him not just for the many books, which were his <u>contribution</u> to American literature, but for his sense of humor. When he appeared in public, reporters crowded around, hoping Clemens would make a funny remark about current events in his famous slow, <u>deliberate</u> drawl. (About the death of one public figure, he said, "I didn't attend the funeral, but I sent a nice letter saying I approved of it.")

Outgoing, <u>sociable</u>, and not particularly modest, Clemens enjoyed his popularity. Though he sometimes found the endless round of dinners and events <u>monotonous</u>, he loved being the center of attention. Still, he poked fun at his own inability to accept fame <u>humbly</u>. Compliments, he said, "always embarrass me—I always feel that they have not said enough."

Clemens refused to take seriously anything he thought was foolish, such as the expectations of polite society. However, he adored his gentle, well-bred wife, Olivia, and tried to behave "properly" in <u>compliance</u> with her wishes. Often his efforts failed, as this <u>narrative</u> shows: One day, Clemens returned from a brief visit to their neighbor, the writer Harriet Beecher Stowe. Greeting him, his wife was horrified to see that he'd forgotten to put on a tie. Unable to <u>withstand</u> her pleading, he went straight up to his room in search of a tie. When he found one, he sent it over to Stowe's house. Attached was a note explaining that the rest of him had come to finish the visit.

1. Circle the word that tells what Twain's <u>contribution</u> to American literature was. What else could be a ***contribution*** to literature?

2. Circle the word that means something similar to <u>deliberate</u>. What would be the opposite of a ***deliberate*** way of speaking?

3. Circle the word that means almost the same as <u>sociable</u>. Do you think being ***sociable*** is an advantage for a celebrity?

4. Underline what Clemens found <u>monotonous</u>. What is a word that means the opposite of ***monotonous***?

5. Circle the word that tells what Clemens did not accept <u>humbly</u>. Then, tell what ***humbly*** means.

6. Underline what Clemens tried to do in <u>compliance</u> with his wife's wishes. What other type of person might require ***compliance***?

7. Circle the paragraph that is a <u>narrative</u> about a tie. If it never really happened, would it still be a ***narrative***?

8. Underline what Clemens could not <u>withstand</u>. What else might someone not be able to ***withstand***?

Name ______________________________ Date ______________

Selections by Mark Twain

Reading Warm-up B

Read the following passage. Pay special attention to the underlined words. Then, read it again, and complete the activities. Use a separate sheet of paper for your written answers.

When young Samuel Clemens decided to become a riverboat pilot, he imagined it would be an easy occupation. He pictured himself steering the boat down the wide Mississippi River, passing the time between ports gazing out in awe, admiring the river's grandeur.

In fact, the job proved to be anything but easy; as Clemens soon discovered, being a riverboat pilot required an impressive store of knowledge. A pilot needed to recognize every landmark for twelve hundred miles, by day or by night, and these often turned out to be transient. For instance, a tall old tree might topple over, and then there would be no more landmark.

The river that had looked so tranquil when Clemens was a passenger, he found, was actually filled with hidden hazards. To an ordinary passenger, a "faint dimple" on the water's surface might be practically invisible; to a trained pilot, it was as conspicuous as a red flag, warning that a jagged rock or wrecked boat lay below.

Clemens quickly learned to loathe some of the less romantic aspects of his job, such as being awoken in the middle of the night to take over at the helm. The chief pilot, too, could be ruthless in his mockery of the inexperienced young man. "The idea of you being a pilot—*you*!" he once told Clemens. "Why, you don't know enough to pilot a cow down a lane." Despite these setbacks, Clemens continued to work hard at mastering his trade, and at last he was accepted as a riverboat pilot. Though he realized he had become rather indifferent to the scenic beauty of the Mississippi, he had gained as much as he had lost, for he had learned to read the river—"a wonderful book," he wrote, with "a new story to tell each day."

1. Circle two words that suggest that grandeur is something good. Then, tell what *grandeur* means.
2. Underline an example of the impressive knowledge needed by a pilot. What makes it so *impressive*?
3. Circle an example of a transient landmark. What other kind of landmark might be *transient*?
4. Underline the words that tell you that the river is not as tranquil as it appears. What could be *tranquil* besides a river?
5. Underline what was as conspicuous as a red flag to a pilot. Describe something that would be *conspicuous* in a classroom.
6. Underline what Clemens came to loathe about his job. Then, give a word that is the opposite of *loathe*.
7. Circle a word that tells you that ruthless is probably something bad. How would the chief pilot's behavior change if he were not *ruthless*?
8. Underline what Clemens was indifferent to. Then, tell what *indifferent* means.

Name ______________________________ Date ______________

"The Boys' Ambition" ***from*** **Life on the Mississippi** and **"The Notorious Jumping Frog of Calaveras County"** by Mark Twain

Literary Analysis: Humor

Humor in literature is writing that is intended to evoke laughter. Western American humorists use a variety of techniques to make their writing amusing. Mark Twain, for example, commonly uses exaggeration, regional dialects, and colorful metaphors.

DIRECTIONS: *Decide whether the following passages are humorous because they contain exaggeration, dialect, colorful metaphor, or a combination of these elements. Write your answer on the lines following each passage.*

1. "He was the curiousest man about always betting on anything that turned up you ever see. . . ."

   ____

   ____

2. "If he even see a straddle bug start to go anywheres, he would bet you how long it would take him to get to . . . wherever . . . and if you took him up, he would foller that straddle bug to Mexico. . . ."

   ____

   ____

3. " . . . and *always* fetch up at the stand just about a neck ahead, as near as you could cipher it down."

   ____

   ____

4. 'He'd spring straight up and snake a fly off'n a counter there, and flop down on the floor ag'in as solid as a gob of mud."

   ____

   ____

Name ______________________ Date ______________

"The Boys' Ambition" ***from*** **Life on the Mississippi** and **"The Notorious Jumping Frog of Calaveras County"** by Mark Twain

Reading Strategy: Understand Regional Dialect

Regional dialect is the informal language people use in everyday speech. Sometimes fiction writers use regional dialect to give readers a picture of certain characters. If you find it hard to understand this language, when you're reading, try reading it aloud.

DIRECTIONS: *Read the following excerpts from "The Notorious Jumping Frog of Calaveras County." Write in your own words what you think each one means.*

1. ". . . he was the curiousest man about always betting on anything that turned up you ever see, if he could get anybody to bet on the other side; and if he couldn't he'd change sides."

____

____

____

2. "Thish-yer Smiley had a mare—the boys called her the fifteen-minute nag, but that was only in fun, you know, because of course she was faster than that—and he used to win money on that horse, for all she was so slow and always had the asthma, or the distemper, or the consumption, or something of that kind."

____

____

____

3. ". . . to look at him you'd think he warn't worth a cent but to set around and look ornery and lay for a chance to steal something. But as soon as money was up on him he was a different dog; his under-jaw'd begin to stick out like the fo'castle of a steamboat, and his teeth would uncover and shine like the furnaces."

____

____

____

4. ". . . all of a sudden he would grab that other dog jest by the j'int of his hind leg and freeze to it—not chaw, you understand, but only just grip and hang on till they throwed up the sponge, if it was a year."

____

____

____

Name ______________________________ Date ______________

"The Boys' Ambition" ***from*** **Life on the Mississippi** and **"The Notorious Jumping Frog of Calaveras County"** by Mark Twain

Vocabulary Builder

Using the Prefix *mono-*

A. DIRECTIONS: *The prefix* mono- *means "alone," "single," or "one." Use the clues given and what you know about the prefix* mono- *to figure out these word puzzles.*

1. knowing two languages = *bilingual;*
   knowing one language = ______________________________
2. paralysis of one side of the body = *hemiplegia;*
   paralysis of a single limb = ______________________________
3. a word with four or more syllables = *polysyllable*
   a word with one syllable = ______________________________
4. having three of one type of chromosome = *trisomic*
   having a single chromosome = ______________________________

Using the Word List

transient	prodigious	eminence	garrulous
conjectured	monotonous	interminable	ornery

B. DIRECTIONS: *In the blank, write the letter of the Word List word that is closest in meaning to the numbered word.*

___ 1. guessed	A. transient
___ 2. celebrity	B. prodigious
___ 3. temporary	C. monotonous
___ 4. bad tempered	D. conjectured
___ 5. talkative	E. ornery
___ 6. unvarying	F. interminable
___ 7. enormous	G. garrulous
___ 8. endless	H. eminence

Name ____ Date ____________________

"The Boys' Ambition" ***from*** **Life on the Mississippi** and **"The Notorious Jumping Frog of Calaveras County"** by Mark Twain

Grammar and Style: Double Negatives

A **double negative** is the use of two negative words when only one is needed.

Double negative: They don't have no business here.

Correct: They don't have any business here. or They have no business here.

Double negatives are not acceptable in standard English.

A. PRACTICE: *Rewrite each of the following examples in standard English, eliminating the double negatives.*

1. "There couldn't be no solit'ry thing mentioned."

____

2. "He didn't try no more to win the fight."

____

3. "He hadn't no opportunities to speak of."

____

4. "He never done nothing for three months."

____

5. "I ain't got no frog."

____

B. Writing Application: *Decide if the sentences below contain double negatives. If the sentence is written correctly, write "correct" on the line that follows it. If the sentence contains a double negative, rewrite it correctly.*

1. She cannot have no dog.

____

2. I didn't find any witnesses.

____

3. They had no business there, neither.

____

4. He wouldn't take no bribe from the lawyer.

____

5. The sentence did not contain a single negative.

____

Name ______________________________ Date ______________

"The Boys' Ambition" ***from*** **Life on the Mississippi** and **"The Notorious Jumping Frog of Calaveras County"** by Mark Twain

Support for Writing

Think about Mark Twain's quote: "The humorous story may be spun out to great length, and may wander around as much as it pleases, and arrive nowhere in particular . . . [It] is told gravely; the teller does his best to conceal the fact that he even dimly suspects there is anything funny about it." To gather information for your **analytic essay** about Twain's ideas of humor as they are reflected in "The Notorious Jumping Frog of Calaveras County," use the graphic organizer below.

Twain's Humor in "The Notorious Jumping Frog of Calaveras County"

Spins out at length (takes its time)	Arrives nowhere (doesn't have a point)	Is told gravely (with a serious tone)	Conceals humor (hides suggestions of humor)

On a separate page, draft your essay connecting each of Twain's points about humor with the example you have found in the story. When you revise, add examples to make your connections between Twain's comments and the story clearer.

Name ______________________________ Date ______________

"The Boys' Ambition" ***from*** **Life on the Mississippi** and **"The Notorious Jumping Frog of Calaveras County"** by Mark Twain

Support for Extend Your Learning

Listening and Speaking

Prepare to **interview** someone in a field that interests you. Imagine that you plan to get a job in this field, just as Twain wanted to be a riverboat pilot. Ask these questions of the person you interview, as well as others of your own choosing:

- Why did you choose this career?
- How did you prepare for it?
- What are its responsibilities and rewards?
- What advice would you give about this career?

After the interview, share your findings with your classmates.

Research and Technology

As you work with a group to prepare to create a **multimedia report** on Mississippi riverboats, do research on the Internet and find other sources, such as audio clips or newspapers. Enter the information you find below.

Life on Mississippi Riverboats

Description of Riverboat	What kind of people worked on a Riverboat	Activities on Riverboat

Prepare your report. Include the sounds of boats and other activities on a river.

Name ______________________________ Date ______________

"The Boys' Ambition" ***from*** **Life on the Mississippi** and **"The Notorious Jumping Frog of Calaveras County"** by Mark Twain

Enrichment: Jargon

When Mark Twain writes about life on the Mississippi, he often uses jargon specific to waterways and steamboats. **Jargon** is the collective name for special words and terms used by people in a certain profession.

DIRECTIONS: *Think about a job that you have done or that you are interested in doing someday. Using the following chart, fill in the title of the job and some examples of jargon that are used on the job. Use the second column of the chart to describe what each word of jargon means.*

Job Jargon

Job Title: ______________________________

Term	What the Term Means

Name ______________________________ Date ______________

"The Boys' Ambition" *from* Life on the Mississippi and "The Notorious Jumping Frog of Calaveras County" by Mark Twain

Selection Test A

Critical Reading *Identify the letter of the choice that best answers the question.*

___ 1. Based on "The Boys' Ambition," what did the boys feel toward people who worked on a steamboat?

A. envy
B. admiration
C. happiness
D. boredom

___ 2. What inference can you make from "The Boys' Ambition" about why being a steamboatman was such a desirable goal to Twain and his companions?

A. The boys could leave Hannibal.
B. Steamboatmen could get rich.
C. The steamboat arrival was each day's high point.
D. There were no other jobs in Hannibal at that time.

___ 3. Which statement shows Twain's humor about his father's job in "The Boys' Ambition"?

A. He says it is a better job than steamboating.
B. He says his father can hang anyone he wants.
C. He says his father has a lot of power in town.
D. He says his father has a special occupation.

___ 4. According to "The Boys' Ambition," which job on a steamboat is the best position?

A. engineer
B. mud clerk
C. barkeeper
D. pilot

___ 5. What exaggeration about Jim Smiley does the narrator of "The Notorious Jumping Frog of Calaveras County" make?

A. Smiley has a frog that is a good jumper.
B. Smiley will bet on anything, on any side.
C. Smiley has a dog that wins fights.
D. Smiley is tricked by a stranger.

Name ______________________________ Date ______________

____ 6. In "The Notorious Jumping Frog of Calaveras County," what does this example of regional dialect mean:

"He roused up, and gave me good day"?

A. He woke up and gave me the time.
B. He stood up and greeted me.
C. He went and made some food for us.
D. He showed me around the town.

____ 7. Which aspect of "The Notorious Jumping Frog of Calaveras County" makes the story humorous?

A. The wild story is told in a voice that has no expression.
B. The story is so unbelievable it is not even funny.
C. The narrator believes it is a true story instead of a tall tale.
D. The narrator falls asleep as he is listening to the story.

____ 8. How would you rephrase this sentence from "The Notorious Jumping Frog of Calaveras County":

"And he had a little small bull-pup, that to look at him you'd think he warn't worth a cent but to set around and look ornery and lay for a chance to steal something"?

A. And he had a small dog that was pretty worthless but he kept him around for protection.
B. And he had a small dog that looked like he hadn't cost a thing and had probably been stolen.
C. And he had a small dog whose job was to look fearsome and lie in wait to snatch something for nothing.
D. And he had a small dog that he kept trying to sell for more money than the creature was worth.

____ 9. In "The Notorious Jumping Frog of Calaveras County," why does Smiley act uninterested when the stranger asks about the frog?

A. He wants to trick him into betting.
B. He doesn't want the frog to compete.
C. He has given up betting for good.
D. He is worried about the frog's health.

Name ______________________________ Date ____________________

____ **10.** How would you restate this sentence from "The Notorious Jumping Frog of Calaveras County":

"If there was a horse race, you'd find him flush or you'd find him busted at the end of it"?

A. At the end of a horse race, he'd either be flushed with victory or arrested.
B. At the end of a horse race, he'd either have won or he'd have lost.
C. At the end of a horse race, you couldn't find him to arrest him.
D. At the end of a horse race, he'd be embarrassed because he had lost.

Vocabulary and Grammar

____ **11.** In which of these sentences is the meaning of the word *interminable* suggested?
A. I had a hard time believing his stories.
B. His story seemed to go on forever.
C. He was willing to bet on anything.
D. He was outsmarted by a stranger.

____ **12.** Which of the following sentences contains a double negative?
A. He wore no suspenders.
B. They would not let us go on the river.
C. Well, I ain't got no frog.
D. I did not wait to hear about the cow.

Essay

13. In "The Boys' Ambition," what do you think is the appeal of being a steamboatman? Using your impressions and the text of "The Boys' Ambition," write a brief essay about why Twain and his companions found the idea of being a steamboatman so exciting.

14. Exaggeration is a major element in "The Notorious Jumping Frog of Calaveras County." Write a brief essay to discuss which parts of the stories about the animals seem to be exaggerations. Include an explanation about why writers might use exaggeration.

Name ______________________________ Date ______________

"The Boys' Ambition" ***from*** **Life on the Mississippi** and
"The Notorious Jumping Frog of Calaveras County" by Mark Twain

Selection Test B

Critical Reading *Identify the letter of the choice that best completes the statement or answers the question.*

____ **1.** Which of the following best describes Jim Smiley?
- **A.** bored and annoyed
- **B.** suspicious and aggressive
- **C.** clever and competitive
- **D.** gentle and tranquil

____ **2.** When the apprentice engineer is able to "cut out every boy in the village," he is able to
- **A.** beat any boy in the village in a fight.
- **B.** take a girl away from any boy in the village.
- **C.** ignore any boy in the village.
- **D.** outrun any boy in the village.

____ **3.** For the author as a boy, the Mississippi River was above all
- **A.** a wonder of nature.
- **B.** a pathway to adventure.
- **C.** a means of escape from Hannibal.
- **D.** an opportunity to get rich.

____ **4.** Base your answer on the following excerpt:

"[Smiley's dog] would grab the other dog . . . and hang on till they throwed up the sponge."

In this sentence, the words "throwed up the sponge" mean that the people watching the dog fight would
- **A.** admit that they had lost the bet.
- **B.** bet more money on Smiley's dog.
- **C.** grab Smiley's dog and tie it up.
- **D.** try to help the other dog beat Smiley's dog.

____ **5.** The reader is led to believe that Andrew Jackson, the fighting dog, lost his last fight because of
- **A.** his own stupidity.
- **B.** the other dog's superior strength.
- **C.** a thrown sponge.
- **D.** a broken spirit after being tricked.

____ **6.** What makes the steamboat such a source of fascination for the boys?
- **A.** It is a marvel of modern technology.
- **B.** It is accessible only to the rich and powerful.
- **C.** It is a connection to the world outside Hannibal.
- **D.** It is connected with stories of shady dealings.

Name ______________________________ Date ______________

____ 7. Which of the following does Mark Twain use to add humor to this story?
A. unexpected plot shifts
B. misunderstandings between characters
C. colorful names for characters
D. all of the above

____ 8. Twain uses exaggeration in "The Boys' Ambition" primarily to
A. make the townspeople look ridiculous.
B. emphasize the boys' feelings about steamboating.
C. contrast Hannibal with St. Louis.
D. make the story entertaining.

____ 9. In the sentence "By and by one of our boys went away," the expression "by and by" means
A. after he said 'good-bye'.
B. some time later.
C. after purchasing his contract.
D. mysteriously.

____ 10. Why did Smiley act indifferently when the stranger asked him about Dan'l Webster?
A. Smiley was hoping to convince the stranger to bet on how well Dan'l could jump.
B. Smiley was busy trying to teach Dan'l to jump, and the stranger interrupted.
C. Dan'l looked like he had something wrong with him, and Smiley was worried.
D. Simon Wheeler had cheated on a bet, and Smiley was angry.

____ 11. When Jim Smiley brought Dan'l Webster downtown and "lay for a bet," Twain means that Jim Smiley would
A. talk for a while.
B. put money on the frog.
C. lie down and sleep.
D. wait for someone to make a bet with him.

____ 12. Which of the following sayings best describes the author's attitude toward the boy who becomes an apprentice engineer?
A. Everything comes to him who waits.
B. Pride goes before a fall.
C. Justice is blind.
D. A rolling stone gathers no moss.

____ 13. One aspect of "The Notorious Jumping Frog of Calaveras County" that makes the story humorous is the fact that
A. Simon Wheeler does not recognize how ridiculous his tale is.
B. the narrator believes everything that Simon Wheeler tells him.
C. Smiley refuses to believe that the frog-jumping contest was fair.
D. the stranger thinks that he can actually fool Smiley.

Name ______________________________ Date ______________

Vocabulary and Grammar

____ 14. What is the probable result of a "*monotonous* narrative"?
A. Listeners will be educated.
B. Listeners will be bored.
C. Listeners will either strongly agree or disagree with the speaker.
D. Listeners will be inspired to fight for the speaker's cause.

____ 15. Who is best described as *garrulous* in "The Notorious Jumping Frog of Calaveras County"?
A. the narrator
B. Simon Wheeler
C. Jim Smiley
D. the stranger

____ 16. The double negatives used in Twain's "The Notorious Jumping Frog of Calaveras County" are used to convey
A. ignorance.
B. humor.
C. an emphatic negative.
D. regional dialect.

____ 17. The drayman's "prodigious voice" in "The Boys' Ambition" makes him well suited to
A. alert the town.
B. drive a dray.
C. be an apprentice engineer.
D. pilot the river.

Essay

18. Who is the main character of "The Notorious Jumping Frog of Calaveras County": the jumping frog Dan'l Webster or the storyteller Simon Wheeler? Write an essay stating your opinion. Support your argument with your definition of a main character and its role in a story, and describe how your choice of main character functions in Twain's tale. Use examples from the work to strengthen your essay.

19. Exaggeration, embellishment, and regional dialect are all techniques that can make a story humorous. Write a brief essay about how these techniques lend humor to one or both of these Twain selections. Support your points about the effectiveness of each humorous technique, using examples from the story or stories.

20. One central idea of "The Boys' Ambition" is that the unknown often has a much greater appeal than the familiar. Write a brief essay about the appeal of the unknown. Use examples from both "The Boys' Ambition" and your own life to support your essay.

"The Outcasts of Poker Flat" by Bret Harte

Vocabulary Warm-up Word Lists

Study these words from the selection. Then, complete the activities.

Word List A

associate [uh SOH see it] *n.* colleague or companion
My father is meeting a business associate for lunch.

commiseration [kuh mi ser AY shun] *n.* sympathy
"I don't want commiseration, " she said, "I want you to help!"

frailer [FRAYL er] *adj.* weaker and more delicate
Grandma looked a little frailer, but she was still full of energy.

indications [in di KAY shunz] *n.* signs
He stared up at the sky, searching for indications of the coming storm.

pallid [PAL id] *adj.* pale or colorless
Studying inside all day, year after year, had left Sue pallid.

provisions [pruh VIZH unz] *n.* supplies of food
I will pack the camping stove and tent if you bring the provisions.

significantly [sig NIF i kant lee] *adv.* meaningfully, in an important way
She says she is different, but I do not think she has changed significantly.

worldly [WURLD lee] *adj.* of this Earth; material, not spiritual
Going on retreat took Mark's mind off of worldly matters.

Word List B

advisable [ad VYZ uh bul] *adj.* worthy of being recommended or suggested
Dentists say it is advisable to have a checkup every six months.

consequently [kahn se KWENT lee] *adv.* as a result
Lulu is very tall, and consequently, often bangs her head on doorways.

notorious [noh TOHR ee us] *adj.* famous for negative reasons
Jesse James was a notorious outlaw of the Wild West.

outskirts [OWT skerts] *n.* area on the outside edge
They live on the outskirts of the city, near the county line.

provoked [pruh VOHKT] *v.* caused to do something
What do you think provoked her to run off without her luggage?

retained [ree TAYND] *v.* kept
"I've lost a few friends," he said, "but I've retained my self-respect."

seclusion [se KLOO zhun] *n.* isolation
The cottage is far from any neighbors, but we enjoy the seclusion.

wily [WY lee] *adj.* cunning and sly
Native American folktales often feature a wily trickster.

Name ______________________________ Date ______________

"The Outcasts of Poker Flat" by Bret Harte

Vocabulary Warm-up Exercises

Exercise A *Fill in each blank in the paragraph below with the appropriate word from List A.*

Julie and Dylan sat down for a rest and watched as their [1] ____________ climbed slowly toward them. "Mack is looking [2] ____________ than he did at the beginning of the expedition," Dylan said. Julie nodded, torn between [3] ____________ for Mack and concern that their [4] ____________ would run out before they reached the mountaintop. Already, her pack felt [5] ____________ lighter. Mack's slow movements were just one of several [6] ____________ that he might be suffering from the high altitude; his face was [7] ____________, too, and he seemed to be having trouble breathing. Still, as he puffed up the slope, his face broke into a wide smile. "Isn't it beautiful up here?" he called. "It makes me forget all my [8] ____________ concerns."

Exercise B *Revise each sentence so that the underlined vocabulary word is used in a logical way. Be sure to keep the vocabulary word in your revision.*

1. I want to lose weight, and consequently, I eat a lot of ice cream and cake.
   ____
2. David lives on the outskirts of town, close to the center.
   ____
3. The wily mouse sat out where it could easily be caught.
   ____
4. Because he always retained his wit and charm, people disliked his company.
   ____
5. The bookstore owner is notorious for her good temper.
   ____
6. Falling down and skinning her knee provoked the child to laugh with delight.
   ____
7. If you want straight *A*s, it is advisable never to study.
   ____
8. The hotel's seclusion made it easy for Ivan to visit tourist sites.
   ____

Name ______________________________ Date ______________

"The Outcasts of Poker Flat" by Bret Harte

Reading Warm-up A

Read the following passage. Pay special attention to the underlined words. Then, read it again, and complete the activities. Use a separate sheet of paper for your written answers.

Billy Evans dumped a final load of pay dirt into the second bucket, set his shovel down, and sighed: time to haul the heavy buckets back down to the river yet again.

Carrying the buckets used to be the job of his friend and <u>associate</u>, "Lucky" Jack Lewis. After breaking his back for months without getting <u>significantly</u> richer, however, Lucky Jack had not felt very lucky anymore, and last week he had hightailed it back East, leaving Billy to work their claim alone.

Billy wiped the sweat off of his face. The sight of his forearm, dark and muscular, reminded him how much he had changed from the thin, <u>pallid</u> young man who had left his home and family two years before.

A shadow fell across the sun, and Billy glanced up, thinking for one startled moment that his younger self had stepped out of his imagination. This boy was smaller and <u>frailer</u> than he had been, though, and his ragged clothes and worn-out shoes were <u>indications</u> of a long, hard journey.

"Come to make your fortune, eh?" said Billy.

The boy nodded.

"Staked a claim yet?"

The boy shook his head, and Billy eyed him with <u>commiseration</u>. No money either, by the look of him, and no tools or <u>provisions</u>. How would he survive without any <u>worldly</u> possessions?

Well, it was not his problem, Billy thought, turning away to pick up the buckets. When he turned back, though, the boy was still standing there, silently watching.

"What's your name, kid?" Billy asked.

The answer came in a whisper: "Jack."

Billy stared at him, then, laughing, shook his head and handed him one of the full buckets. The boy staggered under the weight, but he hung on.

"Welcome to California, Jack," said Billy. "Hope you're feeling lucky."

1. Underline the name of Billy's <u>associate</u>. What is the word for an ***associate*** who is a fellow student?
2. Circle the word that means something similar to <u>significantly</u>. How much would you have to grow to feel ***significantly*** taller?
3. Circle the word that means the opposite of <u>pallid</u>. Would you expect a ***pallid*** slice of watermelon to taste good?
4. Circle the word that tells who or what is <u>frailer</u> than Billy. If a friend of yours was looking ***frailer***, what would you advise?
5. Underline what the boy's ragged clothes and worn-out shoes are <u>indications</u> of. What are ***indications*** that someone is feeling cold?
6. Underline the reason that Billy looks at the boy with <u>commiseration</u>. If Billy didn't feel ***commiseration***, what might he say?
7. Circle the three things that the boy lacks, besides <u>provisions</u>. What sort of ***provisions*** would you pack for a picnic?
8. What sort of <u>worldly</u> riches are Billy and Jack hoping to find?

Name ______________________________ Date ______________

"The Outcasts of Poker Flat" by Bret Harte

Reading Warm-up B

Read the following passage. Pay special attention to the underlined words. Then, read it again, and complete the activities. Use a separate sheet of paper for your written answers.

On the outskirts of the town of Independence, Missouri, where the open prairie began, travelers heading west might expect to find their first taste of the loneliness and seclusion of frontier life. If so, they were in for a surprise! The prairie was packed with people, thousands of them, camped with wagons, oxen, and mules. They were waiting for the grass to grow. Once it had grown high enough to provide their animals plenty of grazing, they could be on their way.

Many of these pioneers were city folk with no experience in "roughing it," and consequently, they made mistakes, such as driving in the wrong direction and crashing their wagons into trees. They also packed a great deal more than was advisable, and ended up having to toss out valuable items that were just too heavy for their teams to pull. Those who came along the trail behind them might find anything from a cast-iron cookstove to a ten-ton pile of bacon.

An item all the travelers retained, despite its weight, was drinking water. They knew that ahead of them lay the notorious Nevada desert, where they could die of thirst just a few hundred miles from the end of their long journey. Still, through poor planning or bad luck, many did indeed run out of water. Then they found themselves at the mercy of the wily businessmen who brought barrels of water east from California, charging as much as $100 for a single glass.

One last obstacle remained: the Sierra Nevada mountain range. Crossing the high Sierras meant hauling a loaded wagon up a steep, muddy, boulder-strewn path, praying to be spared a sudden, deadly blizzard. Perhaps it was this final grueling test that provoked one survivor to write to a friend back East, "STAY AT HOME."

1. Underline the words that tell you the outskirts are not in the center of town. What might you find on the *outskirts* of a town today?
2. Circle the word that suggests the meaning of seclusion. Then, explain what *seclusion* means.
3. What other words could you use here instead of *consequently*?
4. Underline what the pioneers did that was not advisable. What would be *advisable* to pack for a modern camping trip?
5. Circle the item that the travelers retained. Name something you have *retained* since you were younger.
6. Underline what made the Nevada desert notorious. Would you want to go to a place that was *notorious* among travelers?
7. Underline what the businessmen did that was wily. Would you advise buying a car from someone who was *wily*?
8. Underline what the survivor was provoked to do. What might have *provoked* the friend to ignore his advice?

Name ______________________________ Date ______________

"The Outcasts of Poker Flat" by Bret Harte

Literary Analysis: Regionalism

Regionalism is a type of literature whose purpose is to display the "local color" of a region, often by showing the distinctive qualities of the people and the physical environment. This is often done through explanation of customs and attitudes, accurate representation of local speech patterns, and a description of the unique environment.

DIRECTIONS: *Read each excerpt below. Explain what it shows about Poker Flat and the old West.*

1. "There was a Sabbath lull in the air which, in a settlement unused to Sabbath influences, looked ominous."

____

____

____

2. "In that advanced season, the party soon passed out of the moist, temperate regions of the foothills into the dry, cold, bracing air of the Sierras."

____

____

____

3. "A wooded amphitheater, surrounded on three sides by precipitous cliffs of naked granite, sloped gently toward the crest of another precipice that overlooked the valley."

____

____

____

4. "Mr. Oakhurst did not drink. It interfered with a profession which required coolness, impassiveness, and presence of mind, and, in his own language, he 'couldn't afford it.'"

____

____

____

Name ____ Date ____________________

"The Outcasts of Poker Flat" by Bret Harte

Reading Strategy: Question the Text

Questioning the text often helps the reader better understand the selection. By asking questions as you read and then looking for answers, you can help yourself get more out of a selection.

DIRECTIONS: *Reread "The Outcasts of Poker Flat" and then write the answer to each question below its excerpt.*

1. "It was experiencing a spasm of virtuous reaction, quite as lawless and ungovernable as any of the acts that had provoked it."
   What was the "virtuous reaction?"

   ____

   ____

2. "With the easy good humor characteristic of his class, he insisted upon exchanging his own riding horse, 'Five Spot,' for the sorry mule which the Duchess rode."
   What significance does the trading of "Five Spot" for the mule have in the selection?

   ____

   ____

3. "At noon the Duchess, rolling out of her saddle upon the ground, declared her intention of going no farther, and the party halted."
   How does this singular act ultimately have a major effect on the story?

   ____

   ____

4. "In the fresh, open face of the newcomer Mr. Oakhurst recognized Tom Simson, otherwise known as the 'Innocent' of Sandy Bar. . . . [H]e had run away with Piney Woods."
   Why does the author introduce Tom Simson and Piney Woods to the story?

   ____

   ____

Name ______________________________ Date ____________________

"The Outcasts of Poker Flat" by Bret Harte

Vocabulary Builder

Using the Root *-bel-*

The word root *-bel-* means "war," and a word that contains this root probably has something to do with warfare or conflict. For example, the word *antebellum* means "before the war," and specifically refers to the period preceding the Civil War. The word *postbellum*, meaning "after the war," specifically refers to the period following the Civil War.

A. Directions: *Read each sentence below and fill in the missing adjective, either* antebellum *or* postbellum.

1. The ____________________ South had a largely agricultural economy and an easy-paced way of life.
2. The ____________________ North already believed in industry and modernization.
3. The ____________________ United States needed to bring together a nation once torn apart.

Using the Word List

expatriated	anathema	bellicose	recumbent
equanimity	vociferation	vituperative	querulous

B. Directions: *Write the Word List word that is closest in meaning to the italicized word or phrase in each sentence.*

1. "It was her last *abusively spoken* attempt, . . ." ____________________
2. "Uncle Billy passed rapidly from a *quarrelsome* state into one of stupor, . . ." ____________________
3. ". . . the *deported* party consisted of . . ." ____________________
4. "'I'm going,' she said, in a voice of *fault-finding* weakness, . . ." ____________________
5. "As he gazed at his *resting* fellow exiles, . . ." ____________________
6. ". . . Uncle Billy included the whole party in one sweeping *curse*." ____________________
7. ". . . sang with great earnestness and *vehement shouting*." ____________________
8. ". . . to that calm *composure* for which he was notorious." ____________________

Name ____________________ Date ____________________

"The Outcasts of Poker Flat" by Bret Harte

Grammar and Style: Coordinating Conjunctions in Compound Sentences

Conjunctions are words that connect words, phrases, clauses, or sentences. **Coordinating conjunctions** (*and, or, nor, for, so,* and *yet*) connect words, phrases, or clauses of equal weight—particularly in compound sentences.

A. Directions: *Identify the coordinating conjunctions in the following sentences, and explain the linking or contrasting function that each performs.*

1. Two or three men, conversing earnestly together, ceased as he approached, and exchanged significant glances.

   ____

2. Mr. Oakhurst knew that scarcely half the journey to Sandy Bar was accomplished, and the party were not equipped or provisioned for delay.

   ____

3. They had been engaged a long time, but old Jake Woods had objected, and so they had run away.

   ____

B. Directions: *Use coordinating conjunctions to combine each of the following groups of sentences into a single compound sentence.*

1. John Oakhurst was escorted to the outskirts of town. Two women and a suspected thief were also escorted out of town.

   ____

   ____

2. When he awakens the next morning, Mr. Oakhurst discovers that it has snowed during the night. He also discovers that Uncle Billy has stolen the mules and horses. Uncle Billy has not stolen the provisions.

   ____

   ____

Name ______________________________ Date ______________

"The Outcasts of Poker Flat" by Bret Harte

Support for Writing

To prepare to write a **critical review** of "The Outcasts of Poker Flat," enter your opinions about the story in the graphic organizer below.

"The Outcasts of Poker Flat"—Critical Responses

Opinions about Setting: ______________________________
Opinions about Plot: ______________________________
Opinions about Characters: ______________________________
Selected passages and opinions about each passage
Passage 1: ______________________________
Passage 2: ______________________________
Passage 3: ______________________________

On a separate page, write a draft of your critical essay, and be sure to connect your evaluation with specifics about the plot, characters, and passages from the story. When you revise, add words that make strong statements of evaluation, whether positive or negative.

Name ______________________________ Date ______________

"The Outcasts of Poker Flat" by Bret Harte

Support for Extend Your Learning

Listening and Speaking

As you prepare your **eulogy** for Mr. Oakhurst, include the following details:

- Colorful, informal "western" language
- Personal experiences you have had with Mr. Oakhurst

Deliver your eulogy as if you were Tom Simson, the single survivor of the group of outcasts.

Research and Technology

Learn about the gold rush from the Internet and library resources, and use the information to prepare a **prospecting and mining report.** Enter the information you find into the chart below.

Prospecting and Mining Gold

Where to go Prospecting	
Steps involved in Mining	
How to Sell Minerals	

Put your information into a flow chart, a poster, or another visual to show the class the results of your research.

Name ______________________________ Date ______________

"The Outcasts of Poker Flat" by Bret Harte

Enrichment: Social Studies

Directions: *In his writing, Bret Harte challenges the stereotypes of "the outcasts" of society. Study each of the "outcasts" and "innocents" in the selection. Then fill in the following chart to tell which character behaviors are stereotypical of "outcast" or "innocent" and which behaviors are not stereotypical. Then use the information from your chart to make a statement describing the society of Poker Flat.*

Character	Outcast or Innocent?	Stereotypical Behaviors	Behaviors That Are Not Stereotypical
Mr. Oakhurst			
The Duchess			
Mother Shipton			
Uncle Billy			
Tom Simson			
Piney Woods			

The Society of Poker Flat:

____

____

____

____

Name ______________________________ Date ______________

"The Outcasts of Poker Flat" by Bret Harte

Selection Test A

Critical Reading *Identify the letter of the choice that best answers the question.*

____ 1. How are Mr. Oakhurst and the "Duchess" described in "The Outcasts of Poker Flat"?

A. in a way that frightens the reader

B. in a way that shows the era's prejudices

C. in a way that provides humor

D. in a way that is uncaring

____ 2. In "The Outcasts of Poker Flat," how do the four outcasts first behave when they are exiled?

A. with friendship

B. with enthusiasm

C. with bitterness

D. with confusion

____ 3. In "The Outcasts of Poker Flat," why is it important to the plot that Billy steals the mules?

A. It shows Billy's character more fully.

B. It gets rid of an unpleasant character.

C. It directs the others' hostility to Billy.

D. It leaves the others with no escape.

____ 4. In "The Outcasts of Poker Flat," what is Mr. Oakhurst's motivation for returning the money he has won at poker from the "Innocent" Tom Simson?

A. He has won the money by cheating.

B. He fears Simson will do him harm.

C. He knows Tom has no skill at poker.

D. He is rich enough without the money.

____ 5. Why does Harte describe the "gloomy walls" and the "ominously clouded" sky in "The Outcasts of Poker Flat"?

A. to entertain readers with description

B. to persuade readers to visit the Sierras

C. to suggest the dangerous surroundings

D. to show that night is approaching

Name ______________________ Date ______________

____ 6. What attitude does the author show toward the outcasts in "The Outcasts of Poker Flat"
A. affection
B. anger
C. puzzlement
D. disbelief

____ 7. What unselfish act does Mother Shipton perform in "The Outcasts of Poker Flat"?
A. She saves her food for the others.
B. She places a sign by Oakhurst's grave.
C. She makes a pair of snowshoes for Tom.
D. She curses the distant view of Poker Flat.

____ 8. What purpose do Piney and Tom Simson serve in "The Outcasts of Poker Flat"?
A. The others are annoyed by their singing.
B. They help others remember their youth.
C. The others want to protect them.
D. They give the others hope for the future.

____ 9. What is ironic about the title "The Outcasts of Poker Flat"?
A. The outcasts are aware of what will happen to them.
B. Very little of the story actually takes place in Poker Flat.
C. Piney and the Innocent do not yet live in Poker Flat.
D. The outcasts are better people than those who exile them.

____ 10. In "The Outcasts of Poker Flat," what gambling theme is suggested by the ending of the story?
A. A full house beats two of a kind.
B. Keep a poker face to your opponents.
C. End the game when your luck runs out.
D. Always bluff when you have bad cards.

Vocabulary and Grammar

____ 11. In which sentence is the meaning of the word *expatriated* suggested?
A. The outcasts were sent away from home.
B. Mr. Oakhurst led the odd group.
C. The Sierras are beautiful but deadly.
D. Tom Simson tells stories to the group.

Name ______________________ Date ______________

____ 12. Which of these sentences correctly uses coordinating conjunctions?

A. The townsfolk did not want bad women or gamblers in Poker Flat.

B. Uncle Billy ran off with the company's mules, and he left the food behind.

C. Mr. Oakhurst hoped that Tom would be able to reach town.

D. The outcasts sang, told stories, and kept each other hoping.

Essay

13. In "The Outcasts of Poker Flat," the gambler Mr. Oakhurst says: "Luck . . . is a mighty queer thing. All you know about it for certain is that it's bound to change." Who in the story is lucky or unlucky? Write a brief essay about what Mr. Oakhurst's words mean to the story.

14. In "The Outcasts of Poker Flat," do you think Mr. Oakhurst's suicide makes sense in terms of Mr. Oakhurst's occupation as a gambler? Write a brief essay to address this question. Support your response with examples from the story.

Name ______________________________ Date ______________

"The Outcasts of Poker Flat" by Bret Harte

Selection Test B

Critical Reading *Identify the letter of the choice that best completes the statement or answers the question.*

____ 1. The description of the campsite is given to
A. complete the story.
B. show how well the author writes.
C. help the reader visualize the region.
D. contrast Poker Flat with Sandy Bar.

____ 2. Which of the following best describes the feelings that the four outcasts have about one another immediately after they are driven out of Poker Flat?
A. interest and concern
B. hostility and indifference
C. fear and suspicion
D. kindness and affection

____ 3. What important plot development is brought on by Uncle Billy's stealing of the mules?
A. It strands the rest of the travelers.
B. It establishes Uncle Billy as a thief and "outcast."
C. It causes the rest of the group to distrust Uncle Billy.
D. It removes Uncle Billy from the cast of characters.

____ 4. What is the main message of "The Outcasts of Poker Flat"?
A. Living a life of crime is not always wrong.
B. People who commit crimes will ultimately be punished by society.
C. People's attitudes about criminals change when they learn why criminals turn to a life of crime.
D. Punishment without justice is as bad as the crime.

____ 5. Which is the most likely reason the author includes the character of the Duchess in "The Outcasts of Poker Flat"?
A. to provide a romantic interest for Mr. Oakhurst
B. to represent women as part of the group of outcasts
C. to provide a reason for the group to stop halfway to Sandy Bar
D. to compare and contrast with the character of Piney

____ 6. The fact that Mother Shipton refers to Piney as "the child" suggests that she
A. cares for Piney and wants to help her.
B. wants to become Piney's legal mother.
C. disapproves of Piney's marriage.
D. thinks Piney is behaving selfishly.

____ 7. Which motto best describes Uncle Billy's actions?
A. Every man for himself.
B. All for one and one for all.
C. A bird in the hand is worth two in the bush.
D. Don't put off until tomorrow what you can do today.

Name ______________________ Date ______________

____ 8. Which excerpt gives the reader a sense of the regional aspects of the story?
A. "Two or three men, conversing earnestly together, ceased as he approached, and exchanged significant glances."
B. "Mr. Oakhurst received his sentence with philosophic calmness, none the less coolly that he was aware of the hesitation of his judges."
C. "He bestirred himself in dusting his black clothes, washing his hands and face, and other acts characteristic of his studiously neat habits, and for a moment forgot his annoyance."
D. "But at the head of the gulch, on one of the largest pine trees, they found the deuce of clubs pinned to the bark with a bowie knife."

____ 9. Which word best characterizes the author's attitude toward the outcasts in "The Outcasts of Poker Flat"?
A. resentment
B. superiority
C. sympathy
D. condemnation

____ 10. Which of the following words best describe Mr. Oakhurst's character?
A. intelligent and reserved
B. warm and enthusiastic
C. shy and cautious
D. cruel and cunning

____ 11. Which question would be most helpful to ask after learning that Mother Shipton has died?
A. Why was her character considered expendable?
B. Was she "redeemed" after this unselfish act?
C. Will her death cause any characters to change their plan of action?
D. Will her rations be given only to Piney or shared with the group?

____ 12. Harte tells the reader that before Mr. Oakhurst parted from the group with Tom Simson, "He turned suddenly, and kissed the Duchess, leaving her pallid face aflame and her trembling limbs rigid with amazement." What can the reader infer from this scene?
A. The Duchess did not enjoy being kissed.
B. Mr. Oakhurst had already decided not to return to the camp.
C. The Duchess was angry at Mr. Oakhurst for ridiculing her.
D. The Duchess believed that Mr. Oakhurst planned to marry her.

____ 13. Which element of the story shows most clearly that "The Outcasts of Poker Flat" is an example of regional literature?
A. the point of view from which the story is told
B. the dialect of the narrator
C. the circumstances under which the outcasts become stranded
D. the time of year in which the story is set

Name ______________________________ Date ______________

Vocabulary and Grammar

____ 14. Which term is closest to the meaning of the italicized word in this excerpt?

[T]he lovers . . . sang with great earnestness and *vociferation*.

A. loudness
B. sincerity
C. interpretation
D. melodic accuracy

____ 15. Which word is the coordinating conjunction in this sentence?

They slept all that day and the next, nor did they waken when voices and footsteps broke the silence of the camp.

A. all
B. when
C. nor
D. of

____ 16. Uncle Billy is described as a *bellicose* person who is given to using *anathemas*. Which best describes this character?

A. a mean man given to drinking
B. an ornery man given to cursing
C. a thief given to lying
D. a drunk given to abusing medication

____ 17. Which excerpt from the selection was made by someone with a *querulous* attitude?

A. "Tommy, you're a good little man."
B. "Just you go out there and cuss, and see."
C. "There's one chance in a hundred to save her yet."
D. "You are not going, too?"

Essay

18. A two, or the "deuce," is the lowest ranked card in poker. Why does Mr. Oakhurst choose that card on which to write his eulogy? How is its use in keeping with his character? Write an essay that answers these questions, and use details from the selection to support your statements.

19. Some readers are surprised to learn that Mr. Oakhurst commits suicide at the end of the selection. Did this action seem within or outside of the character's prior behavior? Take a position in your essay, and support it with details about Mr. Oakhurst and other examples from the story.

20. Harte says that Mr. Oakhurst was the strongest yet the weakest outcast of Poker Flat. Do you disagree or agree with this statement? Write an essay stating your position, and use details from the selection to explain it. Give examples of Mr. Oakhurst's actions if you agree, and if you disagree, tell who you think were the strongest and weakest members of the group. (You may cite two different characters, if you wish.) Again, support your explanation with several details from the selection.

"Heading West" by Miriam Davis Colt
"I Will Fight No More Forever" by Chief Joseph

Vocabulary Warm-up Word Lists

Study these words from the selections. Then, complete the activities.

Word List A

consequence [KAHN suh kwens] *n.* result; outcome
I had not studied enough, and as a consequence, I did poorly on the exam.

dingy [DIN jee] *adj.* grimy; run-down; in poor condition
Paul, who had not been able to get a decent job, lived in a dingy apartment.

fulfilled [fuhl FILD] *v.* satisfied; achieved; completed
The art exhibition fulfilled everyone's hopes: it was well laid out and enjoyable.

implements [IM pluh muhnts] *n.* tools
All the farm implements were at hand and ready to use.

pedestrian [pi DES tree uhn] *n.* a person on foot
A pedestrian crossing the street at that intersection should be especially careful.

ravine [ruh VEEN] *n.* long, deep hollow in the earth's surface; large gully
When the horse came to the ravine, he shied away and refused to jump it.

severity [suh VER uh tee] *n.* harshness
The severity of the thunderstorms was reported on the evening newscasts.

shrewd [SHROOD] *adj.* very clever; cunning
Orlando is a shrewd businessman who is very successful.

Word List B

coincide [koh in SYD] *v.* to happen at the same time; to meet or join
Will your arrival coincide with our annual summer cookout?

emigrants [EM i gruhnts] *n.* people who leave their native land to settle elsewhere
Many emigrants from Europe arrived at Ellis Island in New York Harbor.

foremost [FOR mohst] *adj.* most important
The ambassador was a foremost statesman for his country.

genial [JEE ni uhl] *adj.* friendly; good-natured; amiable
Steve had a genial manner, and most of his co-workers liked him.

nonplused [non PLUSD] *adj.* utterly surprised; astonished
We thought our team would win, but the 28-0 loss nonplused us.

profusion [proh FYOO zhuhn] *n.* abundance
The weather had been excellent, and there was a profusion of roses in the garden.

repast [ri PAST] *n.* fine or lavish meal
The hosts of the dinner party served a wonderful repast to their guests.

wields [WEELDZ] *v.* handles and uses; brandishes
In ancient Greek art, Poseidon, god of the sea, wields a trident.

Name ______________________________ Date ______________

"Heading West" by Miriam Davis Colt
"I Will Fight No More Forever" by Chief Joseph

Vocabulary Warm-up Exercises

Exercise A *Fill in each blank in the paragraph below with the appropriate word from Word List A.*

In mid-January, a blizzard hit our town. The [1] ________________ of the storm was amazing; it snowed for two consecutive days and nights. The total snowfall more than [2] ________________ the forecasters' predictions of 30 inches. As a(n) [3] ________________, all business ground to a halt. There was scarcely any traffic on the streets, and most of the time not even a(n) [4] ________________ was in sight. You didn't have to be [5] ________________, just sensible, to heed the mayor's advice to stay indoors. The day after the storm was over, people gradually began to appear outside, armed with shovels and other [6] ________________ to clear sidewalks and driveways. You should have seen our driveway lined with huge snow banks! It looked like the plow had cut a(n) [7] ________________ through the snow! A week later, much of the snow had melted, and what was left looked grimy and [8] ________________.

Exercise B *Revise each sentence so that the underlined vocabulary word is logical. Be sure to keep the vocabulary word in your revision.*

Example: Because that item was <u>superfluous</u>, we included it in our report.
Because that item was <u>superfluous</u>, we omitted it from our report.

1. We will both be in Chicago in different weeks in July, so our visits there will <u>coincide</u>.

   ____

2. Groups of <u>emigrants</u> remain in their native countries for many different reasons.

   ____

3. The newspaper editors omitted their <u>foremost</u> reason for endorsing the governor's plan.

   ____

4. He was so <u>genial</u> that most people took care to avoid him.

   ____

5. Stan was <u>nonplused</u> when he heard the news, remarking that it was entirely predictable.

   ____

Name ______________________________ Date ______________

"Heading West" by Miriam Davis Colt
"I Will Fight No More Forever" by Chief Joseph

Reading Warm-up A

Read the following passage. Pay special attention to the underlined words. Then, read it again, and complete the activities. Use a separate sheet of paper for your written answers.

Many pioneers to the American West made their journey in a vehicle called the Conestoga Wagon. This wagon was named for a valley in eastern Pennsylvania. It seems to have been developed in the early 1700s for trade between the colonists and the Indians. The wagons would haul such items as gunpowder, rum, salt, lead, kettles, and other implements or tools. A clever, shrewd trader would exchange these items for furs, which would be shipped to England. Demand for fur hats and coats was high. As a consequence, a busy trader might make a handsome profit.

Early Conestoga Wagons were probably small, since roads at that time were primitive and barely wider than trails. The wagons had no seats, so the driver would walk beside his horses as a pedestrian. Crossing a river or going up or down a steep ravine was especially tricky. The only brake was a wheel lock chain attached to the wagon's back wheel. Later wagons, which were as much as 25 feet long, were pulled by a team of six large horses. In Miriam Colt's day, a Conestoga Wagon could carry 5,000 pounds.

For the pioneers, the severity of the journey west must have been difficult and challenging. It is sometimes hard today to appreciate the hardships they encountered. The roads were dingy, sometimes even nonexistent, and travelers had to endure constant anxiety about their health and safety. Still, an optimistic spirit sustained them with the hope that they would find a better life at the end of the trail. For their great migration, the Conestoga Wagon fulfilled its mission as the mobile container of all their worldly goods.

1. Underline the words in this sentence that give a clue to the meaning of implements. Use the word ***implements*** in a sentence.
2. Circle the word that is a clue to shrewd. What is a synonym for ***shrewd***?
3. Underline the words that hint at the meaning of the word consequence. What is a synonym for ***consequence***?
4. Circle the words that offer a clue to the meaning of pedestrian here.
5. Circle the words that offer clues to the meaning of ravine. What are two synonyms for ***ravine***?
6. Underline the words that give a clue to the meaning of severity. What are two antonyms for ***severity***?
7. Circle the words in this and the previous sentence that give a clue to the meaning of dingy. Use the word ***dingy*** in an original sentence.
8. Underline the words in this sentence hinting at the meaning of fulfilled. What is a synonym for ***fulfilled***?

Name ______________________ Date ______________

"Heading West" by Miriam Davis Colt
"I Will Fight No More Forever" by Chief Joseph

Reading Warm-up B

Read the following passage. Pay special attention to the underlined words. Then, read it again, and complete the activities. Use a separate sheet of paper for your written answers.

In 1848, at the end of the Mexican War, California became a territory of the United States, and the same year would coincide with the discovery of gold there. John A. Sutter had built a fort on the American River, not far from San Francisco. When Sutter's construction manager, James Marshall, found gold there, California almost immediately became the foremost destination in the West for people eager to make their fortune.

The California Gold Rush, as it became known, attracted not only Americans, but emigrants from all over the world—Europe, China, Mexico, and Australia—poured into California. This profusion of new arrivals numbered 100,000 in 1849 alone. For the most part, these "Forty-niners" did not intend to make California their permanent home; they only wanted to strike it rich as soon as possible.

The Gold Rush involved considerable ethnic diversity, since people of many different races and national origins were brought together. Nevertheless, life in the mining camps of the day was seldom friendly or genial; greed and jealousy often erupted into violence. The very same tools that a miner wields could, as many prospectors found out, be used as dangerous weapons. One American army general named Persifor Smith was nonplused in his astonishment that foreigners were allowed to take part in the Gold Rush, and he used words as his weapons, calling on the government to limit the Gold Rush to U.S. citizens.

The Gold Rush had a lasting effect on the city of San Francisco. If you visit Chinatown there today, perhaps sitting down to a lavish repast in one of the neighborhood's fine restaurants, remember that many of the original Chinese settlers came to California as laborers providing goods and services. The miners didn't want to work there; they only wanted to get rich. Therefore, the market for Chinese labor greatly expanded.

1. Underline the words that give a clue to coincide. Use the word *coincide* in a sentence.
2. Circle the words that is a clue of foremost. What is a synonym for *foremost*?
3. Underline the words in this sentence hinting at the meaning of emigrants. Use the word *emigrants* in an original sentence.
4. Underline the words in this sentence that give a clue to the meaning of profusion. What is a synonym for *profusion*?
5. Circle the words that give a clue to genial. Use an antonymn of *genial* in a sentence.
6. Underline the words in this sentence that hint at the meaning of wields. What is a synonym for *wields*?
7. Underline the words that might mean nonplused. What kind of event would cause you to feel *nonplused*?
8. Circle the words in this sentence that mean repast. What is a synonym for *repast*?

Name ______________________________ Date ______________

"Heading West" by Miriam Davis Colt
"I Will Fight No More Forever" by Chief Joseph

Literary Analysis: Tone

Tone is usually revealed through word choice, treatment of characters and events, and—especially in a speech—voice and body language. It is usually described by adjectives such as angry, humorous, or sympathetic.

A. DIRECTIONS: *Read each of the following passages; On the line, write the letter of the adjective that best describes the tone.*

___ 1. "I want to have time to look for my children and see how many I can find. Maybe I shall find them among the dead."—Chief Joseph

A. warlike B. despairing C. questioning D. calm

___ 2. "There is no retreat but in submission and slavery! Our chains are forged! Their clanging may be heard on the plains of Boston! The war is inevitable—and let it come! I repeat, sir, let it come!—Patrick Henry, "Speech in the Virginia Convention"

A. sarcastic B. objective C. annoyed D. challenging

___ 3. "The grave was made beneath the shade of some noble oaks. It had been carefully watched to the present hour by the Pawnees of the Loup, and is often shown to the traveler and the trader as a spot where a just white man sleeps."—James Fenimore Cooper, *The Prairie*

A. respectful B. gloomy C. critical D. bitter

B. DIRECTIONS: *Imagine that you are Miriam Davis Colt. On the lines provided, write an entry for "Heading West" that reflects the tone of one of the following the adjectives. Title your entry using the adjective you choose.*

despairing amused gloomy annoyed critical

____

____

____

____

____

____

____

____

____

____

Name ______________________________ Date ______________

"Heading West" by Miriam Davis Colt
"I Will Fight No More Forever" by Chief Joseph

Reading Strategy: Respond

Effective readers connect what they read with their own experiences, feelings, and ideas. Taking time to notice how you respond to what you are reading not only will increase your enjoyment, but also improve your understanding.

DIRECTIONS: *Use the chart below to track your responses to your reading. In the first column, note specific words, phrases, and passages from the selections that had a strong effect on you. In the second column, list ideas, emotions and images that the words evoked. In the third column note how your response added to your understanding.*

Words, Phrases, Passages	Ideas, Emotions, Images	Improved Understanding

Name ______________________________ Date ______________

"Heading West" by Miriam Davis Colt
"I Will Fight No More Forever" by Chief Joseph

Vocabulary Builder

Using the Latin Term *terra firma*

The Latin words *terra firma* mean "firm earth" or "solid ground." *Terra* can also mean "land," or "territory," as in words like *terra incognita* ("unknown territory"), or "earth" as in *terra cotta* ("baked earth"), unglazed fired clay or pottery.

A. DIRECTIONS: *For each situation below, write a descriptive sentence that contains the term* terra firma, terra incognita, *or* terra cotta.

1. discoveries made by archaeologists digging up an ancient city

   ____

2. an astronaut arriving back on earth after six months in a space station

   ____

3. where the Nez Percé were when the government exiled them

   ____

Using the Word List

genial	pervading	terra firma	emigrants
profusion			

B. DIRECTIONS: *Rewrite each sentence below, replacing the italicized word or phrase with an appropriate word from the Word List.*

1. There were *people who moved* from many lands to America.

   ____

2. As far as the eye could see, the prairie was covered by a *great abundance* of wild flowers.

   ____

3. The settlers hoped to find new land with a *mild* climate.

   ____

4. The feeling *prevalent throughout* the Nez Percé camp was despair.

   ____

5. The weary travelers were happy to disembark and find *firm earth* under their feet.

   ____

Name ______________________________ Date ______________

"Heading West" by Miriam Davis Colt
"I Will Fight No More Forever" by Chief Joseph

Grammar and Style: Sentence Fragments

Many of the entries in Miriam Colt's journal are **sentence fragments**—incomplete sentences that lack a subject, verb, or both. Although sentence fragments are acceptable for taking notes or making quick, informal journal entries, they are not acceptable in finished writing.

Sentence fragment missing subject:	Have driven 18 miles today.
Sentence fragment missing verb:	The lovely day.
Sentence fragment missing subject and verb:	In the far west.

A. Practice: *These sentences and sentence fragments are from "Heading West." Read each one. If a sentence is complete, write "correct" in blank following it. If it is a fragment, rewrite it as a complete sentence.*

1. "We are making every necessary preparation for our journey, and our home in Kansas."

____

2. "Go up, up, up, and upstairs to our lodging rooms."

____

3. "On board steamer 'Cataract,' bound for Kansas City."

____

B. Writing Application: *Rewrite each of these passages from "Heading West" to eliminate all sentence fragments.*

1. "Found ourselves in this miserable hotel before we knew it. Miserable fare—herring boiled with cabbage—miserable, dirty beds, and an odor pervading the house that is not at all agreeable. Mistress gone."

____

____

____

2. "One mile, from the city, and Dr. Thorn has broke his wagon tongue; it must be sent back to Kansas City to be mended: Fires kindled—women cooking—supper eaten sitting around on logs, stones, and wagon tongues."

____

____

____

Name ______________________________ Date ______________

"Heading West" by Miriam Davis Colt
"I Will Fight No More Forever" by Chief Joseph

Support for Writing

Prepare to write a **position paper** explaining why you support or oppose the development of an open space into a mall. Use your imagination to think of how the change would affect people. Enter your pro or con opinions into the chart below.

Why The Open Space Should/Should Not Be Turned into a Mall

Statement for or against Development	
Reason 1 and support or details	
Reason 2 and support or details	

On a separate page, write your draft. Be sure to use persuasive language in supporting your opinion. As you revise, check for smooth transitions from one paragraph and main idea to the next paragraph and main idea.

Name ________________________________ Date ____________________

"Heading West" by Miriam Davis Colt
"I Will Fight No More Forever" by Chief Joseph

Support for Extend Your Learning

Listening and Speaking

Prepare to deliver an **oral interpretation** of Chief Joseph's speech as if you were Chief Joseph, speaking to both his chiefs and the American officials. As you rehearse, use these tips:

- Identify the tone of Chief Joseph's voice as he gave his speech.
- Think about how he stood or gestured when he spoke.

Imagine Chief Joseph in your mind as you give your speech. Ask classmates for feedback on your presentation.

Research and Technology

As you do Internet research into utopian communities for a **marketing brochure,** enter information you find into the chart below.

Western Utopian Communities

Example 1 of Utopian Community	
Why someone would want to live here	
Example 2 of Utopian Community	
Why someone would want to live here	

As you prepare your brochure, focus on things that would draw settlers to want to live in one of the communities. Use photos and other graphics to show the positive side of living in such a community.

Name ______________________ Date ______________

"Heading West" by Miriam Davis Colt
"I Will Fight No More Forever" by Chief Joseph

Enrichment: Social Studies

The days of pioneers braving unknown frontiers are not over. Modern pioneers, the astronauts, leave the confines of planet Earth to explore and probe the frontiers of space. The modern pioneers may someday be followed by settlers like Miriam Davis Colt or exiles like the Nez Percé.

DIRECTIONS: *Imagine yourself as an astronaut embarking on an exploratory space voyage, part of a family seeking a better life on another planet, or part of a group unjustly exiled from Earth. How would you feel about leaving your home and venturing into the unknown? Using the writing of Chief Joseph and Miriam Davis Colt as a guide, complete the following statements, and then write several diary entries of your own. Describe your imaginary departure from Earth, your journey to a new life, and the world you reach. Concentrate on expressing your feelings and emotions. Use the following lines to record some ideas before you write your journal entries.*

I am ______________________

I am leaving Earth because ______________________

My destination is ______________________

Events of my departure ______________________

My feelings ______________________

Events of the journey ______________________

My feelings ______________________

My new home ______________________

My feelings about my new home ______________________

Name ______________________________ Date ______________

"Heading West" by Miriam Davis Colt
"I Will Fight No More Forever" by Chief Joseph

Selection Test A

Critical Reading *Identify the letter of the choice that best answers the question.*

____ 1. Why is it ironic that Colt says the settlers can have faith that the directors will fulfill their part in "Heading West"?
   - A. The settlers did not pay the directors.
   - B. The settlers did not have good faith.
   - C. The directors did not fulfill their part.
   - D. The directors did not join the settlement.

____ 2. In "Heading West," what does Colt mean when she writes "the last visit we shall have until we meet where parting never comes"?
   - A. until we meet at the settlement
   - B. until we meet again in Heaven
   - C. until we all live in the same town
   - D. until we come back for a visit

____ 3. In "Heading West," how does Colt sound as she begins to prepare for the westward move?
   - A. fearful
   - B. worried
   - C. hopeful
   - D. sad

____ 4. How would readers most likely respond to reading about the "miserable hotel" and "dirty beds" in "Heading West"?
   - A. with boredom
   - B. with weariness
   - C. with curiosity
   - D. with sympathy

____ 5. Which of these passages from "Heading West" warns readers that hard times are ahead?
   - A. " . . . a shadow comes over me, as I try to look away into the future . . ."
   - B. "Last night was a lovely moonlit night . . ."
   - C. "Women and children walk along up the hill."
   - D. "Dined on the prairie, and gathered flowers . . ."

Name ______________________________ Date ____________________

___ 6. How might readers respond to reading about "home-sickness" in "Heading West"?

A. by thinking about a time when he or she fixed up a part of the house
B. by thinking about a time when he or she was too busy to think about things
C. by thinking about a time when he or she missed being home
D. by thinking about a time when he or she was at home with the flu

___ 7. What does the final entry of "Heading West" tell you about the settlers who moved West?

A. They all found better lives.
B. They all became farmers.
C. All their expectations were met.
D. Many met disappointing situations.

___ 8. What general tone pervades Chief Joseph's "I Will Fight No More Forever"?

A. sadness
B. anger
C. fear
D. happiness

___ 9. What does Chief Joseph mean by the phrase "From where the sun now stands" in "I Will Fight No More Forever"?

A. as long as the summer lasts
B. for as long as the sun shines
C. from this time forward
D. during the daylight hours

___ 10. What general historical situation does "I Will Fight No More Forever" reflect?

A. the replacement of older Indian leaders with younger ones
B. the poor shelter and food supply on Indian reservations
C. the transportation of Native Americans to reservations
D. the destruction of Native American nations

Vocabulary and Grammar

___ 11. In which of these sentences is the meaning of the word *profusion* expressed?

A. Early settlers often found that they had paid for things that were not delivered.
B. Settlers traveled by train, riverboat, wagons pulled by oxen, and on foot.
C. Prairie settlers were impressed with the abundance of trees and flowers.
D. Settlers found saying goodbye to family to be a sorrowful experience.

Name ______________________ Date ______________

____ 12. Which of these passages from "Heading West" is a sentence fragment?
A. "Here we are, at Kansas City, all safely again on terra firma."
B. "We leave our wagons and make our way to the large camp-fire."
C. "The ladies tell us they are sorry to see us come to this place."
D. "On board steamer 'Cataract,' bound for Kansas City."

Essay

13. Pioneers who moved West faced many risks and dangers. What are some of these, as written about in "Heading West"? Write a brief essay that describes at least two of the dangers Miriam Colt mentions in her diary, and include how you think these dangers affected the settlers.

14. "I Will Fight No More Forever" expresses a sense of sadness and loss. Suppose you are Chief Joseph. In a brief essay, describe how you are feeling about the deaths of the old chiefs and the knowledge that your people are dying and unprotected.

Name ______________________________ Date ____________________

"Heading West" by Miriam Davis Colt

"I Will Fight No More Forever" by Chief Joseph

Selection Test B

Critical Reading *Identify the letter of the choice that best completes the statement or answers the question.*

____ 1. Which word best characterizes Miriam Colt's tone in the following passage?

our "noble lords" complained of the great weight of the wagons

A. respect
B. sarcasm
C. impatience
D. pity

____ 2. Why might it be dangerous for Miriam Colt's husband to let the Georgians know that he is a Free States man?

A. Georgia is a slave state, and the Georgians are against anyone who opposes slavery.
B. The Colts do not want to get friendly with the Georgians.
C. The Georgians are well known for stealing from rich easterners.
D. The Georgians oppose bringing the Vegetarian Company to the western territories.

____ 3. Why does this sentence at the beginning of Miriam Colt's diary turn out to be ironic?

We can have, I think, good faith to believe, that our directors will fulfill on their part:

A. The directors did not build the mills they promised they would.
B. The site of the new city is covered with tents.
C. The families who left the settlement made it impossible for the directors to fulfill their part.
D. The directors did not send an escort to welcome the Colts and other settlers into the new city.

____ 4. Which passage from "Heading West" best conveys a tone of apprehension?

A. "The women and children, who slept in their wagons last night, got a good drenching from the heavy shower."
B. " . . . we wonder if we shall be neighbors to each other in the great 'Octagon City.'"
C. "I said to myself—'Is that what I have got to come to?'"
D. "Found ourselves in this miserable hotel before we knew it."

____ 5. Which of the following responses to this passage from "Heading West" would probably be the most helpful to a reader?

One mile from the city, and Dr. Thorn has broke his wagon tongue; it must be sent back to Kansas City to be mended.

A. wondering why a mechanic couldn't just come out to fix the wagon
B. trying to picture what a wagon with a tongue would look like
C. remembering the feeling of frustration when the car broke down on a vacation
D. guessing about what kind of doctor Dr. Thorn is

Name ______________________ Date ______________

____ 6. What do the situations in "Heading West" and "I Will Fight No More Forever" share that make them likely to evoke strong responses in the reader?
A. They are life-changing.
B. They involve violence.
C. They picture Native Americans.
D. They are terrifying.

____ 7. What is the tone of Chief Joseph's speech "I Will Fight No More Forever"?
A. down but not out
B. zealous and promising
C. wrathful and angry
D. mournful and conceding

____ 8. When Chief Joseph says "It is the young men who say yes and no," he means
A. it is not up to the young men to make the decision about fighting.
B. the young men understand the situation.
C. all the power rests in the hands of the young men.
D. the young men lack the experience and decisiveness to lead.

____ 9. Words such as *sad, sick, cold,* and *tired* establish what element of Chief Joseph's speech?
A. paradox
B. personification
C. tone
D. rhythm

____ 10. Which most clearly expresses the meaning of Chief Joseph's phrase "From where the sun now stands"?
A. from this time on
B. in this exact place
C. today
D. while there is still light

____ 11. Chief Joseph's speech, addressed to his chiefs, is using which approach to elicit a response?
A. the tradition of the Nez Percé tribe
B. a carefully argued position
C. strong emotional appeal
D. his authority as the tribe's leader

____ 12. "I Will Fight No More Forever" possesses historical value because it
A. is the only Native American text that we have.
B. parallels General Howard's account.
C. details Native American rituals.
D. provides some insight into the mind and heart of a key Native American chief.

Name ______________________________ Date ______________

____ 13. Feeling sorrow and pity as you read the words of Chief Joseph is an example of
A. the tone of the speech.
B. a response to the speech.
C. the emotion of the speech.
D. the historical value of the speech.

Vocabulary and Grammar

____ 14. Which quotation from "Heading West" is best characterized by the word *genial*?
A. "The town looks new, but the hue is dingy."
B. "as we leave the smoking embers of our camp-fire this morning."
C. " . . . what a beautiful country is spread out before us!"
D. "We ladies, or rather, 'emigrant women,' . . . around the camp-fire."

____ 15. Why do the settlers in "Heading West" feel *nonplussed* to find that the Secretary of the company was out walking in the rain with his wife on the evening they arrive at the settlement?
A. The Secretary's treatment of his wife is cause for anger among the settlers.
B. The settlers have everything they want and don't need to talk to him.
C. The settlers don't like the Secretary's wife and are relieved she isn't there to greet them.
D. The Secretary's behavior is strange, and the settlers don't know what to make of it.

____ 16. What word best suggests the actions of the directors of the Vegetarian Company regarding the money they have received from the members to build mills?
A. terra firma
B. profusion
C. depredations
D. emigrants

____ 17. Which of these quotations from "Heading West" is a sentence fragment missing its verb?
A. "A hot summer day."
B. "Dined on the prairie, and gathered flowers . . ."
C. "Here too came in the Santa Fe and Indian trade . . ."
D. "Bade our friends good bye, in Potsdam, this morning at the early hour of two o'clock."

Essay

18. Chief Joseph's speech of surrender, reported by newspapers all across the country, made a tremendous impression on Americans. Why do you think people were so moved by Chief Joseph's words? Write an essay discussing people's reactions to the speech and the reasons for it.

19. Settlers ventured into the American West in the hope of making a better life for themselves and their families. The personal costs and dangers of such an undertaking could be great. Write an essay describing the costs and dangers of moving west for Miriam Colt and her family. Cite examples from the selection to support your observations.

20. As Chief of the Nez Percé tribe, Chief Joseph had a deep attachment to and love for his people. Write an essay in which you discuss how Chief Joseph's message and choice of words in "I Will Fight No More Forever" conveys his feelings for his people. Develop your discussion by citing evidence from the selection.

Vocabulary Warm-up Word Lists

Study these words from the selection. Then, complete the activities.

Word List A

aggressively [uh GRES iv lee] *adv.* boldly or energetically
When the magician called for a volunteer, Lucy's hand shot up aggressively.

circulation [ser kyoo LAY shun] *n.* the movement of blood around the body
Does aerobic exercise improve the circulation?

floundered [FLOWN derd] *v.* move in an awkward, stumbling way
Everyone cleared out of Big Bill's way as he floundered around the dance floor.

imperative [im PE ruh tiv] *adj.* urgent and necessary
It is imperative that you return the shirt you borrowed.

likewise [LYK wyz] *adv.* in the same way; also
Kyle is leaving at six; will you be leaving early likewise?

methodically [me THAH dik lee] *adv.* in an orderly, systematic way
Mandy plays chess methodically, while Lisa does not seem to think ahead at all.

panicky [PAN ik ee] *adj.* out of control with fear
His expression turned panicky as the bear lumbered toward him.

undesirable [un de ZY ruh bul] *adj.* not wanted; not pleasing
A large anthill is an undesirable spot for a picnic.

Word List B

agitation [aj i TAY shun] *n.* emotional disturbance or excitement
The man hopped around, wringing his hands, his agitation obvious.

arctic [AHRK tik] *adj.* very cold
Stepping into the air-conditioned house felt like an arctic blast.

asserted [uh SERT id] *v.* insisted on being recognized
If I had not asserted my rights, he would have kept that remote control forever.

capsizing [KAP syz ing] *v.* overturning
Returning to port prior to the storm kept the boat from capsizing.

entanglement [en TAYN gul ment] *n.* state of being tangled
The dog owners let go of their leashes to avoid entanglement.

immortality [im mohr TAL i tee] *n.* lasting fame
That book may be popular now, but do you think it will achieve immortality?

penalty [PEN ul tee] *n.* punishment or unfortunate result
The penalty for her lateness was that all the good seats had been taken.

yearned [YERND] *v.* longed
He yearned for a cold soda, but he had left his wallet at home.

Name ______________________________ Date ______________

"To Build a Fire" by Jack London

Vocabulary Warm-up Exercises

Exercise A *Fill in each blank in the paragraph below with the appropriate word from Word List A.*

I was sitting in the field, watching the cows peacefully and [1] ______________ chewing the grass, when suddenly I noticed a large, angry-looking bull moving [2] ______________ in my direction. I do not exagerate when I say that the blood froze in my veins; it really felt as if my [3] ______________ had actually stopped. Suddenly, it seemed [4] ______________ that I be on the other side of the fence. I began to run. Then, looking over my shoulder, I saw that the bull was doing [5] ______________, only faster. That was when I really started feeling [6] ______________. As I [7] ______________ my way clumsily over the fence, I decided that a field with a bull is an [8] ______________ place to relax, unless you are a cow.

Exercise B *Decide whether each statement below is true or false. Circle* T *or* F, *and explain your answer.*

1. Getting three flat tires in one week would tend to cause a driver agitation.
   T / F ______________________________
2. A smart fly tries to avoid entanglement in a spider's web.
   T / F ______________________________
3. If you go to Texas in July, you will be sure to suffer arctic temperatures.
   T / F ______________________________
4. Football players are especially happy when their team gets a penalty.
   T / F ______________________________
5. Shakespeare achieved immortality through his great cooking.
   T / F ______________________________
6. Cruise tickets might be a good gift for someone who has always yearned to travel.
   T / F ______________________________
7. Capsizing the life boat is a good idea for shipwrecked passengers.
   T / F ______________________________
8. When Rosa Parks refused to give up her seat on a bus, she asserted her rights.
   T / F ______________________________

Name ______________________ Date ______________

"To Build a Fire" by Jack London

Reading Warm-up A

Read the following passage. Pay special attention to the underlined words. Then, read it again, and complete the activities. Use a separate sheet of paper for your written answers.

Imagine being lost alone in the wilderness, hungry, cold, and unprepared—no cozy sleeping bag, no packets of belly-warming cocoa to heat over a campstove. If you should find yourself in this undesirable situation, would you know what to do?

According to survival experts, the first and most important thing is not to become panicky. Sit down, take a deep breath, and think carefully and methodically about your options. What equipment or supplies do you have with you? Even a plastic garbage bag can be extremely useful for keeping you warm and dry. Likewise, you can find natural shelter in unexpected spots—even in deep snow, for instance, there may be a dry, clear area under the lowest branches of a big evergreen tree.

To survive cold weather, it is imperative that you keep your body temperature up. Instead of sitting directly on the ground or in the snow, make a pile of branches or find a fallen tree. Be sure your head is covered—thanks to extra blood circulation around the brain, you can lose forty percent of your heat through your head. If possible, stuff your clothes with dry leaves for insulation, but first check the leaves for bugs! Then, curl yourself up into a ball to conserve your body heat.

Aside from staying alive, your main responsibility is to be found, so *stay in one place*. Searchers are more likely to discover you if you have not floundered around getting even more lost. Also, try to make yourself easy to see: stay out in the open, or use sticks and rocks to make a sign pointing to your shelter. Lastly, if a helicopter flies overhead, wave wildly and aggressively with *both* arms so they know you are in trouble and not just saying hello!

1. Underline what is undesirable about the situation. Then, describe another situation that would be ***undesirable***.
2. Underline what to do to keep from getting panicky. What is the opposite of ***panicky***?
3. Circle a word that means something similar to methodically. How could a pencil and paper help you think ***methodically***?
4. What word could you substitute for *likewise* in this sentence?
5. Underline what is imperative for survival in cold weather. What would be ***imperative*** to know before riding a bicycle downhill?
6. Underline what circulation in the head has to do with keeping warm. What words mean the same as ***circulation***?
7. Underline what could happen if you floundered around rather than stayed put. Would you use the word ***floundered*** for someone who moved with grace and purpose?
8. Circle what you should do aggressively if you see a helicopter. What else might someone do ***aggressively***?

Name ______________________________ Date ______________

"**To Build a Fire**" by Jack London

Reading Warm-up B

Read the following passage. Pay special attention to the underlined words. Then, read it again, and complete the activities. Use a separate sheet of paper for your written answers.

On a cold March morning in 1985, Libby Riddles waited at the starting line of the Iditarod, the "Last Great Race on Earth." Her fifteen sled dogs—Binga, Bug-man, Brownie, Stewpot, and the rest—were barking madly, and Riddles worked hard to hide her own agitation.

All the mushers had good reason to be nervous; after all, the race would cover more than a thousand miles of harsh, dangerous arctic terrain, from rugged mountain peaks to frozen rivers. For Riddles, though, the stakes were extra high. No woman had ever won the Iditarod—if she crossed the finish line first, she would win not just this year's race, but immortality.

Disaster struck, however, before she even got out of Anchorage, the city where the race began. Her excited dog team decided to take a "shortcut" through the woods. Ignoring her shouts, they dragged her through the brush, nearly capsizing the sled as Riddles struggled to keep the lines clear and avoid entanglement. She quickly asserted her authority, though, and soon she and her team were off again, this time for real.

Bitter subzero temperatures, sleepless nights, even briefly losing her dogs when they took off without her—nothing stopped Riddles, and soon she was in the lead. Then, a huge storm blew up, a raging, blinding blizzard with seventy-mile-an-hour winds. While her competitors hung back in the safety of a village, Riddles pushed on into the blizzard with her team.

It was a risky move, and she might very well have paid the ultimate penalty for her decision. Instead, thanks to her courage and skill—not to mention good luck—Riddles achieved the goal she yearned for: she became the first woman to win the "Last Great Race on Earth."

1. Underline the way the dogs showed agitation. How does a baby show ***agitation***?
2. Circle the word that means something similar to arctic. Why would ***arctic*** terrain be dangerous?
3. Underline why winning the race would bring Riddles immortality. Name someone you admire who earned ***immortality*** through his or her achievements.
4. Underline what the dogs did that nearly resulted in capsizing the sled. Why would ***capsizing*** the sled be a bad thing for Riddles?
5. Underline what Riddles did to avoid entanglement. Then, describe another kind of ***entanglement***.
6. How do you think Riddles asserted her authority over the dogs?
7. What would be the "ultimate penalty" that Riddles might have paid?
8. Underline what Riddles yearned to do, and did. Name another achievement that someone might ***yearn*** for.

Name ______________________________ Date ______________

"To Build a Fire" by Jack London

Literary Analysis: Conflict

Conflict is the struggle between two opposing forces or characters. An **internal conflict** is a struggle between conflicting thoughts and emotions within a character's mind. You face an internal conflict, for example, when you want to spend time studying for a test, yet you also want to go to the movie with your friends. An **external conflict** is a struggle between a character and an outside force, such as another character, society, nature, or fate. A pilot trying to land an airplane in strong winds is engaged in an external conflict—person against nature.

DIRECTIONS: *Following are brief excerpts from "To Build a Fire." Identify the conflict in each as internal or external. Then name the opposing forces—person against internal self, or person against nature, fate, another character, or society—and briefly explain the conflict.*

1. "It was seventy-five below zero. Since the freezing point is thirty-two above zero, it meant that one hundred and seven degrees of frost obtained."

   ____

2. "There was nobody to talk to; and, had there been, speech would have been impossible because of the ice-muzzle on his mouth."

   ____

3. "He tried to keep this thought down, to forget it, to think of something else, he was aware of the panicky feeling that it caused and he was afraid of the panic."

   ____

4. "He spoke to the dog . . . but in his voice was a strange note of fear that frightened the animal. . . . As it came within reaching distance, the man lost his control."

   ____

5. "High up in the tree one bough capsized its load of snow . . . it grew like an avalanche, and it descended without warning upon the man and the fire, and fire was blotted out!"

   ____

6. "He was very careful. He drove the thought of his freezing feet, and nose, and cheeks, out of his mind, devoting his whole soul to the matches."

   ____

7. ". . . it was a matter of life and death. This threw him into a panic, and he turned and ran up the creekbed along the old, dim trail."

   ____

8. "Well, he was bound to freeze anyway, and he might as well take it decently."

   ____

Name ______________________________ Date ________________

"To Build a Fire" by Jack London

Reading Strategy: Predict

Making predictions about what you are reading based on clues in the text and on your own previous experience can increase your enjoyment of a literary work and help you be a more effective reader. Of course, not all your predictions will match the outcomes in the text. You may have to change your predictions as you read further and discover additional clues.

DIRECTIONS: *As you read "To Build a Fire," watch for clues that can help you predict what will happen next. In the chart below, list the clues, your predictions based on those clues, and the actual outcomes from the text.*

CLUE	PREDICTION	OUTCOME

Name ______________________________ Date ______________

"To Build a Fire" by Jack London

Vocabulary Builder

Using the Latin Root *-ject-*

The Latin root *-ject-* comes from a verb meaning "to throw" and appears in many English words.

A. DIRECTIONS: *Read the list of prefixes and their meanings. Then read each sentence and explain how the prefix and the root* -ject- *influence the meaning of the underlined word.*

de- = "down"
e- = "out of"
ob- = "in the way"; "against"

1. The pilot saved himself by ejecting from the cockpit as the plane went down.

____

2. We were sure that the coach would object to our missing practice.

____

3. Jillian became dejected when she learned that she had failed the history test.

____

Using the Word List

conjectural	unwonted	conflagration	peremptorily

B. DIRECTIONS: *Each question consists of a related pair of words in CAPITAL LETTERS, followed by four lettered pairs of words. Choose the lettered pair that best expresses a relationship* similar *to that expressed in the numbered pair and circle the letter of your choice.*

1. CAMPFIRE : CONFLAGRATION::
   A. car : truck
   B. spark : match
   C. flurry : blizzard
   D. sun : desert
2. CONJECTURAL : CERTAIN ::
   A. guess : fact
   B. generous : charitable
   C. delicious : tasty
   D. shifting : fixed
3. COMMANDS : PEREMPTORILY::
   A. awakes : retires
   B. sings : ballads
   C. moves : forward
   D. dances : gracefully
4. UNWONTED : SURPRISING ::
   A. undesired : hating
   B. cruel : frightening
   C. sparse : meager
   D. routine : unusual

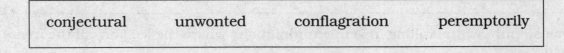

Name ______________________________ Date ______________

"To Build a Fire" by Jack London

Grammar and Style: Adverb Clauses

Adverb clauses are subordinate clauses that modify verbs, adjectives, or other adverbs. They explain or describe *how, when, where, why, under what circumstances,* and *to what extent.*

Adverb clause telling when:	When he touched a twig, he had to look and see whether or not he had hold of it.
Adverb clause telling why:	He ran because he was afraid.

A. Practice: *Some of these sentences from "To Build a Fire" contain an adverb clause. Read each sentence, and when you find an adverb clause, underline it. Then note whether it tells* how, when, where, why, under what circumstances, *or* to what extent. *For sentences that do not contain an adverb clause, write* none.

1. "If he fell down it would shatter itself, like glass, into brittle fragments."
   ____
2. "It knew that it was no time for traveling."
   ____
3. "So long as he walked four miles an hour, he pumped that blood, willy nilly, to the surface."
   ____
4. "When all was ready, the man reached in his pocket. . . ."
   ____
5. "It was all pure white, rolling in gentle undulations where the ice jams of the freeze-up had formed."
   ____

B. Writing Application: *Combine each pair of simple sentences below into one complex sentence containing an adverb clause. Underline the adverb clause.*

1. Spring water lay hidden under the snow. The man tried to avoid walking there.
   ____
   ____
2. The man built a fire right under a snow-laden tree. The snow fell and extinguished the flame.
   ____
   ____
   ____

Name ______________________________ Date ______________

"To Build a Fire" by Jack London

Support for Writing

Prepare to write your **literary analysis** of how the elements of "To Build a Fire" work together to communicate the story's message. Enter your thoughts and opinions in the chart below.

"To Build a Fire" — Analysis

Message of "To Build a Fire"	
Setting : Details supporting message	
Characters: Details supporting message	
Plot: Details supporting message	

On a separate page, write a draft of your literary analysis. State your thesis, as well as a main idea in each paragraph from your chart. When you revise, make sure you have supported your thesis, and add more details if you need to.

Name ______________________________ Date ______________

"To Build a Fire" by Jack London

Support for Extend Your Learning

Listening and Speaking

As you prepare to write an **enactment** of the dog talking about the man in "To Build a Fire," imagine what he would say about what the man is doing and how he is behaving. As you work, keep these things in mind:

- Refer to the text of the story for accuracy.
- Include details that reflect the dog's highly developed senses of smell and hearing.

As your write, create a character for the dog that makes him an individual. After you read your enactment to the class, ask for feedback.

Research and Technology

As you prepare to create a **booklet** of safety guidelines for avoiding hypothermia (body temperature that is below normal), do research on the Internet. Enter your findings in the chart.

Hypothermia and How to Avoid It

Hypothermia: Definition	
Symptoms/Dangerous Situations	
How to Avoid It	
How to Treat It	

Create a word-processed booklet that explains how to avoid this dangerous condition of cold weather. As you create your booklet, think about the people who would benefit from it.

Name ______________________________ Date ______________

"To Build a Fire" by Jack London

Enrichment: Films About Survival

Stories of survival under challenging conditions abound in literature, in film, and on television. Although the main character in "To Build a Fire" does not survive, his behavior functions as a kind of negative guide to living through the rigors of a winter journey in the Arctic. The story probably also led you to think about the kind of characteristics that enable people to adapt to adverse conditions and, thus, to survive.

DIRECTIONS: *Consult a knowledgeable person or a guide to movies and videos to find one that deals with survival under challenging conditions. Here are a few examples:* Air Force One, Cool Hand Luke, Incredible Journey, Lord of the Flies, Return of the Jedi, *and* Swiss Family Robinson. *View one of these survival films or another of your choice. As you watch, note how the survivors adapt to conditions, and how this adaptability helps them survive. Then write a profile of a person with character traits that would prepare him or her to adapt to difficult situations. Support your points by citing evidence from the film you view and "To Build a Fire." Use the following lines to record some ideas before you write your profile.*

Movie and surviving characters: ______________________________

____

____

How does each character adapt and survive? ______________________________

____

____

____

____

____

____

How do survivors differ from those who die? ______________________________

____

____

____

____

Some character traits that allow people to adapt: ______________________________

____

____

____

____

Name ______________________ Date ______________

"To Build a Fire" by Jack London

Selection Test A

Critical Reading *Identify the letter of the choice that best answers the question.*

____ **1.** What is the external conflict in "To Build a Fire"?
A. between human and dog
B. between human and nature
C. between human and human
D. between human and God

____ **2.** What information appears toward the beginning of "To Build a Fire" that helps readers predict that the man will soon be in trouble?
A. It will take him all day to reach camp.
B. The sun has not come above the horizon.
C. It is much colder than he thinks it is.
D. He has heavy whiskers on his face.

____ **3.** How does the dog in "To Build a Fire" express his anxiety about the situation?
A. by running around in circles
B. by drooping his tail
C. by burrowing under the snow
D. by running back to the camp

____ **4.** In "To Build a Fire," what can you predict when the man comes across a hidden spring?
A. The dog will fall into a hidden spring.
B. The man will fall into a hidden spring.
C. The man will follow the spring to camp.
D. The man will drink from the spring.

____ **5.** What does London suggest when he writes: "The dog did not know anything about thermometers . . . But the brute had its instinct" in "To Build A Fire"?
A. The man is smarter than the dog.
B. The dog does not need a device to measure the cold.
C. A man's brain and a dog's brain are not the same.
D. Only man has awareness about danger.

Name ______________________________ Date ______________

____ 6. Which element of "To Build a Fire" best reflects the main external conflict of the story?

A. the man's refusal to heed the advice of the old-timer

B. the man's choice to smoke his pipe after eating his lunch

C. the man's choice to try to reach the camp by nightfall

D. the man's refusal to pay attention to the dog's behavior

____ 7. Which of these states a central message of "To Build a Fire"?

A. To survive in the wilderness, pay attention to your surroundings.

B. To survive in the Arctic, know when summer is due to arrive.

C. To survive in extreme cold, dress in warm clothing and boots.

D. To survive in extreme conditions, be sure to carry enough food.

____ 8. Which of these details emphasizes the central message of "To Build a Fire" most clearly?

A. The man keeps his food from freezing by storing it near his skin.

B. The man keeps watching to avoid falling into a hidden spring.

C. The man runs as fast as he can to keep his body from freezing.

D. The man builds a fire under a tree with snow-covered branches.

____ 9. Why does the man in "To Build a Fire" finally put aside his panic about freezing to death?

A. He realizes he cannot light a fire if he is feeling panic.

B. He wants to die with dignity if he cannot survive the cold.

C. He does not want his panic to frighten his dog companion.

D. He realizes he cannot run well if he is feeling panic.

____ 10. Which internal conflict does the man experience toward the end of "To Build a Fire"?

A. hope versus acceptance

B. summer versus winter

C. anger versus sadness

D. life versus death

Vocabulary and Grammar

____ 11. In which sentence is the meaning of the word *unwonted* suggested?

A. The old-timer warned the man about the cold.

B. The man did not realize he was feeling unusual cold.

C. The dog understood cold and tried to warn the man.

D. When the man froze to death, the dog went to find warmth.

Name ______________________________ Date ______________

____ 12. Which of these sentences contains an adverb clause?

A. "The man sat up in the snow for a moment and struggled for calmness."

B. "At last, when he could endure no more, he jerked his hands apart."

C. "The sight of the dog put a wild idea into his head."

D. "Twenty times he scratched before he succeeded in lighting it."

Essay

13. Neither the man nor the dog in "To Build a Fire" have names. Why do you think the author did this? What do nameless characters suggest to a reader? Write a brief essay to give your opinion about why the man and the dog have no names in this story.

14. At the beginning of "To Build a Fire," London describes the man in this way: "The trouble with him was that he was without imagination. He was quick and alert in the things of life, but . . . not in the significances." Write a brief essay to show how this description predicts what will happen to the man.

Name ________________________________ Date ________________

"To Build a Fire" by Jack London

Selection Test B

Critical Reading *Identify the letter of the choice that best completes the statement or answers the question.*

____ 1. In "To Build a Fire," there is an external conflict between
A. the beauty of nature and the cruelty of nature.
B. society and the individual.
C. human beings and nature.
D. instinct and civilization.

____ 2. Which of the following character flaws brings about the man's tragic end?
A. cowardice
B. carelessness
C. overconfidence
D. greed

____ 3. Toward the end of "To Build a Fire," the man has an internal conflict between his
A. body and his will.
B. short-term goals and his long-term goals.
C. conscience and his needs.
D. animal nature and his spiritual nature.

____ 4. Which of the following themes is expressed by the contrasting ways in which the dog and the man cope with the cold?
A. Animals are naturally superior to humans.
B. Animals are unable to have or express emotions.
C. Humans need to be as well attuned to nature as animals in order to survive in it.
D. Humans are so closely tied to civilization that they cannot return to nature.

____ 5. Until the story's end, the man's attitude toward the advice provided by the old-timer of Sulphur Creek was one of
A. respect.
B. curiosity.
C. confusion.
D. ridicule.

____ 6. Which passage from the beginning of the story gives the strongest clue to the attitude that contributes to the man's death?
A. "It was a steep bank, and he paused for breath at the top, excusing the act to himself by looking at his watch."
B. "He was used to the lack of sun. It had been days since he had seen the sun, and he knew that a few more days must pass before that cheerful orb, due south, would just peep above the skyline and dip immediately from view."
C. "The man flung a look back along the way he had come."
D. "He was a newcomer in the land, a *chechaquo,* and this was his first winter."

Name ______________________________ Date ______________

____ 7. Which example best reflects the main external conflict of the story?
A. the encounter between the old timer and the man
B. the hostility between the man and the dog
C. the opposing emotions of the man near the end of the story
D. the conflict of the man's animal nature and his spiritual nature

____ 8. Which of the following details reflects the story's central theme most clearly?
A. The fire was put out by an avalanche of snow from the branches that the man had inadvertently agitated.
B. Even though it was high noon, there was no sun in the sky.
C. At precisely the expected time, the man arrived at the forks of the creek.
D. While attempting to build a fire, the man burned his hands.

____ 9. Which internal conflict does the man experience toward the end of the story?
A. terror versus faith
B. reality versus hope
C. sorrow versus stoicism
D. regret versus rage

____ 10. In "To Build a Fire," London's attitude toward the Alaskan wilderness can best be described as
A. nostalgic.
B. respectful.
C. apprehensive.
D. affectionate.

____ 11. Which of the following clues is most likely to lead a reader to predict that the man will make it to camp?
A. "For the moment, the cold of space was outwitted."
B. "He had forgotten to build a fire and thaw out."
C. "He was pleased at the speed he had made. If he kept it up, he would certainly be with the boys by six."
D. "Once in a while the thought reiterated itself that it was very cold and that he had never experienced such cold."

____ 12. Which of following is the correct way to predict while reading a story?
A. Don't try to correct your first prediction, but just read on quickly to the end of the story.
B. Start making predictions about the end of the story about halfway through it.
C. Check your predictions as you read, and revise them if necessary.
D. Avoid using your own experience when making predictions about your reading.

Vocabulary and Grammar

____ 13. Choose the correct vocabulary word to complete the sentence.
If the man had been more given to __________ thoughts from the beginning, he might have survived.
A. unwonted
B. peremptory
C. conjectural
D. none of the above

Name ______________________________ Date ________________

____ 14. Which of the following quotations contains an adverb clause explaining *under what circumstances*?
A. "When all was ready, the man reached in his pocket for a second piece of birch bark."
B. "If he had only had a trail mate he would have been in no danger now."
C. "As he looked apathetically about him, his eyes chanced on the dog. . . ."
D. "He could not pick and choose, for he had to lift the fuel between the heels of his hands."

____ 15. What does the adverb clause in the following quotation tell?
His theory of running until he reached camp and the boys had one flaw in it.
A. when
B. where
C. under what circumstances
D. to what extent

____ 16. What best explains this ironic quotation from the story?
and the moccasin strings were like rods of steel all twisted and knotted as by some conflagration.
A. The moccasin laces are so twisted and frozen that they are like steel rods contorted by a hot, destructive fire.
B. The soft moccasin laces are now frozen and hard like steel.
C. The man is trying to do the right thing by taking off his moccasins, but he can't.
D. The tied laces are as tangled as if they had been blown around in a high wind.

____ 17. Which word best suggests the way the man treats the dog in the story?
A. unwonted
B. conjectural
C. peremptorily
D. none of the above

Essay

18. The man in "To Build a Fire" has taken on a great challenge by choosing to work in a very remote and cold place. If you had to choose a great physical challenge of some type, what would you choose to do? Write an essay describing what your own challenge would be like. What do you think you might gain from such an experience? How would you use the experience of the man in the story to help you survive your challenge?

19. Sometimes an author will include a minor character who has virtues that the protagonist lacks. In Jack London's "To Build a Fire," that minor character is a dog. The dog consistently displays more innate common sense and wisdom than the man. Write an essay in which you compare and contrast the dog's and the man's attitudes toward the dangerously cold journey they are taking. Include at least three specific actions of the dog that show its instincts, under the circumstances, to be superior to the man's judgment.

20. To maintain suspense, authors may provide clues that lead readers to predict the outcome but also give readers details that make them uncertain about the outcome. In some cases, the outcome may be predictable, but how the ending works out keeps readers in suspense. When you first read "To Build a Fire," were you uncertain about the outcome, or did you know what would happen, but not how? What clues made you respond to the story the way you did? Write an essay relating your thought and prediction process as you read "To Build a Fire." Use examples from the selection where necessary.

"The Story of an Hour" by Kate Chopin

Vocabulary Warm-up Word Lists

Study these words from the selection. Then, complete the activities.

Word List A

absolutely [ab suh LOOT lee] *adv.* totally; without exception
Jody is a vegetarian, so she eats absolutely no meat.

countless [KOWNT les] *adj.* too many to count
Uncle Pete has driven here countless times, and yet he still gets lost.

intention [in TEN shun] *n.* purpose
My intention was to draw a puppy, but it came out looking like a cow.

paralyzed [PAR uh lyzd] *adj.* unable to move
The deer stared into the headlights, as if paralyzed by fear.

perception [per SEP shun] *n.* awareness or understanding
Lee's perception of what happened is completely different from mine.

powerful [POW er ful] *adj.* strong; mighty
The weightlifter flexed his powerful arms.

revealed [ri VEELD] *v.* made known
Her so-called best friend revealed her secret to the whole school.

significance [sig NIF i kans] *n.* meaning
I read the motto on her T-shirt, but its significance was unclear to me.

Word List B

eaves [EEVZ] *n.* overhanging edge of a roof
Have you noticed the vines growing underneath the eaves?

illumination [i loo mi NAY shun] *n.* enlightenment
Reading the instructions turned my confusion to illumination.

imploring [im PLOHR ing] *v.* begging
"Please, I am imploring you," she said. "Don't wear that ugly shirt!"

inability [in uh BIL i tee] *n.* lack of ability
Jen loves to sing but gets frustrated by her inability to carry a tune.

persistence [per SIS tens] *n.* stubborn refusal to give up
She did not want to lend him the CD, but his persistence wore her down.

striving [STRY ving] *v.* trying very hard
I am striving to be nicer to my brother, but I don't always succeed.

subtle [SUH tul] *adj.* not obvious
There was a subtle sweetness in the air—roses, perhaps?

trivial [TRI vee ul] *adj.* unimportant
Charlie tends to get overexcited about trivial things.

Name ______________________________ Date ______________

"The Story of an Hour" by Kate Chopin

Vocabulary Warm-up Exercises

Exercise A *Fill in each blank in the paragraph below with the appropriate word from Word List A.*

When I went downtown, my only [1] ______________ was to return a book to the library. Honestly, I had [2] ______________ no plan to go in the dumpling shop. When I walked by, though, I smelled the [3] ______________ aroma of fried dumplings and my stomach growled. A moment's thought [4] ______________ the obvious [5] ______________ of that growl: I had not had lunch. I stood there, [6] ______________ by indecision. Should I save my money and go home and make a sandwich, or give in to the temptation as I had done [7] ______________ times before? Of course, I gave in. All right, maybe I have no willpower, but it is not my fault—the dumplings made me do it. At least, that is my [8] ______________ of what happened!

Exercise B *Decide whether each statement below is true or false. Circle* T *or* F, *and explain your answer.*

1. If you do not know the meaning of a word, a dictionary can provide illumination.
   T / F ______________________________
2. Dumping an entire shakerful of salt into your food will give the dish a subtle flavor.
   T / F ______________________________
3. The inability to tell green from red is a sign of color blindness.
   T / F ______________________________
4. Persistence is advised by the saying, "If at first you don't succeed, try, try again."
   T / F ______________________________
5. The eaves of a house are usually found in the basement, behind the furnace.
   T / F ______________________________
6. If begging and pleading do not get you what you want, imploring might work better.
   T / F ______________________________
7. Happy, easygoing people tend to lose their temper over trivial problems.
   T / F ______________________________
8. People who read a lot of self-help books may be striving to improve themselves.
   T / F ______________________________

Name ______________________________ Date ______________

"The Story of an Hour" by Kate Chopin

Reading Warm-up A

Read the following passage. Pay special attention to the underlined words. Then, read it again, and complete the activities. Use a separate sheet of paper for your written answers.

You may have heard irony mentioned countless times: "Isn't it ironic?" Yet, as you will discover if you ask for a definition, many people who talk about irony do not really understand the significance of the word.

One reason for this confusion is that *irony* can mean several different things. For instance, there is *verbal irony*, in which the speaker's intention is the opposite of what he or she is saying. "Can't wait to run out and buy *that*," your friend says after a commercial. Her tone of voice, however, makes it clear that she has absolutely no desire to do so.

Have you ever sat motionless in a movie theater, staring in paralyzed horror at the screen as the main character strolls into danger? "Watch out!" you want to scream. "The bad guy's right behind that door!" This is an example of *dramatic irony*, in which there is a conflict between the character's perception of events and that of the audience (or reader). You see things differently than the character, because more has been revealed to you: an earlier scene showed the "bad guy" in his hiding place.

Dramatic irony often has a strong impact on our emotions, but a third type, *situational irony*, can be even more powerful. Situational irony occurs when something happens that contradicts our expectations.

In the classic novel *Howard's End*, a dying woman writes a note in which she leaves her home to a young friend, Margaret. Her rich widower and children burn the note and keep the house. Since nobody else knows about the note, we do not expect that the friend will ever own the house. Ironically, however, the widower later falls in love with Margaret. In the end, he marries her and gives her the house that should have been hers all along.

1. Circle a word in this paragraph that means something similar to countless. What is an antoymn *countless*?
2. Circle a word that, like significance, has to do with meaning. If you wanted to know the *significance* of a word, what would you do?
3. Underline what shows the friend's true intention. If your *intention* was to spend money, where would you start?
4. Underline what the friend has absolutely no wish to do. Would somebody who was *absolutely* full order dessert?
5. Circle the word that means almost the same as paralyzed. If you were *paralyzed* with laughter, would you be rolling around on the floor?
6. Underline the words that mean "You have a different perception." What could change your *perception* of someone?
7. Circle the word that means revealed. How do you feel when the ending of a movie is *revealed* before you see it?
8. Circle the word that means the same as powerful. What else might be described as *powerful*?

Name ______________________________ Date ______________

"The Story of an Hour" by Kate Chopin

Reading Warm-up B

Read the following passage. Pay special attention to the underlined words. Then, read it again, and complete the activities. Use a separate sheet of paper for your written answers.

"Kevin," my mother reminded me, "don't forget you promised to take Blue to his appointment at the vet this afternoon, okay?"

I grunted a reply and went off to search for the dog, wondering why I always got stuck with these trivial chores when I had so many more important things to do.

Blue lay in his usual spot by the porch, resting in the shade under the eaves. When he saw me, he sprang up and dashed over with his ratty old tennis ball. "Not now," I told him, but he dropped it at my feet, then pushed at me with his nose. Annoyed at his persistence, I snapped on his leash, kicked the ball away, and pulled him to the car.

The visit to the veterinarian went fine, as usual, and I'd forgotten all about it when the phone rang a week later. It was the vet, saying a routine blood test had turned up a problem.

"But he seems perfectly normal!" I protested.

"Early symptoms can be subtle," she explained. "We'll repeat the test, but if the results are consistent, Blue may be seriously ill."

I wandered outside, striving to grasp the meaning of this news. Blue trotted over and flopped down beside me, imploring me to pet him with a gaze that made me feel about two inches tall. How long had it been since I'd responded to that look by rubbing him behind the ears, instead of telling him to quit bothering me? Suddenly, it seemed obvious that tossing a ball took less energy than getting irritated over Blue's inability to take a hint.

The story has a happy ending—Blue wasn't sick after all. But that moment of illumination stayed with me, and I knew I would never take my dog for granted again.

1. Circle the word that means the opposite of trivial. Do you think taking a pet for a checkup is a *trivial* task?

2. Underline the words that hint at where you might find eaves. Then, name a kind of dwelling that does not have *eaves*.

3. Underline the words that show Blue displaying persistence. Describe a time when you or someone else showed *persistence*.

4. Would you describe the symptoms of a bad cold as subtle? Explain.

5. Underline the news that Kevin is striving to grasp. What would be the opposite of *striving*?

6. Circle what Blue is imploring Kevin to do. Then, give another word for *imploring*.

7. Earlier in the passage, how did Blue show his inability to take a hint? (Look for lines you already underlined, but answer in your own words.)

8. Circle the paragraph in which Kevin experiences a moment of illumination. If you wanted to learn how to care for a pet, where would you go for *illumination*?

Name ________________________________ Date ________________

"The Story of an Hour" by Kate Chopin

Literary Analysis: Irony

Irony is a contrast or a difference between what is stated and what is meant, or between what is expected to happen and what actually happens. **Situational irony** occurs when a result turns out differently than expected. For example, from the actions of Mrs. Mallard and her friends, readers expect that she will be overcome with grief at the news of her husband's death. Instead she exults in her freedom. **Dramatic irony** occurs when readers know something a character does not know. Readers know a few seconds before Mrs. Mallard, for example, that her husband is actually alive. Think of other stories you have read that use irony.

DIRECTIONS: *On the lines provided, identify stories you have read that use irony. Quote or summarize a passage that is an example of situational irony and one that is an example of dramatic irony. Then explain the irony in each passage.*

1. **Situational irony:** Students should choose a passage that illustrates how the outcome of an action or situation is different from what the reader expects.

2. **Dramatic irony:** Students should choose a passage that illustrates how the readers are aware of something that a character in the story does not know.

Name ______________________________ Date ______________

"The Story of an Hour" by Kate Chopin

Reading Strategy: Recognize Ironic Details

In literature, as in life, **irony** occurs when there is a contrast between what is stated and what is intended, or between expectations and reality. Authors create irony by supplying details that lead us to expect an outcome different from what actually happens.

DIRECTIONS: *Think about "The Story of an Hour" in terms of the ironic details that Chopin has provided—words that led you to think one thing about the events and the characters when actually something else was true. List four of these details below and tell what they led you to expect and what the ironic result was.*

Ironic details	What you expected	What actually happened

Name ______________________________ Date ______________

"The Story of an Hour" by Kate Chopin

Vocabulary Builder

Using the Prefix *fore-*

The prefix *fore-* means "before" in the sense of time, place, or condition.

A. DIRECTIONS: *Write the letter of the best definition of each of the following words having the prefix* fore.

___ 1. foreleg

___ 2. forenoon

___ 3. forecast

___ 4. forewarn

___ 5. foreword

___ 6. foreclosure

A. action taken before a loan is lost

B. part of a book that comes before the main section

C. front leg of any animal having four or more legs

D. prediction made before a weather system arrives

E. another word for the morning, the part of the day before 12 o'clock P.M.

F. give notice before a bad event occurs

Using the Word List

forestall	repression	elusive
tumultuously	importunities	

B. DIRECTIONS: *Select the Word List word that relates best to each situation, and write the word on the line.*

1. Mrs. Mallard's previous actions regarding her feelings about her marriage

____

2. Josephine's whispered pleas at her sister's bedroom door

____

3. the way Mrs. Mallard's imaginings about the free days ahead of her went through her mind

____

4. Richards's attempt to keep the shock of seeing her husband alive from Mrs. Mallard

____

5. the mysterious, unsolvable nature of love

____

Name ______________________________ Date ______________

"The Story of an Hour" by Kate Chopin

Grammar and Style: Appositives and Appositive Phrases

An **appositive** is a noun or pronoun placed near another noun or pronoun to give additional information about the first usage. An appositive that can be dropped from a sentence without changing the meaning of the sentence must be set off with commas or dashes. If the appositive is essential to the meaning of the sentence, it is not set off by commas. When an appositive has its own modifiers, it is an **appositive phrase.**

Appositive: Her husband's friend Richards was there. (Richards is essential to the meaning of the sentence because we need to know which of her husband's friends is meant. No commas are used.)

Appositive phrase: Louise's joy—a feeling of complete freedom from repression—almost overwhelmed her. (The appositive phrase is not essential to the meaning of the sentence. Dashes are used.)

A. Practice: *Underline the appositive or appositive phrase in each sentence. Where necessary, add commas.*

1. A breeze a delicious breath of rain swept through the house.
2. The well-known author Kate Chopin gave the opening address at the meeting.
3. Louise Mallard felt trapped by marriage a repressive institution.
4. The announcement of Mallard's death was a mistake a serious error with dire consequences.
5. One Victorian author Kate Chopin had strong opinions about the place of women in society.

B. Writing Application: *Combine each pair of sentences into one sentence containing an appositive.*

1. Mrs. Mallard found herself whispering a single word over and over. That word was "free."

   ____

2. An oak barrier kept Josephine from seeing what her sister was doing. The bedroom door was the barrier.

   ____

3. She felt unfettered by the restraints of time. She felt like a soaring eagle.

   ____

Name ____________________ Date ____________________

"The Story of an Hour" by Kate Chopin

Support for Writing

Prepare to write a **reflective essay** about a time in which your life changed dramatically, such as a move from one home to another. Enter your memories and reflections on the event in the graphic organizer below.

Sometimes Life Changes Quickly

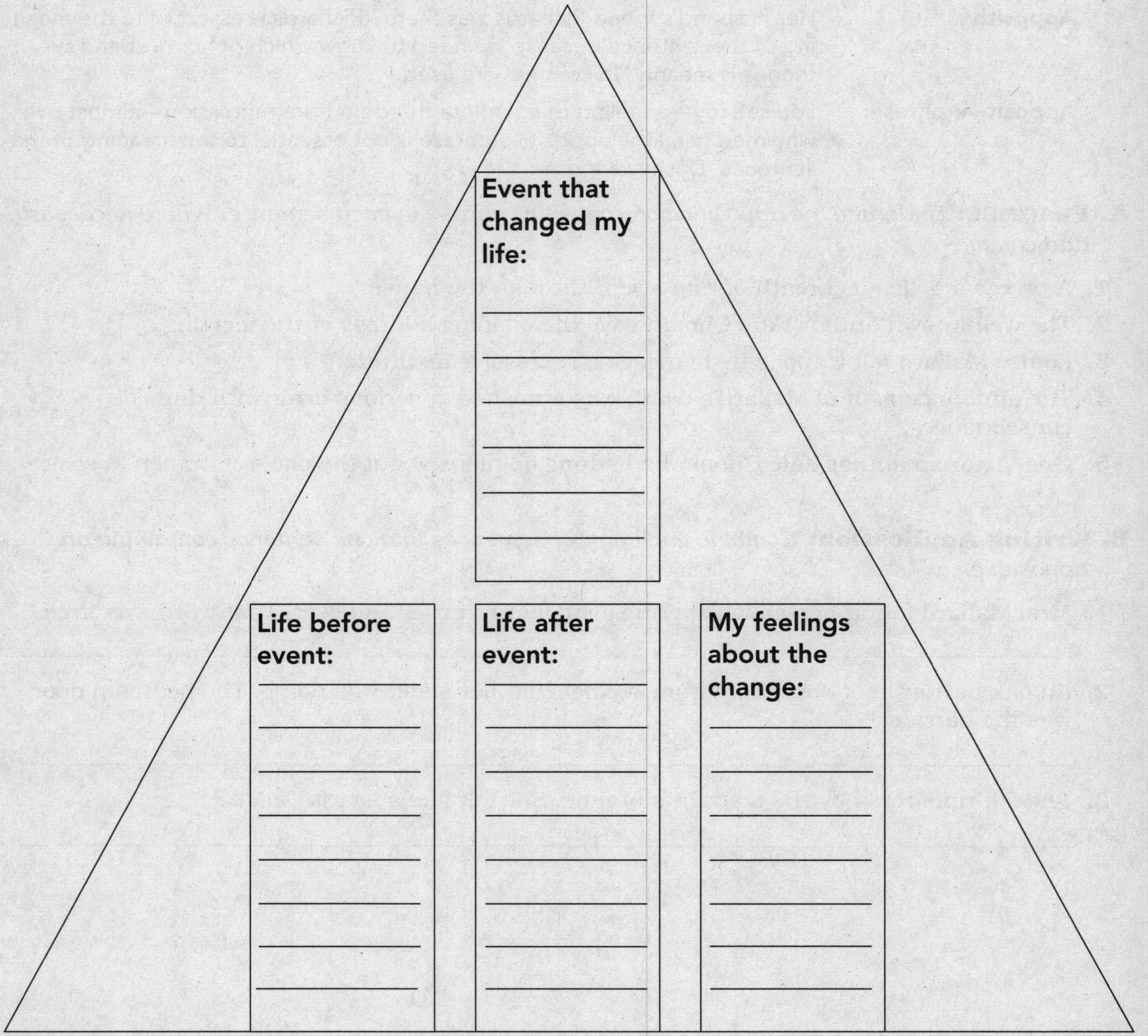

On a separate page, write a draft of your reflective essay. Organize your thoughts either in chronological order in or in their order of importance. When you revise your essay, be sure your thoughts and feelings about the dramatic event have been made clear to the reader. Add or eliminate information to strengthen the impression you wish to make.

Name ______________________________ Date ______________

"The Story of an Hour" by Kate Chopin

Support for Extend Your Learning

Listening and Speaking

As you imagine that Mr. Mallard did not return, and think about how Mrs. Mallard might have lived her life, prepare a **soliloquy** by Mrs. Mallard. As she reflects on her life ten years later, keep these things in mind:

- Has Mrs. Mallard's heart trouble improved, or not?
- What has it meant to "live for herself"?

Present your soliloquy as though you are Mrs. Mallard. Reread the story to find details for your characterization.

Research and Technology

As you do research on women in another culture for an **oral report,** enter your findings into the table below.

Women in (choose another country/culture) ______________
Compared with Women in U.S.

Cultural Factor	Women in ______________	Women in U.S.
Social		
Political		
Economic		

Present your report and ask for feedback. Compare your findings about women in other cultures with those of your classmates.

Name ______________________ Date ______________________

"The Story of an Hour" by Kate Chopin

Enrichment: Social Studies

DIRECTIONS: *Form a group with some classmates to discuss "The Story of an Hour." First, research society's attitudes toward love and marriage in the late 1800s. Then, prior to your discussion, answer the first three questions, using an extra sheet of paper if needed.*

1. In what ways, if any, is the story dated?

   ____

   ____

2. In what ways, if any, does it represent universal feelings and attitudes?

   ____

   ____

3. Imagine that the roles are reversed—the husband is told that his wife has been killed. How might he react to the message?

   ____

   ____

Hold the discussion with your group. Start by comparing your answers to the questions above. Share your research with other group members. Try role-playing some of the ideas about the relationship that come out of the discussion. After the discussion, answer these questions:

1. What were the group's consensus answers to the first three questions?

   ____

   ____

2. How did your own answers differ from the group's answers?

   ____

   ____

3. Were there any gender differences in the responses? If so, what were they?

   ____

   ____

4. What insights did reading and discussing the story give you into the relationship of marriage and what it takes to make it succeed?

   ____

   ____

Name ______________________________ Date ______________

"The Story of an Hour" by Kate Chopin

Selection Test A

Critical Reading *Identify the letter of the choice that best answers the question.*

___ 1. In "The Story of an Hour," why is Josephine afraid to tell Mrs. Mallard that her husband died?

A. Mrs. Mallard has a mental problem.
B. Mrs. Mallard has a heart condition.
C. Mrs. Mallard is expecting a baby.
D. Mrs. Mallard is planning to leave him.

___ 2. In "The Story of an Hour," what is ironic about the sounds Mrs. Mallard hears after she has been told of her husband's death?

A. They are all sounds of ongoing life.
B. They are all sounds from outdoors.
C. They are all sounds from faraway.
D. They are all sad and lonely sounds.

___ 3. In "The Story of an Hour," the thing that Mrs. Mallard feels approaching her is described as "creeping" and as something that will "possess her." Why are these words ironic?

A. It is her sudden death she feels coming.
B. It is her widowhood she feels coming.
C. It is her mourning she feels coming.
D. It is her freedom she feels coming.

___ 4. Which moment in "The Story of an Hour" is an example of situational irony?

A. when Mrs. Mallard wishes to be alone after hearing the news of her husband's death
B. when Mrs. Mallard weeps wildly after hearing the news of her husband's death
C. when Mrs. Mallard whispers, "free, free, free," after hearing of her husband's death
D. when Mrs. Mallard says, "Go away," after hearing the news of her husband's death

___ 5. When Mrs. Mallard says "free, free, free" in "The Story of an Hour," what becomes clear?

A. Mr. Mallard has not been killed in an accident.
B. Mrs. Mallard does not have heart trouble.
C. Mrs. Mallard is happy to be free of her husband.
D. Mrs. Mallard's sister is worried about her.

Name ______________________ Date ______________

___ 6. What is a major theme of Chopin's "The Story of an Hour"?
A. personal freedom
B. open marriage
C. sad widowhood
D. loss of love

___ 7. In "The Story of an Hour," whom does Mrs. Mallard believe she will live for when she thinks her husband has been killed?
A. for his memory
B. for her sister
C. for Mr. Richards
D. for herself

___ 8. In "The Story of an Hour," what is ironic about these words: "She breathed a quick prayer that life might be long . . . only yesterday she had thought with a shudder that life might be long"?
A. Yesterday she thought she would die young.
B. She gets her wish after she stops wishing for it.
C. She has never had a prayer answered before.
D. Her wishes changed after her husband died.

___ 9. What happens toward the end of "The Story of an Hour" that changes the entire story?
A. Richards says he loves Mrs. Mallard.
B. Mr. Mallard walks through the door.
C. Josephine comes down the stairs.
D. Mrs. Mallard goes downstairs.

___ 10. In "The Story of an Hour," what is ironic about the death of Mrs. Mallard after she sees her husband still alive?
A. Her heart problem should have been cured by now.
B. Her sister and Mr. Mallard are in love with each other.
C. She had thought she had accepted the fact of his death.
D. She had thought she had her whole life ahead of her.

___ 11. Why might readers interpret the title "The Story of an Hour" as an ironic title?
A. A character gains her freedom and loses her life in a single hour.
B. A character loses her husband in a single hour.
C. A character learns that her heart disease is fatal in a single hour.
D. A character dies from a severe emotional reaction in a single hour.

Name ______________________________ Date ______________

Vocabulary and Grammar

____ 12. In which of these sentences is the meaning of the word *tumultuously* suggested?
A. Mr. Richards checked the news before he went to see Mrs. Mallard.
B. Mrs. Mallard wept wildly in her sister's arms at the bad news.
C. The sounds from outside spoke of new life to Mrs. Mallard.
D. Mr. Mallard was not killed in the accident after all.

____ 13. Which sentence below contains an appositive?
A. There were patches of blue sky showing.
B. She sat with her head thrown back.
C. It was her sister Josephine who told her.
D. She knew that she would weep again.

Essay

14. The final words of "The Story of an Hour," are these: "When the doctors came they said she had died of heart disease—of joy that kills." In what way do these words suggest the opposite of what really happens? Write a brief essay to explain the irony of the story's final sentence.

15. Reread this passage from "The Story of an Hour": "There would be no powerful will bending hers in that blind persistence with which men and women believe they have a right to impose a private will upon a fellow creature." What view of marriage do you think Chopin is communicating in this story? Write a brief essay to give your response.

Name ______________________ Date ______________

"**The Story of an Hour**" by Kate Chopin

Selection Test B

Critical Reading *Identify the letter of the choice that best completes the statement or answers the question.*

____ 1. Readers in Kate Chopin's time must have found "The Story of an Hour" particularly shocking because of the contrast between Mrs. Mallard's response to her husband's death and
A. the response that society would consider appropriate.
B. the love that Mr. Mallard feels for his wife.
C. her response to the discovery that he is actually alive.
D. her professions of affection for her husband.

____ 2. When Mrs. Mallard reflects that, "It was only yesterday she had thought with a shudder that life might be long," she becomes aware of the irony that she
A. had worried about a life that she now knows will be short.
B. has not been punished for such unacceptable thoughts.
C. now desired something she has previously feared.
D. had not valued her husband properly until she lost him.

____ 3. Mrs. Mallard's reflection that she had recently wished for a short life soon has additional irony for the reader because
A. the reader knows that she still wants her life to be short.
B. she gets what she wanted after she stopped wanting it.
C. the reader sees her as a less worthy person than her husband.
D. she has too much intensity of feeling to wish for a short life.

____ 4. Why does Mrs. Mallard refuse her sister Josephine's offer to keep her company?
A. Mrs. Mallard does not want to upset her sister.
B. Mrs. Mallard prefers not to display emotion to others.
C. Mrs. Mallard needs privacy to confront her true feelings.
D. Mrs. Mallard wants Josephine to keep Richard company.

____ 5. How does Mrs. Mallard "hear the story" of her husband's death?
A. with a paralyzed inability to accept its meaning
B. with sudden, wild weeping
C. with a shriek of joy and relief
D. with a sigh and a dull stare in her eyes

____ 6. What is the meaning of the following passage from the story?

A kind intention or a cruel intention made the act seem no less a crime as she looked upon it in that brief moment of illumination.

A. Mrs. Mallard finally realizes that her husband had been cruel to her when she thought he was being kind.
B. She hadn't known until now whether her husband's intention had been cruel or kind.
C. She now understands that imposing your own will on someone is a crime, no matter whether the intention is cruel or kind.
D. She suddenly understands that her self-assertion is a crime, whether her intention was cruel or kind.

Name ______________________ Date ______________

___ 7. Under which type of irony would you classify Josephine's fear that her sister will "make herself ill" by grieving alone in her room?
A. situational
B. dramatic
C. verbal
D. none of the above

___ 8. In "The Story of an Hour," Kate Chopin is primarily concerned with the
A. sacrilege of rejoicing at someone's death.
B. importance of confirming reports of tragic events.
C. difficulty of distinguishing between illusion and reality.
D. individual's right to self-expression.

___ 9. After the initial storm of tears, Mrs. Mallard's response to the news of her husband's death is motivated largely by a wave of
A. self-assertion.
B. anger.
C. self-pity.
D. vengeance.

___ 10. Which of the following excerpts from "The Story of an Hour" best illustrates the author's use of irony?
A. "She wept at once, with sudden, wild abandonment, in her sister's arms."
B. "She was young, with a fair, calm face, whose lines bespoke repression and even a certain strength."
C. "And yet she had loved him—sometimes. Often she had not. What did it matter!"
D. "'Louise, open the door! I beg; open the door—you will make yourself ill.'"

___ 11. Kate Chopin's "The Story of an Hour" is a powerful illustration of the
A. cruel irony of fate.
B. tragedy of thwarted love.
C. emptiness of marriage.
D. injustice of life.

___ 12. What is the best reason for considering the title "The Story of an Hour" ironic?
A. The events in the story take much longer than an hour.
B. It is really a story about people.
C. The title is deceptively undramatic compared to the events.
D. The words suggest the opposite of their usual meaning.

___ 13. What word best characterizes this statement about Louise's feeling for her husband?
And yet she had loved him—sometimes.
A. joyful
B. sorrowful
C. ironic
D. insincere

Name ______________________________ Date ______________

Vocabulary and Grammar

____ 14. Which of the following sentences contains an appositive phrase?
A. Louise's sister Josephine tried to comfort her.
B. Her fair, calm face bore lines that reflected repression and even a certain strength.
C. Her husband's friend Richards had learned of the tragedy at the newspaper office.
D. One strong impulse ruled her, an overwhelming feeling of self-assertion.

____ 15. Which vocabulary word best suggests Mrs. Mallard's emotional state regarding her marriage before she hears of her husband's death?
A. elusive
B. repression
C. tumultuously
D. importunities

____ 16. What was the result of Josephine's *importunities* outside her sister's door?
A. They gave support to Mrs. Mallard's feelings of self-assertion.
B. They made Mrs. Mallard impatient and annoyed with her.
C. They persuaded Mrs. Mallard to leave her room.
D. They led her to overhear Mrs. Mallard weeping.

____ 17. When Kate Chopin refers to the feeling stealing over Louise Mallard as *elusive*, she means the feeling is
A. terrifying to face.
B. painful to imagine.
C. necessary to escape.
D. difficult to grasp.

Essay

18. Do you admire Mrs. Mallard for daring to take joy in this revelation of freedom, or do you condemn her for reacting with such callousness to her husband's death? Explain your answer in an essay, and cite details from the selection to support it.

19. How might Josephine and Richards have reacted if they had learned about Mrs. Mallard's true feelings regarding her husband's death? Imagine their reactions and write an essay describing and explaining them. Cite examples from the selection to explain what you know about each character, as well as the attitudes of the period. Use these examples to support your conclusions.

20. The Victorian world in which Kate Chopin lived and wrote was one of strong social restraints. The rules and expectations of marriage, the exaltation of romantic love, and the dominance of the husband over the wife prevented many Victorian women from viewing their circumstances honestly. Do you think Mrs. Mallard is a victim of Victorian attitudes toward marriage? Why or why not? Write an essay in which you give your opinion of Mrs. Mallard and her circumstances. Support your argument with evidence from Mrs. Mallard's thoughts in the aftermath of her husband's presumed death.

"Douglass" and "We Wear the Mask" by Paul Laurence Dunbar

Vocabulary Warm-up Word Lists

Study these words from the selections. Then, complete the activities.

Word List A

devious [DEE vee uhs] *adj.* deceptive; crooked
We mistrusted Dana, since we had heard that he had proved to be devious before.

grins [GRINZ] *v.* smiles widely
When Mom points the camera and says, "Say cheese," everybody grins.

harsh [HARSH] *adj.* severe; cruel
The winters in Canada can be harsh, with sub-zero temperatures and much snow.

mask [MASK] *n.* covering that conceals the face
Clowns usually wear a mask that covers their face.

passionate [PASH uh nuht] *adj.* full of emotion
Bill is a passionate follower of baseball.

swarm [SWORM] *v.* to gather or collect in large numbers; to throng
Bees have been known to swarm on that cherry tree in springtime.

tempest [TEM puhst] *n.* bad storm
Last year's category-4 hurricane was a tempest we will never forget.

tortured [TOR choord] *adj.* tormented; violently injured
Tortured by his conscience, the traitor finally confessed to the authorities.

Word List B

bark [BARK] *n.* boat or ship
A Spanish fleet surrounded the pirate bark as it tried to escape.

dissension [di SEN shuhn] *n.* disagreement; conflict
There was a lot of dissension among the members of the political party.

ebb [EB] *n.* flow of water back toward the sea, as the tide falls
When we noticed the ebb of the tide, we moved closer to the water.

guile [GYL] *n.* slyness; trickery
Guile was not part of his nature; he was totally open and honest.

myriad [MIR ee uhd] *adj.* very numerous
When we looked through the telescope, we could see myriad stars.

salient [SAY lee uhnt] *adj.* prominent; very important
A salient part of the governor's philosophy was her belief in human rights.

subtleties [SUT uhl teez] *n.* fine distinctions; delicately skillful or clever points
It took some time for me to appreciate the subtleties of Professor Coburn's argument.

vile [VYL] *adj.* vicious; corrupt; hateful
Several newspapers denounced the recent kidnapping of a child as a vile crime.

Name ______________________________ Date ______________

"Douglass" and **"We Wear the Mask"** by Paul Laurence Dunbar

Vocabulary Warm-up Exercises

Exercise A *Fill in each blank in the paragraph below with the appropriate word from Word List A.*

Some people are hard to figure out. They are not really deceptive or [1] ______________, but they seldom let their guard down or reveal their true opinions. My friend Ken is an example. He is always cheerful and outgoing and never seems [2] ______________ or even saddened by conflicts or disappointments. Whatever the situation, Ken [3] ______________ happily and never passes up a chance to use his quick wit. I can't escape the feeling, though, that Ken lives behind a happy-go-lucky [4] ______________. He doesn't seem [5] ______________ about anything: school, sports, or future careers. Lots of my classmates envy him for his good looks and trouble-free attitude, and they [6] ______________ to be his friends. Maybe Ken is lucky. I wonder, though, how he might react to a storm or [7] ______________ of real trouble: a setback that would teach him that life sometimes contains [8] ______________ realities.

Exercise B *Decide whether each statement below is true or false. Circle* T *or* F, *and explain your answer.*

1. The proper place to look for a bark is on the water.
   T / F ______________________________
2. The opposite of "harmony" is dissension.
   T / F ______________________________
3. The tide's ebb occurs when the water is advancing up the beach.
   T / F ______________________________
4. People with guile can generally be trusted.
   T / F ______________________________
5. The adjective myriad refers to a very small number.
   T / F ______________________________
6. A salient argument typically receives a lot of emphasis and attention.
   T / F ______________________________
7. The subtleties of a literary work are conspicuous and readily apparent.
   T / F ______________________________
8. It makes sense to avoid associating with people who are known to be vile.
   T / F ______________________________

Name ______________________________ Date ______________

"Douglass" and **"We Wear the Mask"** by Paul Laurence Dunbar

Reading Warm-up A

Read the following passage. Pay special attention to the underlined words. Then, read it again, and complete the activities. Use a separate sheet of paper for your written answers.

As Karen swings her leg in front of her and leans on her crutches, she nods to the other cheerleaders on their way to practice, and grins happily as if nothing in the world was wrong. She has been going through each day wearing the mask of brave cheerfulness ever since the accident at the cheering competition, where she broke her leg and shattered her squad's hopes for earning the state title.

Inside her, however, rages a tempest of painful emotions. Though the other girls have been kind and concerned only about her recovery, she feels responsible for the loss of the championship, and full of guilt. She often scolds herself in harsh tones when she is alone, "How could you have been so clumsy? We had practiced that throw hundreds of times! You knew it perfectly! How could you have managed to land so badly?" Time after time, the words have filled the air like a swarm of angry bees, and time after time she has cried with frustration.

As she sits on the sidelines of the gym, watching her friends warming up, and wishing she could join them, the coach comes over and sits next to her.

"You look tortured, Karen. You have to stop punishing yourself."

Karen looks away so the coach cannot see her eyes. She does not want to be devious and try to trick the coach, but she is afraid she is going to cry.

"I know you are passionate about cheerleading, it is something you truly love, and you are one of the best."

"Was, maybe," Karen whispers.

"Are," replies the coach. "Present tense. And remember, Karen, no one blames you but yourself. All the rest of us admire your courage."

Karen looks at the coach and smiles, genuinely smiles, for the first time in two weeks.

1. Underline the words that give a clue to the meaning of grins. What is a synonym for *grins*?
2. Circle the words that give a clue to the meaning of mask. Is this word used literally or figuratively here?
3. Underline the words in this sentence that hint at the meaning of tempest. Name a synonym for *tempest*.
4. Circle the word that gives a clue to the meaning of harsh. What are two synonyms for *harsh*?
5. Circle the words that offer clues to the meaning of swarm. Name something else that might *swarm*.
6. Underline the word that is close in meaning to tortured. Rewrite the sentence using a synonym for *tortured*.
7. Underline the phrase that has almost the same meaning as devious. Write an original sentence using the word devious.
8. Circle the words in this sentence that give a clue to the meaning of passionate. Name two antonyms for *passionate*.

Name ______________________________ Date ______________

"Douglass" and **"We Wear the Mask"** by Paul Laurence Dunbar

Reading Warm-up B

Read the following passage. Pay special attention to the underlined words. Then, read it again, and complete the activities. Use a separate sheet of paper for your written answers.

Masks have been used by myriad cultures, probably beyond counting, throughout the world. Mask makers have used an astonishing variety of materials, including wood, metal, clay, shells, paper, cloth, fiber, ivory, horn, stone, leather, and feathers. One of the most important, salient features of a mask, of course, is that it covers the face, hiding a person's identity. Simultaneously, however, a mask may establish another identity, suggesting both a personality and a mood.

Occasions and functions for mask wearing are as varied as the materials used. In some African cultures, the first masks are believed to have been used for disciplining children. A mother, for example, might paint a hideous, vile face at the bottom of her water gourd. The face would warn her child not to follow her to the well. Other masks have been used to call on the spirits of ancestors, to initiate young people, to help in hunting, or to protect or frighten troops in battle. On Roman warships, for instance, a terrifying mask was sometimes fixed to the prow of the bark to frighten opponents.

In other cultures, judges have worn masks to protect themselves from people seeking revenge and to reduce conflict, or dissension. The elaborate, complex subtleties of masks used to protect people from disease are striking features of Sri Lankan "devil masks." Masks used at festivals, such as Halloween and Mardi Gras, are often linked with humor, guile or cunning, and naughty pranks.

The ebb and flow of masks used in the theater are especially interesting. With origins in ancient Greek religion, masks in western theater have been popular in a number of periods, including the Middle Ages and the Renaissance. On Java and Bali in Indonesia, masks have been used in dance dramas ever since the eighteenth century.

1. Underline the words in this sentence that give a clue to the meaning of myriad. Use the word *myriad* in an original sentence.
2. Circle the words in this sentence that give a clue to the meaning of salient. Use a word meaning the opposite of *salient* in a sentence of your own.
3. Underline the word in this sentence that hints at the meaning of vile. What are two antonyms for *vile*?
4. Underline the words in this sentence that give a clue to the meaning of bark.
5. Circle the words in this sentence that give a clue to the meaning of dissension. Use a word meaning the opposite of *dissension* in a sentence of your own.
6. Underline the words in this sentence that hint at the meaning of subtleties. Use the word *subtleties* in an original sentence.
7. Underline the words in this sentence that give a clue to the meaning of guile.
8. Circle the words in this sentence that hint at the meaning of the word ebb. Is this word used literally or figuratively here?

Name ______________________________ Date ______________

"Douglass" and **"We Wear the Mask"** by Paul Laurence Dunbar

Literary Analysis: Rhyme

Rhyme is the repetition of sounds in the accented syllables of two or more words appearing close to each other. A **true rhyme** consists of words whose vowel sounds and final consonants are the same (*fall, squall*). A **slant rhyme** consists of words whose final consonant sounds match but whose vowel sounds are similar but not exact (*prove, love*). A rhyme that occurs at the ends of lines is called an **end rhyme.** If the rhyme occurs within a single line, it is called an **internal rhyme.**

DIRECTIONS: *Read the following lines from the poems. For each item, circle two kinds of rhyme the italicized words form.*

1. "This debt we pay to human *guile;*
With torn and bleeding hearts we *smile,*"
A. true rhyme B. slant rhyme C. end rhyme D. internal rhyme

2. "We sing, but oh the clay is *vile*
Beneath our feet, and long the *mile;*"
A. true rhyme B. slant rhyme C. end rhyme D. internal rhyme

3. "Ah, Douglass, we have fall'n on evil *days,*
Saw, salient, at the cross of devious *ways,*"
A. true rhyme B. slant rhyme C. end rhyme D. internal rhyme

4. "Such days as thou, not even thou didst *know,*
Not ended then, the passionate ebb and *flow.*"
A. true rhyme B. slant rhyme C. end rhyme D. internal rhyme

5. "Saw, salient, at the *cross* of *devious* ways,"
A. true rhyme B. slant rhyme C. end rhyme D. internal rhyme

6. "And all the *country* heard *thee* with amaze."
A. true rhyme B. slant rhyme C. end rhyme D. internal rhyme

7. "When thee, the eyes of that harsh long *ago*
The awful tide that battled to and *fro;*"
A. true rhyme B. slant rhyme C. end rhyme D. internal rhyme

8. "Now, when the waves of swift dissension *swarm,*
Oh, for thy voice high-sounding o'er the *storm,*"
A. true rhyme B. slant rhyme C. end rhyme D. internal rhyme

Name ______________________________ Date ______________

"Douglass" and **"We Wear the Mask"** by Paul Laurence Dunbar

Reading Strategy: Interpret

When reading a poem, you often need to **interpret** the meaning of the poet's words and lines, or "read between the lines"—carefully examining the words for what they say and imply. Interpreting is often easier if you ask yourself questions after every few lines.

DIRECTIONS: *Answer these interpretive questions about specific words and lines of Dunbar's poetry. Remember to read into the poet's meaning of every line and word. Refer to the selection if you need to.*

1. In "Douglass," who is the "we" in the excerpt "Ah, Douglass, we have fall'n on evil days"?

____

____

2. In "Douglass," what is the "awful tide that battled to and fro"?

____

____

____

3. In "Douglass," what does the "shivering bark" signify?

____

____

4. In "Douglass," what is the "lonely dark"?

____

____

5. Why does Dunbar address the poem "Douglass" to Frederick Douglass, an American abolitionist?

____

____

____

6. What is the mask hiding in "We Wear the Mask"?

____

____

7. Why does Dunbar want to "hide our cheeks" and "shade our eyes" in "We Wear the Mask"?

____

____

____

Name ______________________________ Date ______________

"**Douglass**" and "**We Wear the Mask**" by Paul Laurence Dunbar

Vocabulary Builder

Related Words: Forms of *guile*

The word *guile* means "craftiness." The word *beguile* means "to mislead by craftiness or deceit." *Guile* and *beguile* are related words.

A. DIRECTIONS: *Form other words from* guile *and* beguile *by adding the suffixes listed. Write the meaning of each word on the lines.*

1. *beguile + -ed* ______________________________

____

2. *guile + -less* ______________________________

____

3. *beguile + -er* ______________________________

____

4. *beguile + -ing* ______________________________

____

Using the Word List

salient	tempest	stark
guile	myriad	

B. DIRECTIONS: *Circle the word that best completes each sentence.*

1. The error was salient and stood ________ all the rest.
   A. out from B. below C. by D. to the right
2. The tempest that occurred was more violent than any ________.
   A. game B. criminal C. color D. windstorm
3. The stark trees stood out ________ against the rest of the landscape.
   A. boldly B. subtly C. darkly D. colorfully
4. The guile shown by the con artist demonstrated her level of ________.
   A. brashness B. trickiness C. perkiness D. voicelessness
5. The myriad colors made the room seem like a ________.
   A. paintbrush B. airbrush C. rainbow D. gray color

Name ______________________ Date ______________

"Douglass" and **"We Wear the Mask"** by Paul Laurence Dunbar

Grammar and Style: Punctuation of Interjections

An **interjection** is a part of speech that expresses emotion. It is always set off from the rest of a sentence by a comma or an exclamation point, depending on the degree of emotion being expressed. For example, the sentence *Yes! I like it very much* indicates excitement, whereas *Yes, I like it very much* indicates acceptance.

A. PRACTICE: *The following four excerpts from the selection contain interjections. Change the expression of emotion in each excerpt by rewriting it with different punctuation.*

1. "Ah, Douglass, we have fall'n on evil days,"

____

____

2. "Nay, let them only see us,"

____

____

3. "Now, when the waves of swift dissension swarm,"

____

____

4. "Oh, for thy voice high-sounding o'er the storm,"

____

____

B. Writing Application: *Use the following interjections to create new sentences from each sentence in the list. Punctuate your sentences properly.*

Ah Hey No Oh Yes

1. I didn't like the movie. ______________________
2. Why not? ______________________
3. We met the new neighbor. ______________________
4. The sky is blue. ______________________
5. He enjoys playing baseball. ______________________
6. She cut her hair very short. ______________________
7. I've been to Mexico. ______________________
8. I want to go to dinner. ______________________

Name ______________________________ Date ______________

"Douglass" and **"We Wear the Mask"** by Paul Laurence Dunbar

Support for Writing

After you've chosen a historic figure to honor with a **poem,** use the graphic organizer below to document the person's life in comparison with today's world.

Poem for (choose a name) ______________ in Today's World

Name of historical figure:		
Accomplishments	**Personal Characteristics**	**How He or She Would Challenge Today's Problems**
Sensory images I could use to describe this person:		

On a separate page, write a draft of your poem. Use the sensory images combined with the other details from your chart. When you revise your work, be sure you have left a sharp impression of your historical figure. Give your poem a title.

Name ________________________________ Date ________________

"**Douglass**" and "**We Wear the Mask**" by Paul Laurence Dunbar

Support for Extend Your Learning

Listening and Speaking

Choose one of the Dunbar poems to use for your **oral interpretation.** Analyze each line for meaning and form, and use these tips:

- Look for interjections and imagery that emphasize tone and rhythm.
- Read the poem aloud several times to evoke emotion.

Present your poem to the class and ask for feedback. If there is time, pair with a classmate who has chosen the other poem, and present your readings as a team.

Research and Technology

To prepare to write a **report,** search the Internet for critical response to Dunbar's poetry, and enter details in the chart below.

Critical Response to Dunbar's Poetry

Positive responses to Dunbar's poetry	Negative responses to Dunbar's poetry

On a separate page, write your report. Summarize the information you have found in your research. Then, make a statement of your own about the value of Dunbar's poetry.

Name ______________________________ Date ______________

"Douglass" and **"We Wear the Mask"** by Paul Laurence Dunbar

Enrichment: Art

Dunbar's "We Wear the Mask" suggests that he and others like him wear a mask for the rest of the world to see. Masks are a common way to convey certain images or emotions—they have been used for this purpose in ancient Greek dramas and African ceremonies as well as in modern celebrations such as Mardi Gras.

DIRECTIONS: *Analyze your reaction to one of the poems. Describe an image or emotion that reflects this reaction. Think of how certain facial images can be used to portray that emotion. Use the questions below to guide your thinking. Then design a mask that portrays that image or emotion. Draw your mask in the space provided.*

The image or emotion I would like to portray with my mask is:

____

____

Characteristics of my mask:

____

____

____

____

____

____

Drawing of my mask:

Name ______________________________ Date ______________

"**Douglass**" and "**We Wear the Mask**" by Paul Laurence Dunbar

Selection Test A

Critical Reading *Identify the letter of the choice that best answers the question.*

___ **1.** What does Dunbar mean in these opening lines of "Douglass," when he writes:

"Ah, Douglass, we have fall'n on evil days, / Such days as thou, not even thou didst know"?

A. African Americans are better off now than in the days of slavery.
B. African Americans are worse off now than in the days of slavery.
C. Frederick Douglass did not understand the times in which he lived.
D. Frederick Douglass would not understand the new ways.

___ **2.** Which kind of rhymes are found in this passage from "Douglass":

"Such days as thou, not even thou didst know, / When thee, the eyes of that harsh long ago"?

A. slant rhyme and end rhyme
B. end rhyme and internal rhyme
C. slant rhyme and true rhyme
D. end rhyme and true rhyme

___ **3.** Which kinds of rhyme are found in these lines from "Douglass":

"Now, when the waves of swift dissension swarm, / . . . / Oh, for thy voice high-sounding o'er the storm"?

A. end rhyme and slant rhyme
B. slant rhyme and true rhyme
C. end rhyme and internal rhyme
D. internal rhyme and true rhyme

___ **4.** What does the image "Honor, the strong pilot [who] "lieth stark" suggest in "Douglass"?

A. Honor died when Douglass died.
B. A pilot without honor is a liar.
C. Douglass's strength was his honor.
D. The honorable Douglass lies dead.

___ **5.** What image does Dunbar suggest in "Douglass" when he refers to the great man's voice speaking over "the storm" and his "strong arm to guide the shivering bark"?

A. Douglass had a loud voice.
B. Douglass was physically strong.
C. Douglass was like the captain of a ship.
D. Douglass kept people warm.

Name ______________________________ Date ______________

____ 6. Which kinds of rhyme are found in these two lines from "We Wear the Mask": "We wear the mask that grins and lies. / It hides our cheeks and shades our eyes -"?
A. slant rhyme and end rhyme
B. true rhyme and internal rhyme
C. internal rhyme and end rhyme
D. true rhyme and end rhyme

____ 7. According to "We Wear the Mask," when is the only time that the white world is willing to see African Americans?
A. when they are crying
B. when they hide their feelings
C. when they are praying
D. when they are wounded

____ 8. In "We Wear the Mask," what does Dunbar say is shown on the masks worn by African Americans?
A. anger
B. blood
C. happiness
D. frustration

____ 9. What image does Dunbar convey with the line "And mouth with myriad subtleties" from "We Wear the Mask"?
A. a mouth that can only smile or frown
B. a mouth that can express subtle feelings
C. a mouth that makes speeches
D. a mouth that is covered by a mask

____ 10. In "We Wear the Mask," why do the speakers wear masks?
A. They are attending a costume party.
B. They are going skiing.
C. They are cold in the winter.
D. They are hiding their feelings.

Vocabulary and Grammar

____ 11. In which sentence is the meaning of the word *tempest* suggested?
A. People wear masks to hide feelings.
B. Douglass guides people through a storm.
C. The poet wants Douglass to be alive.
D. The people sing but their hearts are sad.

Name ______________________________ Date ______________

___ **12.** Which of these sentences contains a correctly punctuated interjection?

A. "We smile, but O great Christ our cries"

B. "Not ended then, the passionate ebb"

C. "Why should the world be otherwise,"

D. "Oh, for thy voice o'er the storm,"

Essay

13. In "We Wear the Mask," why does Dunbar say that African Americans feel they have to wear masks when they deal with white people? Write a brief essay to give your response. Support your ideas with examples from the poem.

14. The second stanza of "Douglass" reads like this:

> Now, when the waves of swift dissension swarm,
> And Honor, the strong pilot, lieth stark,
> Oh, for the voice high-sounding o'er the storm,
> For thy strong arm to guide the shivering bark

What central image of Douglass and African Americans does Dunbar set up? What are the people in the poem doing? Write a brief essay to explain the images in this stanza.

Name ____ Date ______________________

"Douglass" and **"We Wear the Mask"** by Paul Laurence Dunbar

Selection Test B

Critical Reading *Identify the letter of the choice that best completes the statement or answers the question.*

___ **1.** In "We Wear the Mask," Dunbar suggests the world sees his fellow African Americans
A. in a harsh and honest light.
B. only when they hide their feelings.
C. when they are filled with "tears and sighs."
D. as they are praying to Christ.

___ **2.** What is symbolized in these lines from "We Wear the Mask"?
but oh the clay is vile
Beneath our feet, and long the mile;
A. an evil person
B. a long, hard life
C. a broken promise
D. an act of revenge

___ **3.** In "Douglass," Dunbar uses the image of a boat in a stormy sea mainly to symbolize the
A. joy and excitement of African Americans immediately after slavery was abolished.
B. parallel between nature's power and the enduring quality of African American culture.
C. seafaring traditons of many African cultures.
D. turnmoil and hardships African Americans still faced after emancipation.

___ **4.** The speaker in "We Wear the Mask" believes that wearing the mask is
A. evil.
B. foolish.
C. impossible.
D. essential.

___ **5.** In "We Wear the Mask," the overall emotional tone that Dunbar uses is one of
A. aggression.
B. defeat.
C. hopefulness.
D. bitterness.

___ **6.** Which words are an example of a slant rhyme?
A. *pilot* and *lieth*
B. *thou* and *know*
C. *tide* and *ride*
D. *mask* and *mile*

___ **7.** Which definition most closely distinguishes a slant rhyme?
A. The words appear within a single line.
B. The words appear within a single sentence.
C. The vowel sounds are similar.
D. The beginning consonants must be the same.

Name ______________________________ Date ______________

____ 8. In "We Wear the Mask," Dunbar suggests that the mask shows
A. anger.
B. despair.
C. happiness.
D. strength.

____ 9. What is an appropriate interpretation of the following lines from "We Wear the Mask"?

Why should the world be overwise,
In counting all our tears and sighs?

A. We should not think that anyone is able to guess our thoughts.
B. Too much knowledge brings misery and hardship to the world.
C. We must realize that we are really no wiser than anyone else.
D. Why should we think anyone cares what we really feel?

____ 10. According to "We Wear the Mask," why do African Americans wear the mask?
A. to pretend that they were white
B. to convince themselves that they had made more gains than they actually had
C. to hide their feelings about slavery and racial violence
D. to display their material and intellectual success

____ 11. Which of the following presents the most appropriate interpretation of these lines from the first stanza of "Douglass"?

Not ended then, the passionate ebb and flow,
The awful tide that battled to and fro;
We ride amid a tempest of dispraise.

A. When slavery ended, African Americans began to quarrel among themselves as some individuals competed to gain power and influence over the rest of the African American community.
B. The struggle for equality and against prejudice is not over; in fact, it's worse.
C. The Civil War did not end when slavery was abolished but continued for several years afterward.
D. The strength and character of African Americans were not destroyed by slavery but continued to grow in spite of it.

____ 12. In "Douglass," Dunbar leaves the reader feeling
A. that no improvements will happen soon for African Americans.
B. that Frederick Douglass was a great speaker.
C. afraid to travel by ocean because of tempests.
D. the world is slowly getting more racially tolerant.

____ 13. Which definition most closely distinguishes an internal rhyme?
A. The rhyming words appear within a single line.
B. The vowel sounds must be identical.
C. The vowel sounds are similar or identical.
D. The consonants after the vowel sounds in both words are the same.

Name ______________________________ Date ______________

Vocabulary and Grammar

____ 14. In "We Wear the Mask," how does a mouth with *myriad* subtleties help pay a debt to human *guile*?
- A. By saying countless small things, we can be very crafty in how we humans portray ourselves.
- B. By smiling broadly, we can give back something to the human spirit.
- C. By seeing each mouth as a human being, we can better visualize human society.
- D. When communicating in eloquent speech, one can make almost anyone believe in anything.

____ 15. In "Douglass," the line "And Honor, the strong pilot, lieth *stark*" implies that honor is
- A. floating all around us.
- B. angry and seething.
- C. cold, stiff, and dead.
- D. waiting for its soldiers.

____ 16. In "Douglass," the line "We ride amid a *tempest* of dispraise" gives the image of being
- A. lulled by a rocking motion.
- B. swept up by a hurricane.
- C. carried by a bubbling stream.
- D. lifted by a chilly breeze.

____ 17. Which punctuation after the interjection best expresses a calm, pensive emotion?
- A. Ah? Douglass, we have fall'n on evil days.
- B. Ah! Douglass, we have fall'n on evil days.
- C. Ah, Douglass, we have fall'n on evil days.
- D. Ah. Douglass, we have fall'n on evil days.

Essay

18. Restate in an essay Dunbar's sentiments as expressed in "We Wear the Mask" to a person unfamiliar with the poem. Use details from the poem to support your interpretation of it.

19. Paul Laurence Dunbar was the son of former slaves. His father escaped to Canada but returned to the United States to fight in the Union army. Dunbar was the first African American to make a significant attempt to earn his living as a writer. Knowing this, reread one or both of the poems and write an essay explaining how you think Dunbar looked upon the position of African Americans in post-Civil War society. Use details from one or both of the poems in your essay, as well as historical facts of the era.

20. One critic has stated that Paul Laurence Dunbar's "We Wear the Mask" is a poem "about concealed racial fire." Write an essay in which you argue either for or against that viewpoint. Is Dunbar's poem about race, or is it more universal? Support your opinion with evidence from one or both of the poems, as well as facts from Dunbar's life and work.

Name ______________________ Date ______________

Unit 4: Division, Reconciliation, and Expansion

Benchmark Test 6

MULTIPLE CHOICE

Literary Analysis and Reading Skills *Read the selection. Then, answer the questions that follow.*

Thish-yer Smily had a mare—the boys called her the fifteen-minute nag, but that was only in fun, you know, because, of course, she was faster than that—and he use to win money on that horse, for all she was so slow and always had the asthma, or the distemper, or the consumption, or something of that kind. They use to give her two or three hundred yards' start, and then pass her under way; but always at the fag-end of the race she'd get excited and desperate-like, and come cavorting and spraddling up, and scattering her legs around limber, sometimes in the air, and sometimes out to one side amongst the fences, and kicking up m-o-r-e dust, and raising m-o-r-e racket with her coughing and sneezing and blowing her nose—and always fetch up at the stand just about a neck ahead, as near as you could cipher it down.

from "Jim Smily and His Jumping Frog" [bartleby] by Mark Twain

1. Which phrase from the selection is an example of regional dialect?
   A. Thish-yer Smily
   B. the fifteen-minute nag
   C. something of that kind
   D. kicking up m-o-r-e dust

2. What does the phrase *thish-yer* mean?
   A. fissure
   B. this here
   C. it's your
   D. farmer

3. Which is the most accurate paraphrase of "scattering her legs around limber"?
   A. breaking her legs because they were too weak
   B. losing her legs
   C. tripping over lumber
   D. flailing her legs awkwardly

4. If you find regional dialect difficult to understand, what is most likely to help you figure it out?
   A. using a dictionary
   B. reading it aloud
   C. ignoring words you don't understand
   D. asking a friend what the words mean

5. What is the main technique Twain uses to create humor in the selection?
   A. a narrator who doesn't know how ridiculous he is
   B. exaggeration
   C. joke telling
   D. puns and word play

Name ______________________ Date ______________

6. How important is the setting of a selection, such as this one, to the literary movement known as regionalism?
   A. unimportant
   B. not very important
   C. important
   D. very important

7. What is the best question to ask yourself to increase your understanding of the selection?
   A. Why am I reading this selection?
   B. What other selections has the author written?
   C. What is happening in this part?
   D. To whom is the narrator telling this story?

8. What is the tone of the selection?
   A. pessimistic
   B. confused
   C. humorous
   D. matter-of-fact

9. What is the difference between tone and mood?
   A. Tone is created by theme and mood by characters, setting, and plot.
   B. Tone is a writer's attitude and mood is the feeling the reader gets from a selection.
   C. Tone has to do with the language used in a selection and mood has to do with the reader's attitude toward the selection.
   D. Tone refers to serious works, while mood refers to humorous selections.

10. Which is an example of internal conflict?
   A. A character struggles with the guilt he feels about a crime he committed as a child.
   B. A character struggles to distinguish herself from her many siblings.
   C. A character struggles against the restrictions of traditional gender roles.
   D. A character struggles to keep her faith in God after a tragic accident.

11. What is the best description of the conflict in dramatic irony?
   A. A character's words do not express what she means.
   B. A character's actions are unexpected.
   C. A character's words or actions contradict what the reader knows to be true.
   D. A character believes something that the reader knows to be untrue.

12. Which of the following elements often reveals irony?
   A. details
   B. plot
   C. descriptions
   D. climax

Name ______________________ Date ______________

13. How does predicting increase a reader's comprehension?
   A. Predicting sharpens the reader's intellect.
   B. Predicting makes the reader pay attention to all the details.
   C. Predicting forces the reader to identify cause and effect relationships.
   D. Predicting focuses attention as the reader attempts to confirm the prediction.

Read the selection. Then, answer the questions that follow.

Dead Men Tell No Tales

THEY say that dead men tell no tales!

Except of barges with red sails
And sailors mad for nightingales;

Except of jongleurs stretched at ease
Beside old highways through the trees;

Except of dying moons that break
The hearts of lads who lie awake;

Except of fortresses in shade,
And heroes crumbled and betrayed.

But dead men tell no tales, they say!

Except old tales that burn away
The stifling tapestries of day:

Old tales of life, of love and hate,
Of time and space, and will, and fate.

—Haniel Long

14. Why is the poem ironic?
   A. because the title and refrain contradict the meaning
   B. because the speaker displays verbal irony
   C. because the tone of the poem is wry
   D. because readers are aware of information that the speaker does not know

15. What is the relationship of the title to the theme of the poem?
   A. The title expresses the theme.
   B. The title contradicts the theme.
   C. The title is unrelated to the theme.
   D. The title illuminates an aspect of the theme.

16. Which is the best summary of the theme of the poem?
   A. Dead people have no place in the memory of the living.
   B. The dead are more imaginative than the living.
   C. The dead live on in history.
   D. The dead are best forgotten.

Name ______________________ Date ____________

17. What kind of rhyme did Haniel Long use in this poem?
   A. exact
   B. slant
   C. internal
   D. blank verse

18. What is the most reasonable interpretation of the meaning of this line from the poem?

   The stifling tapestries of day:

   A. cares and worries of the working day
   B. difficulties of weaving tapestries
   C. polluted atmosphere created by factories
   D. oppressive everyday reality

19. On what should a reader depend when responding to a poem such as this one?
   A. vocabulary and usage
   B. the emotions the poem evokes
   C. the reader's ability to intellectualize
   D. logic and reason

20. Which word best describes the tone of the poem?
   A. humorous
   B. angry
   C. celebratory
   D. grim

21. What type of rhyme does the word pair *good* and *food* demonstrate?
   A. exact
   B. slant
   C. end
   D. internal

22. Which of the following creates tone?
   A. word choice
   B. figures of speech
   C. length
   D. sentence structure

Vocabulary

23. Based on your knowledge of the Greek prefix *mono-* and the meaning of the word *travelogue*, what does *monologue* mean?
   A. unvarying
   B. one topic
   C. single destination
   D. speech by one person

Name ________________________________ Date ________________

24. Based on your knowledge of the words *rebellion* and *belligerent,* to what concept does the Latin word part *-bel-* relate?
   A. beauty
   B. truth
   C. war
   D. speech

25. In which of these sentences is the Latin term *terra firma* used correctly?
   A. The police officer requested a writ of terra firma from the judge.
   B. After a month at sea, I was grateful to be on terra firma.
   C. We demonstrated terra firma when we all voted for the same candidate.
   D. Explorers needed terra firma to circumnavigate the globe.

26. Based on your knowledge of the meaning of the Latin root *-ject-,* what does the verb *subject* mean?
   A. complain
   B. act as a role model
   C. demonstrate proficiency
   D. cause to experience

27. Based on your knowledge of the meaning of the Anglo-Saxon prefix *fore-,* what does the noun *forebear* mean?
   A. ancestor
   B. minister
   C. winner
   D. hunter

Grammar

28. Which sentence has a double negative?
   A. Under no circumstances can he attend this year's conference.
   B. According to the log, he was never in the building on Wednesday.
   C. You told me not to, so I didn't leave home.
   D. He couldn't never make a soufflé that didn't fall.

29. Which of these is a properly punctuated compound sentence?
   A. You may feel certain that you are right but still be completely wrong.
   B. Look carefully in the upper branches, or you will miss the nuthatch.
   C. For health reasons, Jorge never eats meat.
   D. Under the direction of an expert, anyone can repair a car engine.

30. Which of these is a sentence fragment?
   A. The most elaborate head covering interlaced with turquoise ribbons.
   B. Watch for cars!
   C. Reese woke early that fateful morning.
   D. Tana rarely studies, but she has never failed a test.

Name ______________________ Date ______________

31. Which word does the adverb clause in this sentence modify?

When the alarm blasted and the peacocks screeched, I knew this wouldn't be an ordinary day in paradise.

A. blasted
B. screeched
C. knew
D. ordinary

32. In the sentences below, which appositive phrase is punctuated correctly?

A. The classic song, "Stairway to Heaven," is a genuine masterpiece.
B. Many of the most satisfying Russian novels *War and Peace* for example are the most satisfying.
C. Mr. McIntosh, an elegant dresser, was the first to rent a tuxedo.
D. Bill met his first wife Helen Hobbes at a doctor's office.

33. In the sentences below, which interjection is punctuated correctly?

A. Eek, a mouse!
B. Oh, I don't know what I want to do tonight.
C. Sure! I'll baby sit on Saturday.
D. Uh! Where's the dish soap?

ESSAY

34. Write about someone who has played an important role in your life. You may write either a reflective essay or a poem. Describe the person and that person's effect on you. Use specific examples and details that show what the person is like.

35. Write an analytical essay or position paper on an education-related issue. Include facts and specific details that support your position. Organize your essay point-by-point, use transitions to make your argument progress logically and smoothly, and conclude persuasively.

36. Write a critical review of a short selection of your choice. After an introduction in which you describe your opinion of the selection and the reasons you hold it, focus your review by analyzing a particular literary element, such as plot, characterization, or theme. Use details and quotations from the text to support your analysis.

Name ______________________________ Date ______________

Unit 4: Division, Reconciliation, and Expansion

Diagnostic Test 7

MULTIPLE CHOICE

Read the selection. Then, answer the questions that follow.

Sometimes it is impossible to prevent snakebites. When a person accidentally steps on a snake in the woods, disturbing its nest, the snake's first reaction will be to strike and defend itself. Often, it will not only bite, but it will also clutch its victim in its strong jaws, making release difficult.

Protect yourself from becoming the victim of a painful and sometimes extremely dangerous snakebite. Remain on hiking paths, stay alert when climbing rocky terrain, and keep your hands and feet out of leafy, overgrown areas. You should also regard loose rocks and stacks of firewood with caution, because snakes often curl up in small, warm, sunlit places.

Once you spot a snake, refrain from touching it, even if it looks harmless. People have been bitten by poisonous snakes because they mistook them for less hazardous ones. Many harmless snakes have diamond patterns on their backs, but so do rattlesnakes! If you are bitten by a snake, never conclude that it is not a serious wound. Even in the absence of venom, a snakebite can cause infection and allergic reactions. Seek help immediately!

1. According to the selection, what is a snake's first reaction when it is disturbed in its nest?

A. to flee and protect itself

B. to strike and defend itself

C. to protect its young

D. to pretend that it is dead

2. According to the selection, why is it often difficult for an animal to get away, once it is bitten by a snake?

A. The bite causes the animal to become very weak.

B. The snake often wraps itself around its victim.

C. The bite is too painful to allow movement.

D. The snake often clutches its victim in its strong jaws.

3. According to the selection, why should people be on the lookout for snakes in piles of loose rock or firewood?

A. The markings on some snakes make them resemble these natural objects.

B. Snakes often venture into such places, looking for mice and other prey.

C. Such objects are commonly found in the habitats of snakes.

D. Snakes like to curl up in such small, warm, sunlit places.

4. Based on this selection, why would it be a good idea to learn the markings of the snakes in your region before setting off on a hike?

A. People find it difficult to refrain from picking up a snake.

B. Hikers should know enough to be able to tell poisonous snakes from harmless snakes.

C. Rocky terrains occur in almost every North American habitat.

D. Many harmless snakes have diamond patterns on their backs.

Name ______________________________ Date ______________

5. Based on the selection, which is the best definition for *venom*?
   A. the pattern on a snake's back
   B. the teeth, or fangs, of a snake
   C. the poison that some snakes carry
   D. the long, slender, forked tongue of a snake

6. According to the selection, what are some common side effects of the bites of nonpoisonous snakes?
   A. severe muscular spasms
   B. vomiting and high fever
   C. coma or death
   D. infections and allergic reactions

7. According to the selection, what should you do if you are bitten by a snake?
   A. Get immediate medical attention.
   B. Lie down and elevate the bite.
   C. Kill the snake so that it can be examined by medical authorities.
   D. Wash the bite with cold water and bandage it tightly.

Read the selection. Then, answer the questions that follow.

Although many ancient cultures had games that involved hitting balls with sticks, modern golf was developed in Scotland. By the 1400s, the Scots were taking a club, swinging it at a ball, and moving the ball from starting point to finishing hole in as few strokes as possible. Even at that early stage, the game was about skill, not haste. In fact, a complete game of golf, which covers a course of eighteen holes, might take an entire afternoon.

Unlike most games, golf is a sport that players tend to play against themselves. Each time they play, they try to do better than they did the last time. Since the beginning, golf has hooked its players into intensely focusing on making those improvements. They try to put everything else out of their minds while they concentrate on their tee shots, their swings, and their putts. In fact, in 1457, King James II of Scotland issued a ban on the playing of golf, complaining that it kept his archers from practice with their bows and arrows.

The Scottish heath is an ideal landscape for the rolling greens, open spaces, and natural hazards that golf requires. Today, almost every village seems to have its own course. Some are quiet country landscapes, but others boast lavish clubhouses with banquet halls and country-club facilities. Still others, like St. Andrew's, are world-famous because of the championship tournaments that are played there.

8. According to the selection, how is golf similar to other ancient games?
   A. Like them, golf is played by both men and women.
   B. Like them, golf is played by hitting a ball with a stick.
   C. Like them, golf was developed in Scotland.
   D. Like them, golf is played on a rolling green.

9. According to the selection, which statement is true about golf?
   A. Hazards on a course include ponds, streams, and sand traps.
   B. Most courses have clubhouses with banquet halls.
   C. A complete game involves 18 holes.
   D. The best golfers play the game very quickly, but that takes years of practice.

Name ______________________ Date ______________

10. What does the author mean by "players tend to play against themselves"?
   A. Golf is a one-person game, like solitaire.
   B. Golfers try to play the game by hitting the least amount of shots.
   C. Golfers try to avoid hitting the ball into sand traps.
   D. Golfers are always trying to do better than they did the last time they played.

11. Based on the selection, what is one very important character trait that a golfer needs?
   A. ability to concentrate
   B. ability to think quickly
   C. ability to solve difficult problems
   D. ability to make logical generalizations

12. Based on the selection, what does it mean to "issue a ban" on something?
   A. challenge someone to compete
   B. suggest ways to improve something
   C. forbid people from doing something
   D. focus on certain skills

13. Based on the selection, what was the most probable reason that golf kept King James's archers from practicing with their bows and arrows?
   A. Golf provided more exercise than archery did.
   B. They were hooked on trying to improve their golf skills.
   C. They didn't think that King James should tell them how to spend their free time.
   D. Their village, like many others, had its own golf course.

14. What had the greatest effect on the development and spread of golf courses in Scotland?
   A. Early in its development, King James II issued a ban on the playing of golf.
   B. A complete game of golf might take an entire afternoon.
   C. The rolling, green land of Scotland is ideal for golf courses.
   D. People built lavish clubhouses and banquet halls.

15. What is St. Andrew's?
   A. a quiet country landscape in Scotland
   B. a world-famous golf course in Scotland
   C. a large banquet hall for golfers in Scotland
   D. a museum for the history of golf in Scotland

Selections by Edwin Arlington Robinson and Edgar Lee Masters

Vocabulary Warm-up Word Lists

Study these words from the selections. Then, complete the activities.

Word List A

chiseled [CHIZ uhld] *v.* cut or shaped with a chisel (sharp hand tool)
The decoy carver quickly chiseled the wood into the shape of a duck.

discontent [dis kun TENT] *n.* dissatisfaction or displeasure
Seeing my brother's look of discontent, I offered to swap my prize for his.

medicinal [me DIS in uhl] *adj.* having the properties of medicine
Many medicinal herbs can easily be grown in pots indoors.

memorable [MEM er uh buhl] *adj.* worth remembering
What really made that party memorable was the great band that played.

rambled [RAM buhld] *v.* wandered aimlessly
We rambled over the fields and hills, following wherever our feet took us.

repose [ri POHZ] *n.* state of being at rest
He tiptoed through the house, not wanting to disturb his father's repose.

schooled [skoold] *v.* taught or trained
She has been schooled in shiatsu as well as Swedish massage.

weariness [WEER ee nes] *n.* fatigue
My weariness overcame me and I drifted off to sleep.

Word List B

admirably [AD mer uh blee] *adv.* in a way that deserves admiration
Considering what he has been through, I think he has behaved admirably.

arrayed [uh RAYD] *v.* dressed up; decked out
Arrayed in his rented tuxedo, Sam joined his prom date in the limousine.

consistent [kun SIS tent] *adj.* staying the same; steadfast
Mrs. Edwards may be strict, but at least she is consistent in her rules.

crimson [KRIM sun] *adj.* deep red
"That crimson dress makes you look like a movie star," he said.

imperially [im PEER ee uhl ee] *adv.* majestically
The beauty queen sat on the float, waving imperially at the crowd.

influenced [IN floo ensd] *v.* moved or affected
His mother being a lawyer influenced his own choice of career.

pessimistic [pes i MIS tik] *adj.* gloomy; expecting the worst
Macie is sure it will rain on our picnic, but I am feeling less pessimistic.

quench [kwench] *v.* put out (as a fire)
Nothing can quench my burning desire to run away with the circus.

Name ______________________________ Date ______________

Selections by Edwin Arlington Robinson and Edgar Lee Masters

Vocabulary Warm-up Exercises

Exercise A *Fill in each blank in the paragraph below with the appropriate word from Word List A. Use each word only once.*

Some vacations are easily forgotten, but my summer in the country was truly [1] ______________. Every day, with nothing in particular to do, I [2] ______________ over the hills, breathing in air that was so fresh and healthy it seemed to have a [3] ______________ effect. If I ever felt sadness or [4] ______________, all I had to do was walk until the mood passed. When I was overcome by [5] ______________, I found a place to rest. One day, I stopped at an old cemetery, where I read the words [6] ______________ on the overgrown tombstones. One said, "She was [7] ______________ in the ways of these hills, and now she finds [8] ______________ here."

Exercise B *Answer the questions with complete explanations.*

1. Would you expect someone who walked <u>imperially</u> to be shy and modest?

____

2. If someone said, "Hand me the <u>crimson</u> tie," would you give him the red one or the blue one?

____

3. Which would <u>quench</u> a fire better, gasoline or water?

____

4. In a movie, who behaves more <u>admirably</u>, the hero or the villain?

____

5. Would a report card filled with *D*s and *F*s be <u>consistent</u> with plans to go to college?

____

6. Do you think someone who is very <u>pessimistic</u> is a lot of fun to be around?

____

7. If you saw a girl <u>arrayed</u> in her best clothes, would you think she was going to a party or getting ready to take out the garbage?

____

8. Do you think a shopper with only a dollar is likely to be <u>influenced</u> by price?

____

Name ______________________________ Date ______________

Selections by Edwin Arlington Robinson and Edgar Lee Masters

Reading Warm-up A

Read the following passage. Pay special attention to the underlined words. Then, read it again, and complete the activities. Use a separate sheet of paper for your written answers.

When I picture Grandpa Lou, I see his hands—strong, brown, weather-beaten hands. This memorable image in my mind is not a photo, but a video clip, because the hands were always in motion: hammering a board in place on the henhouse, hauling buckets of scraps to the pigs, slapping the rump of a stray cow that had rambled away from the herd.

Grandpa Lou believed in hard work, for himself and for everyone else, especially his grandchildren. Long ago, he had been schooled in the idea that a boy with a few minutes of free time was a boy looking for trouble. "Idle hands find mischief," he would say, and find me yet another chore to do. By dinnertime, I was ready to drop with weariness, but Grandpa Lou, who had been working alongside me all day, showed no sign of exhaustion himself.

He was eighty-five when he had the operation on his heart. It was strange to see him in the hospital room, with its white walls and faint medicinal smell. He rested on his back, eyes closed, his hands folded across his chest in repose. Grandpa Lou was not doing as well as they had hoped, one of my aunts told me in a whisper. "He never complains," she said, "but we know he's unhappy."

Looking at the still hands, I thought I knew the reason for his discontent. "Grandpa," I said, "look what I brought you." He turned his head slowly and opened his eyes without much interest, expecting, I was certain, more chocolates or another flower arrangement. When he saw the small woodcarving set, however, his expression changed.

I still have the wooden cow he chiseled for me during his hospital stay; when I look at it, what I see is Grandpa Lou's hands.

1. Underline the memorable image the writer has of Grandpa Lou. Then, describe a *memorable* feature of someone you have met.
2. Circle what you would call a cow that rambled away from the herd. Then, suggest another word that you could substitute for *rambled* in this sentence.
3. Underline what Grandpa Lou was schooled in. What else might someone be *schooled* in?
4. Circle the word that means the same as weariness. What is a good cure for *weariness*?
5. Underline what had a medicinal smell. Name an item that is *medicinal*.
6. Underline what about Grandpa Lou suggests repose. Is *repose* something Grandpa Lou seems to enjoy?
7. Circle the word that means something similar to discontent. How do you know if someone is feeling a sense of *discontent*?
8. Underline what Grandpa Lou chiseled with his new carving set. What word could you use here instead of *chiseled*?

Name ______________________ Date ______________

Selections by Edwin Arlington Robinson and Edgar Lee Masters

Reading Warm-up B

Read the following passage. Pay special attention to the underlined words. Then, read it again, and complete the activities. Use a separate sheet of paper for your written answers.

As I accept this Academy Award, I would like to thank everyone who contributed to the film and to my career; but, also, I would like to take a moment to express my tremendous gratitude to the person who first influenced me as an actress: my high school drama teacher, Ms. Veronica Graham.

I remember the day I walked into Ms. Graham's class to find her arrayed in a toga for our first reading of *Julius Caesar*. I was a skinny girl who went to any length to avoid showing my legs, so you can imagine my horror when Ms. Graham told us we all had to wear togas, too. As I stood there, blushing crimson with embarrassment, my deepest wish was that I had chosen wood shop or home economics for my elective. Then, Ms. Graham strode imperially out onstage, and my everyday world disappeared; in the way she walked, the way she spoke, she had actually transformed herself into Julius Caesar. At that moment, I knew that I had to be an actress.

Ms. Graham taught as admirably as she acted, and with apologies to my director, I have to say that I learned everything I know about acting from her. The very most important thing she taught me, however, was not to give up. Over the years, the memory of Ms. Graham has been a consistent source of support and encouragement for me. Whenever I felt most pessimistic about my chances in Hollywood, I would think of her favorite saying: "Never let anything quench your fire, and you'll never find yourself out in the cold." So, thank you for everything, Ms. Graham, and I accept this Oscar in your honor.

1. Who might have influenced the speaker, besides her drama teacher? What is a synonym for *influenced*?
2. Circle what Ms. Graham was arrayed in. Then, tell what *arrayed* means.
3. What else might be *crimson* besides a blush?
4. Circle what Ms. Graham did imperially. Who else might behave *imperially*?
5. Circle two things Ms. Graham did admirably. What else might someone do *admirably*?
6. Underline what was a consistent source of support to the speaker. Then, tell what *consistent* means.
7. Why might the speaker have felt pessimistic about her chances as an actress?
8. If you wanted to do the opposite of quench a fire, what would you do?

Name ______________________________ Date ______________

"Luke Havergal" and **"Richard Cory"** by Edwin Arlington Robinson
"Lucinda Matlock" and **"Richard Bone"** by Edgar Lee Masters

Literary Analysis: Speaker

Often, the **speaker** of a poem is the poet, but when the speaker is a fictional character, as in the poems by Edwin Arlington Robinson and Edgar Lee Masters, the poem may not only communicate a message, but also reveal the attitude of the speaker and possibly the development of his or her character. For example, in "Richard Cory," the speaker looks with envy and admiration on Cory for his wealth and breeding. This provides insight into the character speaking the poem—that he or she is not of the same economic or social class.

DIRECTIONS: *In some poems, the speaker's identity is obvious, but in other poems, such as "Luke Havergal," the speaker's identity and purpose are more mysterious. Read "Luke Havergal" again, and then answer the questions below. Cite examples from the poem to support your answers.*

1. What details from "Luke Havergal" provide clues to the speaker's identity?

____

____

2. Do you think the woman whom the speaker mentions is alive or dead? Why or why not?

____

____

____

____

3. Is the speaker of this poem providing advice about a physical journey or a supernatural one? How can you tell?

____

____

4. Does the speaker of this poem expect Luke Havergal to find happiness? How can you tell?

____

____

5. What do you think happened to Luke Havergal before the speaker began speaking?

____

____

Name ______________________________ Date ______________

"Luke Havergal" and **"Richard Cory"** by Edwin Arlington Robinson
"Lucinda Matlock" and **"Richard Bone"** by Edgar Lee Masters

Reading Strategy: Recognize Attitudes

Language in literature is rarely neutral and objective. It usually presents a particular point of view or outlook on life. In a poem, the point of view is normally that of the speaker, who might be the poet, a fictional or nonfictional character, or an element of nature. By analyzing the language the speaker uses, you can make inferences about his or her **attitude.** To help find clues to the speaker's attitude, ask the following questions as you read a poem:

- Who is the speaker?
- What is the subject of the poem?
- What is the speaker's reason for speaking? What does the speaker hope to accomplish by speaking?
- What does the speaker *not* tell you?
- What biases or prejudices are revealed by the speaker's language?
- What emotion does the speaker express? What emotion does the speaker want you to feel?

DIRECTIONS: *Use this chart to help you recognize attitudes in the poems by Edwin Arlington Robinson and Edgar Lee Masters. For each poem, determine who the speaker is and write passages from the poem that express the speaker's attitude in the third column. In the last column, write adjectives that describe the attitude that is illustrated by the clues. An example is provided for you.*

Name of poem	Speaker	Clues to speaker's attitude	Attitude suggested by the clues
"Luke Havergal"	A ghost	"There is not a dawn in eastern skies"; "God slays himself with every leaf that flies, / And hell is more than half of paradise." "There is yet one way to where she is, / Bitter, but one that faith may never miss."	pessimistic, despondent, bitter
"Richard Cory"			
"Lucinda Matlock"			
"Richard Bone"			

Name ______________________ Date ______________

"Luke Havergal" and **"Richard Cory"** by Edwin Arlington Robinson
"Lucinda Matlock" and **"Richard Bone"** by Edgar Lee Masters

Vocabulary Builder

Using the Root *-pose-*

A. DIRECTIONS: *The word root* -pose- *means "rest," "place" or "position." It sometimes carries the meaning of the placing or positioning of parts. Define each underlined word below based on its use in the sentence and what you know about the word root* -pose-.

1. Because the body of the "Iceman" had been buried in snow and ice for thousands of years, it had scarcely begun to <u>decompose</u>.

____

____

2. Anna was nervous before going on stage, but she tried to <u>compose</u> herself.

____

____

3. I <u>suppose</u> we could go to the movies Monday night, if there is an early show.

____

____

4. If you type too fast, you might <u>transpose</u> some letters.

____

____

Using the Word List

imperially	repose	degenerate	epitaph

B. DIRECTIONS: *Above each underlined word in the following paragraph, write a synonym from the Word List.*

During her life, Arliss' accusers claimed she was a <u>corrupt</u> person. But when she died, the community laid her out almost <u>regally</u> in an ornate coffin. Even her enemies maintained a respectful silence as she was lowered into the grave for her final <u>rest</u>. The headstone above her grave bore the <u>legend</u>: "A loyal sister, a wise leader, loved by all."

Name ______________________ Date ______________

"Luke Havergal" and **"Richard Cory"** by Edwin Arlington Robinson
"Lucinda Matlock" and **"Richard Bone"** by Edgar Lee Masters

Grammar and Style: Noun Clauses

A **subordinate clause** contains a subject and verb but cannot stand alone as a sentence. A **noun clause** is a subordinate clause that can function in a sentence as a subject, predicate nominative, direct object, indirect object, or object of a preposition.

Noun clause used as subject:	*What concerned Harry* was that he might lose his place.
Noun clause used as predicate nominative:	He became *what he had always wanted to be.*
Noun clause used as direct object:	Heidi thought *that Peggy would return immediately.*
Noun clause used as indirect object:	Send *whoever wants some* a bottle of maple syrup.
Noun clause used as object of a preposition:	Eileen heard nothing about *where Danny had gone.*

A. Practice: *The passages below are from "Luke Havergal" and "Richard Cory." On the lines provided, identify how the noun clause is used in each excerpt.*

1. ". . . wait for <u>what will come</u>." ______________________

2. "To make us wish <u>that we were in his place</u>." ______________________

3. "God slays Himself with <u>every leaf that flies</u>." ______________________

B. Writing Application: *Complete each sentence by adding a noun clause in the part of speech specified.*

1. Gorillas are ______________________ (predicate nominative).
2. ______________________ (subject) is what you get.
3. I do not know ______________________ (direct object).
4. Please give ______________________ (indirect object) a sample of the new product.
5. I asked him about ______________________ (object of a preposition).

Name ______________________ Date ______________

"Luke Havergal" and **"Richard Cory"** by Edwin Arlington Robinson
"Lucinda Matlock" and **"Richard Bone"** by Edgar Lee Masters

Support for Writing

As you prepare to write a **firsthand biography,** choose a person whom you know well. Enter important information about him or her in the chart below.

Biography of ______________

Personality trait/Event that reflects it: ______________
Personality trait/Event that reflects it: ______________
Personality trait/Event that reflects it: ______________
Personality trait/Event that reflects it: ______________

On a separate page, put the personality traits and events in the order of their importance, and write a draft of your biography. As you revise, add or eliminate details to sharpen the impression of your subject.

Name ______________________________ Date ______________

"Luke Havergal" and **"Richard Cory"** by Edwin Arlington Robinson
"Lucinda Matlock" and **"Richard Bone"** by Edgar Lee Masters

Support for Extend Your Learning

Listening and Speaking

As you listen to Simon and Garfunkel's "Richard Cory," compare it with Robinson's poem. Prepare for a **class discussion** that compares the two works. Follow these suggestions:

- Is the song effective?
- Does it capture the message of the poem?
- In what ways, if any, does the song alter Robinson's meaning?

Discuss the two works with your class. Which work does the class like better? Why? Do you agree?

Research and Technology

As you prepare to create an **illustrated** booklet, review *Spoon River Anthology* to find poems that share a similar theme. Enter images from each in the chart below.

Theme of ________________ in *Spoon River Anthology*

Title of poem:	Details related to theme:
________________ ________________ ________________	________________________________ ________________________________ ________________________________
Title of poem:	**Details related to theme:**
________________ ________________ ________________	________________________________ ________________________________ ________________________________
Title of poem:	**Details related to theme:**
________________ ________________ ________________	________________________________ ________________________________ ________________________________

After you have prepared an illustrated booklet of the poems with a similar theme, write an introduction to explain why you have chosen them and how they are connected.

Name ____________________ Date ____________

"Luke Havergal" and **"Richard Cory"** by Edwin Arlington Robinson
"Lucinda Matlock" and **"Richard Bone"** by Edgar Lee Masters

Enrichment: Dance

Each of the poems in this selection reveals some aspects of the character's personality and values, while other parts remain a mystery. The reader of a poem must often imagine what a character in the poem is like, judging from clues in the poem. For example, Edgar Lee Masters tells us that part of Richard Bone's job is to chisel epitaphs on headstones, but he does not tell us what Richard Bone looks like. However, the reader can surmise that Richard Bone can both lift a heavy headstone and chisel fine details. So, we can guess that he is probably able-bodied and dexterous. From this image we can picture how Richard Bone might move.

DIRECTIONS: *Try to picture each character in each of the poems. (Remember that the speaker is not always the main character of the poem.) Look for the clues in each poem that reveal its main character's personality. What does each character look like while moving? Now think about what each character would look like when dancing. What would he or she dance to—music, sounds of nature, or maybe silence? Weave body movements and sounds together to create a dance that the character might do. Use the space below to plan your dance.*

Poem/Character	Body Movements	Sounds
Luke Havergal		
Richard Cory		
Lucinda Matlock		
Richard Bone		

Name ______________________________ Date ________________

"Luke Havergal" and **"Richard Cory"** by Edwin Arlington Robinson
"Lucinda Matlock" and "Richard Bone" by Edgar Lee Masters

Selection Test A

Critical Reading *Identify the letter of the choice that best answers the question.*

____ **1.** In "Luke Havergal," what does the speaker want Luke to do?
A. to visit her grave
B. to join her in death
C. to climb the western gate
D. to meet her at twilight

____ **2.** In "Luke Havergal," what relationship has existed between Luke and the speaker?
A. They were sweethearts.
B. They were mother and son.
C. They were sister and brother.
D. They were father and daughter.

____ **3.** In "Luke Havergal," how does the speaker show Luke the importance of what she wishes him to do?
A. by describing the eastern dawn
B. by comparing hell and paradise
C. by repeating "Out of a grave I come,"
D. by reminding him of her kiss

____ **4.** In "Richard Cory," whose ideas does the speaker reflect?
A. his own
B. Richard Cory's
C. the townspeople's
D. the Cory family's

____ **5.** In "Richard Cory," what is the general feeling Richard Cory inspires in the townspeople up until the last lines?
A. confusion
B. envy
C. approval
D. pity

Name ______________________________ Date ______________

____ **6.** In “Richard Cory,” what attitude would you expect the speaker to have as he writes the final lines of the poem?
A. satisfaction
B. shock
C. acceptance
D. admiration

____ **7.** In “Lucinda Matlock,” what is the title character’s attitude toward life?
A. She thinks life is hard.
B. She thinks life ends too soon.
C. She thinks life is worthwhile.
D. She thinks life is boring.

____ **8.** Which of these might the title character say to young people at the end of “Lucinda Matlock”?
A. Life will get better as you get older.
B. All life has some sorrow.
C. You can sleep after you die.
D. It takes strength to engage in life.

____ **9.** In “Lucinda Matlock,” what attitude can you assume she would have toward young complaining people?
A. sympathy
B. disgust
C. relief
D. agreement

____ **10.** What job does the title character have in “Richard Bone”?
A. He is an undertaker.
B. He is an epitaph carver.
C. He is a stonecutter.
D. He is a historian.

____ **11.** Why does the speaker in “Richard Bone” carve lies about the dead?
A. He does not know they are lies.
B. He does not care about truth or lies.
C. He is paid to carve what he is told.
D. He wants to make survivors feel better.

Name ______________________ Date ______________

Vocabulary and Grammar

____ 12. In which sentence is the meaning of the word *repose* suggested?

A. A ghost called from the grave to Luke Havergal.

B. Everyone thought Richard Cory lived a charmed life.

C. Lucinda Matlock rested only when she died.

D. Richard Bone questioned the value of his life's work.

____ 13. Which key word helps you to recognize the noun clause in this line: "In fine, we thought that he was everything"?

A. fine

B. we

C. that

D. he

Essay

14. Why do you think the speaker and the townspeople in "Richard Cory" had a picture of Richard Cory that was different from the real person? Write a brief essay to suggest reasons why the townspeople might have been so wrong about someone they saw every day.

15. Richard Bone in the poem of the same name compares himself to a historian. How could a person who carves epitaphs be like a person who writes history? Write a brief essay using your own ideas and the material from the poem to give your opinion on Richard Bone's belief.

Name ______________________ Date ______________

"**Luke Havergal**" and "**Richard Cory**" by Edwin Arlington Robinson
"**Lucinda Matlock**" and "**Richard Bone**" by Edgar Lee Masters

Selection Test B

Critical Reading *Identify the letter of the choice that best completes the statement or answers the question.*

____ **1.** What is the speaker's main motive for talking to Luke Havergal in this poem?
A. to comfort Luke
B. to convince Luke to act on his feelings
C. to chastise Luke for being overly emotional
D. to provide Luke with hope for a brighter future

____ **2.** Which of the following best describes the tone of "Luke Havergal"?
A. angry
B. hopeful
C. indifferent
D. brooding

____ **3.** Which of the following most likely explains the relationship between Luke Havergal and the woman mentioned in the poem?
A. The woman was Luke's lover, but she died.
B. The woman was Luke's enemy, and she destroyed his life.
C. The woman was a homeless vagrant whom Luke saw and pitied.
D. The woman was a murderer who killed Luke's family.

____ **4.** Who is the speaker of "Luke Havergal"?
A. Luke Havergal
B. a living woman
C. a ghost
D. Edwin Arlington Robinson

____ **5.** Who is the speaker of "Richard Cory"?
A. Richard Cory
B. a person in the town
C. a member of Richard Cory's family
D. Edwin Arlington Robinson

____ **6.** Why did the speaker of "Richard Cory" envy Richard Cory?
A. because he was wealthy and admirable
B. because he had a large family
C. because he led a happy life
D. because he was a community leader

____ **7.** Which of the following passages from "Richard Cory" shows that the speaker admired Richard Cory's character and manners?
A. "He was a gentleman from sole to crown,"
B. "But still he fluttered pulses when he said, / 'Good-morning'"
C. ". . . and he glittered when he walked."
D. "And he was rich—yes, richer than a king—"

Name ______________________________ Date ______________

___ 8. Which sentence best describes Lucinda Matlock's view of life?
A. The parties and explorations of youth are the best part of life; old age is full of pain, suffering, and loneliness.
B. You need anger to get you through the hardships of life; the angrier you are, the more likely you are to survive to an old age.
C. You must work hard and you may encounter sorrow, but life is basically fulfilling and rewarding.
D. People's lives are determined by fate, and no one really cares about what you think or how you feel.

___ 9. Which of the following best describes the tone of Masters's "Lucinda Matlock"?
A. contented
B. despairing
C. self-righteous
D. disappointed

___ 10. Which of the following excerpts gives the best insight into the personality of Lucinda Matlock?
A. "One time we changed partners,"
B. "Enjoying, working, raising the twelve children,"
C. "And by Spoon River gathering many a shell,"
D. "Anger, discontent, and drooping hopes?"

___ 11. Which of the following passages from "Richard Bone" shows that the speaker feels uncomfortable about chiseling deceptive epitaphs?
A. "I did not know whether what they told me/Was true or false."
B. "And I chiseled them whatever they wished,/All in ignorance of its truth."
C. "I knew how near to the life/Were the epitaphs that were ordered . . ."
D. "And made myself party to the false chronicles/Of the stones,"

___ 12. What does this passage from "Richard Bone" suggest about the speaker's attitude?

But still I chiseled whatever they paid me to chisel
And made myself party to the false chronicles

A. He is indifferent to the truth.
B. He has been influenced to hide the truth.
C. He prefers not to know the truth.
D. He will chisel only true epitaphs.

Vocabulary and Grammar

___ 13. How does the italicized noun clause function in the following line from "Richard Bone"?

And I chiseled for them whatever they wished. . . .

A. as a direct object
B. as an indirect object
C. as a predicate nominative
D. as the object of a preposition

Name ______________________________ Date ______________

____ **14.** Which of the following words could be substituted for *imperially* in the following passage from "Richard Cory" without changing the meaning of the sentence?

He was a gentleman from sole to crown,
Clean favored, and *imperially* slim.

A. surprisingly
B. majestically
C. beautifully
D. shockingly

____ **15.** Which of the following statements most accurately paraphrases the following excerpt from "Lucinda Matlock"?

At ninety-six I had lived enough, that is all
And passed to a sweet *repose*.

A. At age ninety-six, I moved into a nursing home.
B. At age ninety-six, I stopped working and started having fun.
C. At age ninety-six, I decided to stop working and retire.
D. At age ninety-six, I died and got a long overdue rest.

____ **16.** In the following passage from "Richard Bone," what does the word *epitaph* mean?

They would bring me the *epitaph*
And stand around the shop while I worked

A. inscription
B. headstone
C. grave marker
D. dead body

____ **17.** A noun clause is a subordinate clause that

I. has a subject and a verb.
II. cannot stand alone as a sentence.
III. is used as a noun in a sentence.

A. I and II
B. II and III
C. I and III
D. I, II, and III

Essay

18. Choose one of the poems in this selection and write a short biographical essay on the title character. Draw conclusions about the life the character led or is leading, and support those conclusions with details from the poem. Consider the tone of the poem you choose, and use that as a clue to the kind of life the person led.

19. How would you describe Lucinda Matlock's attitude toward younger people? Write an essay describing how she comes to give the advice she does in the poem. Do you think she despises people who are younger than she, or is she motivated by a desire to ensure that they do not miss out on life? Support your conclusions with details from the poem.

20. What do you think the speaker of "Luke Havergal" wants Luke Havergal to do? Write an essay, using evidence from the poem to answer the question and support your answer.

"A Wagner Matinée" by Willa Cather

Vocabulary Warm-up Word Lists

Study these words from the selection. Then, complete the activities that follow.

Word List A

alight [uh LYT] *v.* to get down or set foot on a platform or sidewalk
As the train slowed to a stop, I prepared to alight on the platform.

comprehend [kahm pree HEND] *v.* to understand
That theory is so complex that it is difficult to comprehend.

conjuror [KUN juh ruhr] *n.* magician
The entertainer was a famous conjuror, who performed magic tricks.

eluding [i LOOD ing] *adj.* evading; escaping
Eluding the police, the cat burglar slipped away in the night.

haggard [HAG uhrd] *adj.* drawn; pale
Sam looked haggard, as if he hadn't slept for days.

legacy [LEG uh see] *n.* inheritance; anything handed down from the past
Grandmother's stories about her own youth are a precious family legacy.

pitiless [PIT ee les] *adj.* without pity or compassion
The weather has been pitiless, with extremely cold winters and very hot summers.

vainly [VAYN lee] *adv.* to no effect; emptily
Mark tried vainly to persuade Mom, but she would not accept his arguments.

Word List B

absurdities [ab SERD uh teez] *n.* irrational or illogical things or situations
Among other absurdities, the comedian introduced a hilarious talking parrot.

characteristically [ka rak ter IST ik uh lee] *adv.* typically; in a predictable fashion
Cyrus was characteristically melancholy, seldom cracking a smile.

frenzy [FREN zee] *n.* state of great excitement or madness
The cornered cat shrieked in a frenzy of fear.

harmonious [har MOH nee uhs] *adj.* in tune or harmony with
Sue's neighbors are a harmonious group of people.

immobility [im oh BIL i tee] *n.* motionless state
Do not be fooled by the possum's immobility; it is still very much alive!

pathetic [puh THET ik] *adj.* pitiful; worthy of compassion
The condition of the refugees was pathetic; many of them even lacked shoes.

pedestal [PED uhs tuhl] *n.* base for a statue or sculpture
The statue stood on a magnificent pedestal of polished granite.

wholly [HOL ee] *adv.* entirely
Trent's story was wholly unbelievable, and we dismissed it out of hand.

Name ______________________________ Date ______________

"A Wagner Matinée" by Willa Cather

Vocabulary Warm-up Exercises

Exercise A *Fill in each blank in the paragraph below with the appropriate word from Word List A.*

After his parents took him to see a magic show, Lenny decided he wanted to become a magician, or [1] ______________. He imagined himself preparing his performances and getting ready to [2] ______________ on stage in front of the audience. They would try desperately but [3] ______________ to [4] ______________ the secrets of his tricks, and Lenny, [5] ______________ all their efforts, would remain mysterious as ever. He would work hard to keep up with new trends in the magic business. Putting up with a harsh and [6] ______________ schedule in tour might make him so tired that he would look weary, or even [7] ______________. However, he would have the greatest magic show in the country, and a lasting reputation for unbelievable tricks would be his [8] ______________ to future generations.

Exercise B *Decide whether each statement below is true or false. Circle* T *or* F, *and explain your answer.*

1. Absurdities are worth taking seriously.
   T / F ______________________________
2. If someone is characteristically optimistic, he or she generally looks on the bright side.
   T / F ______________________________
3. A person in a frenzy might act wildly and unpredictably.
   T / F ______________________________
4. Nations that sign a peace treaty expect that their relations will not be harmonious.
   T / F ______________________________
5. Paralysis causes a state of immobility.
   T / F ______________________________
6. A pathetic state of affairs often inspires pity.
   T / F ______________________________
7. A pedestal often supports a statue or sculpture.
   T / F ______________________________
8. If a house has been wholly renovated, parts of it remain to be refurbished.
   T / F ______________________________

Name ______________________________ Date ______________

"A Wagner Matinée" by Willa Cather

Reading Warm-up A

Read the following passage. Pay special attention to the underlined words. Then, read it again, and complete the activities. Use a separate sheet of paper for your written answers.

In the late nineteenth and early twentieth centuries, millions of immigrants streamed off ships from Europe to alight on American soil for the first time. The majority of these newcomers settled in eastern cities, such as New York, Philadelphia, Boston, and Baltimore. Many of them joined relatives who were already here. These family members could help the new arrivals comprehend the challenges of building a new life. They could assist with learning an unfamiliar language, finding a place to live, and securing a job.

A number of immigrants, however, traveled westward to the Great Plains. In return for cheap land, these settlers were prepared to endure a pitiless climate of scorching summers and freezing winters. Many of these Midwestern farmers were from Scandinavia and central Europe.

In many of her novels, Willa Cather celebrated the Czech and Slovak farmers of Nebraska. She thought of them as unsung heroes. Their legacy of courage and endurance, passed down to their descendants, deserved commemoration, Cather believed. In his book, *Giants in the Earth,* published in 1927, the novelist Ole Edvart Rölvaag wrote about the Norwegian homesteaders of the Dakota Territory.

Both Cather and Rölvaag were realistic in their portrayals of the immigrants' farm life. The farmers' existence was so harsh that many homesteaders became haggard—worn out with fatigue. Some of the characters struggle vainly against misfortune and are crushed by the obstacles they encounter. Other characters are luckier, eluding disaster and disappointment. In the end, for both authors, a person winning out in this challenging environment is almost like a conjuror, whose magical abilities suffice to build a new life full of hope and promise.

1. Underline the words in this sentence that give a clue to the meaning of alight. Use the word ***alight*** in an original sentence.
2. Circle the words in this and the next sentence that give a clue to the meaning of the word comprehend. What is a synonym for ***comprehend***?
3. Underline the words that give a clue to the meaning of pitiless. What is an antonym for ***pitiless***?
4. Circle the words that offer a clue to the meaning of legacy here. What is a synonym for the word ***legacy***?
5. Circle the words in this sentence that offer clues to the meaning of haggard. Use a word meaning the opposite of ***haggard*** in a sentence.
6. Underline the words in this sentence that give a clue to the meaning of vainly. What are two antonyms for ***vainly***?
7. Circle the words in this sentence that give a clue to the meaning of eluding. Use the word ***eluding*** in an original sentence.
8. Underline the words in this sentence hinting at the meaning of conjuror. Use the word ***conjuror*** in an original sentence.

Name ______________________________ Date ______________

"A Wagner Matinée" by Willa Cather

Reading Warm-up B

Read the following passage. Pay special attention to the underlined words. Then, read it again, and complete the activities. Use a separate sheet of paper for your written answers.

As an art form, opera is over 400 years old. Developed in Italy in the early 1600s, operas are unique fusions of song, orchestral accompaniment, and stage effects. These effects include costumes, scenery, and lighting. In an ideal performance, all these elements exist in a harmonious, balanced combination.

Many people find opera difficult to understand, however. Some critics mock operatic works as absurdities that no reasonable person can take seriously. Critics claim that operas characteristically possess unrealistic plots, which depend on coincidence so much that they are wholly unbelievable. According to these skeptics, operatic characters exemplify ridiculous extremes. At some points, they exhibit a frenzy of wild emotions, and at others they lapse into static immobility.

Opera's fans, on the other hand, claim that no other art form contains such rich possibilities of expression. Without unduly glorifying opera, or putting it on a pedestal, it must be acknowledged that the form afforded great composers like Richard Wagner and Giuseppe Verdi wonderful artistic opportunities. For example, two or more characters singing together could express varying or conflicting emotions at the same time. Orchestral themes could function like flashbacks or foreshadowing in literature, signaling a memory of the past or a hint about the future. Profound emotions could be illustrated on stage, ranging from the triumphant to the pathetic.

In the end, opera has not turned out to be everybody's cup of tea. People like Aunt Georgiana in Willa Cather's story, "A Wagner Matinée," are still in the minority, and oper a has never been hugely popular, at least in America. Let there be no doubt, however, that opera's fans are passionate, if they are anything!

1. Underline the words in this sentence that give a clue to the meaning of harmonious. Use a word meaning the opposite of ***harmonious*** in a sentence.
2. Circle the words in this sentence that give a clue to the meaning of absurdities. Are ***absurdities*** logical or illogical?
3. What is a synonym for characteristically? What is an antonym for ***characteristically***?
4. Underline the words in this sentence that give a clue to the meaning of wholly. What is a synonym for ***wholly***?
5. Circle the words in this sentence that give a clue to the meaning of frenzy. Use a word meaning the opposite of ***frenzy*** in a sentence of your own.
6. Underline the word in this sentence that hints at the meaning of immobility. What is a synonym for ***immobility***?
7. Underline the words in this sentence that give a clue to the meaning of pedestal. Is this word used literally or figuratively here?
8. Circle the words in this sentence that hint at the meaning of the word pathetic.

Name ______________________ Date ______________

"A Wagner Matinée" by Willa Cather

Literary Analysis: Characterization

Most readers enjoy a story more when they feel as if they know the characters as people. **Characterization** is the way in which a writer reveals a character's personality. A writer can make direct statements about a character, give a physical description, describe the character's actions, and/or tell the character's thoughts and comments.

DIRECTIONS: *Read each excerpt from the selection, and write down what each tells you about the character of Aunt Georgiana.*

1. "Whatever shock Mrs. Springer experienced at my aunt's appearance she considerately concealed."

2. ". . . a plain, angular, spectacled woman of thirty."

3. ". . . she eloped with him, eluding the reproaches of her family and the criticism of her friends by going with him to the Nebraska frontier."

4. ". . . in those days I owed to this woman most of the good that ever came my way, . . ."

5. "Don't love it so well, Clark, or it may be taken from you."

6. "When the violins drew out the first strain of the Pilgrims' chorus, my Aunt Georgiana clutched my coat sleeve."

7. "Poor old hands! They were stretched and pulled and twisted into mere tentacles to hold, and lift, and knead with; . . ."

8. "She burst into tears and sobbed pleadingly, 'I don't want to go, Clark, I don't want to go!'"

Name ______________________________ Date ______________

"A Wagner Matinée" by Willa Cather

Reading Strategy: Clarify

As you read, it is important to **clarify,** or check your understanding, of the details in what you read. You can clarify the details by reading a footnote, looking up a word in the dictionary, rereading a passage to refresh your memory, or reading ahead to find additional details.

DIRECTIONS: *Read each phrase from the selection. Answer the question using one clarifying strategy.*

1. ". . . the gangling farmer boy my aunt had known, scourged with chilblains . . ."
   What is a chilblain?

   ____

   ____

2. "[Aunt Georgiana] had come all the way in a day coach. . ."
   What was the origin and destination of Aunt Georgiana's trip?

   ____

   ____

3. "One summer, which she had spent in the little village in the Green Mountains where her ancestors had dwelt for generations, . . ."
   Where are the Green Mountains?

   ____

   ____

4. "I suggested our visiting the Conservatory and the Common before lunch, . . ."
   Why would Aunt Georgiana be interested in the Conservatory?

   ____

   ____

5. ". . . with the bitter frenzy of the Venusberg theme and its ripping of strings, . . ."
   What is the significance of the term *Venusberg*?

   ____

   ____

6. "Soon after the tenor began the 'Prize Song,' I heard a quick-drawn breath, and turned to my aunt. Her eyes were closed, but the tears were glistening on her cheeks, . . ."
   Why did the "Prize Song" make Aunt Georgiana cry?

   ____

   ____

Name ______________________________ Date ______________________

"A Wagner Matinée" by Willa Cather

Vocabulary Builder

Using Words from Music

Words from music can often have two meanings—one specific musical meaning and one for use in a nonmusical context.

A. DIRECTIONS: *Each sentence below contains a word from music. On the line below the sentence, write either* musical *or* nonmusical *to show how the word is used in the sentence.*

1. The team practiced as a prelude to the big game.

____

2. His key didn't fit in the new lock.

____

3. When we heard the prelude, we knew the performance had just started.

____

4. They played the song in a minor key.

____

Using the Word List

reverential	tremulously	semi-somnambulant
inert	prelude	jocularity

B. DIRECTIONS: *Each sentence includes a word or phrase that means about the same as one of the words in the Word List. Underline that word or phrase and write the Word List word in the blank.*

1. The orchestra began with the overture to the opera. ______________
2. Aunt Georgiana was emotional and spoke with a quivering voice. ______________
3. In the concert hall, she seemed somewhat less unable to move. ______________
4. The trip left Aunt Georgiana feeling as though she were partly sleepwalking.

____

5. Clark's attempts at light-hearted joking seemed lost on Aunt Georgiana.

____

6. Clark had very respectful feelings for his aunt. ______________

Name ______________________________ Date ______________

"A Wagner Matinée" by Willa Cather

Grammar and Style: Reflexive and Intensive Pronouns

Pronouns that end in *-self* or *-selves* are either reflexive or intensive pronouns, depending on how they are used in a sentence. A **reflexive pronoun** refers to the subject of the sentence and is necessary to complete the meaning of the sentence. An **intensive pronoun** simply adds emphasis to the noun or pronoun for which it stands; it can be deleted without changing the meaning of the sentence.

Reflexive pronoun: . . . she had surrendered herself unquestioningly into the hands of a country dressmaker.

Intensive pronoun: . . . her fingers worked mechanically upon her black dress, as though of themselves they were recalling the piano score they had once played.

A. Practice: *In the following sentences, identify each pronoun ending in* -self *or* -selves *as reflexive or intensive.*

1. Sometimes I write myself notes to help me remember things. ______________
2. We ourselves want to go to the game. ______________
3. The little boy likes to try to tie his shoes himself. ______________
4. The children watch themselves in the mirror as they practice dancing. ______________
5. Mr. and Mrs. Perez just bought themselves a new house. ______________
6. We gave ourselves too little time for the trip. ______________

B. Writing Application: *Rewrite each of the following sentences using a reflexive or intensive pronoun correctly.*

1. The boys did the work without help from anyone else.

____

2. Lakisha bought a new jacket with her own money.

____

3. Now that you have bought a present for your sister, what will you get?

____

4. We wanted a treat, so we went on a boat ride.

____

5. Sometimes I really like to be alone.

____

Name ______________________ Date ____________

"A Wagner Matinée" by Willa Cather

Support for Writing

As you prepare to write an **editorial** on Willa Cather's portrayal of Nebraska, enter your arguments in the chart below. Keep in mind that you will be writing as though you are the editor of a Nebraska newspaper.

Why Willa Cather's "A Wagner Matinée" is Fair/Not Fair to Nebraskans

Example from story: Why it supports my opinion
Example from story: Why it supports my opinion
Example from story: Why it supports my opinion

On a separate page, put your examples in order of importance and write a draft of your editorial. When you revise your work, make sure you have used persuasive language to make your point of view clear and powerful.

Name ______________________________ Date ______________

"A Wagner Matinée" by Willa Cather

Support for Extend Your Learning

Listening and Speaking

As you work with a partner to prepare **monologues** by the two characters about the effect of the music on Aunt Georgiana, consider the following elements:

- What memories were drawn out?
- What were the physical reactions?

Present your monologues to the class and ask for feedback. Ask your classmates whether they think your respective portrayals of Clark and Aunt Georgiana were believable.

Research and Technology

Take notes on the Wagner opera you listen to in preparation for a **musical presentation** of one of the passages. Do background research on the Internet about the opera you chose.

________________ **by Richard Wagner**

Characters	
Setting	
Plot	

Use the information from your chart to help your classmates understand what is going on in the musical passage you chose and how the passage is important to the rest of the opera.

Name ______________________________ Date ______________

"A Wagner Matinée" by Willa Cather

Enrichment: Music

Identity in Song

DIRECTIONS: *Among some African tribes, a baby's mother develops a song for the child. The mother teaches the song to the rest of the village, and the music becomes the child's song. The village sings the song at important times throughout the child's life—celebrations of achievement, recovery from wounds or illness, and other ceremonies.*

Find or write a song that represents you as a person—your song. Write the name of your song and describe it. Tell why you identify with the song.

My Song: ______________________________

This is my song because:

____

____

____

____

____

____

____

____

Some lines from the song that best describe me are:

____

____

____

____

____

____

____

____

____

____

____

____

____

Name ______________________________ Date ______________

"A Wagner Matinée" by Willa Cather

Selection Test A

Critical Reading *Identify the letter of the choice that best answers the question.*

___ 1. In "A Wagner Matinee," which method of characterization does the author use here to describe Aunt Georgiana:

"... her linen duster had become black with soot"?

A. a character's thoughts and words
B. a physical description of the character
C. comments made by other characters
D. the character's statements

___ 2. In "A Wagner Matinee," how would a reader clarify the meaning of:

"He requested me to meet her at the station, and render her whatever services might prove necessary"?

A. use a map to find the station
B. find out what city the station is in
C. look up the meaning of the word *prove*
D. look up the meaning of the word *render*

___ 3. In "A Wagner Matinee," what can the reader infer about Aunt Georgiana from reading that she "would often stand until midnight at her ironing board . . . gently shaking me when my drowsy head sank down over a page of irregular verbs"?

A. She preferred ironing to learning.
B. She started her working-day late.
C. She disliked the study of Latin verbs.
D. She cared about her nephew's schooling.

___ 4. In "A Wagner Matinee," how does the narrator feel about how his aunt once cared for him?

A. unhappy
B. bored
C. grateful
D. angry

___ 5. Which answer describes Aunt Georgiana's adult life on the farm in "A Wagner Matinee"?

A. full of life
B. quiet and lonely
C. comfortable
D. city-like

Name ______________________ Date ______________

____ **6.** In "A Wagner Matinee," which life event causes the most pain?

A. the realization of one's loss
B. the failure of prairie farming
C. the insensitivity of youth
D. the absence of dreams

____ **7.** In "A Wagner Matinee," what do readers learn by reading that Aunt Georgiana was worried because she had not told her daughter to cook the mackerel in the cellar so it wouldn't spoil?

A. She often neglects her daughter.
B. She takes her responsibilities seriously.
C. She hates to use any food that isn't fresh.
D. She has trouble enjoying her travels.

____ **8.** In "A Wagner Matinee," how can a reader clarify this passage:

"When the musicians came out . . . she . . . looked with quickening interest down over the rail . . . perhaps the first wholly familiar thing that had greeted her eye since she had left old Maggie and her weakling calf"?

A. do research on musicians
B. look up the word *familiar*
C. reread to identify who Maggie is
D. find information on calves

____ **9.** In "A Wagner Matinee," how would a reader clarify the information in this passage:

"Shortly afterward he had gone to town on the Fourth of July, lost his money at a faro[14] table, ridden a saddled Texas steer . . . and disappeared with a fractured collarbone"?

A. read the information in footnote 14
B. do research on Texas gambling
C. look up the meaning of *steer*
D. do research on the Fourth of July

____ **10.** In "A Wagner Matinee," which of these is used to express Aunt Georgiana's emotional state?

A. her hair
B. her hands
C. her love of music
D. her love for her nephew

Name ______________________________ Date ______________

Vocabulary and Grammar

____ 11. In which sentence is the meaning of the word *inert* suggested?
A. Aunt Georgiana arrived flustered on the morning train.
B. I remembered her constant work at the farm in Nebraska.
C. She sat motionless as we listened to the Wagner music.
D. She cried when she had to leave and return to Nebraska.

____ 12. Which of the following sentences uses an intensive pronoun?
A. I saw that it was my aunt herself.
B. The musicians began to play.
C. She worried about the weakling calf.
D. I studied music with others and alone.

Essay

13. In "A Wagner Matinee," Aunt Georgiana says to Clark, "Don't love it so well Clark, or it may be taken from you." What do you think she means by this? Write a brief essay to discuss this quote. Use what you have learned about Aunt Georgiana in the story in your discussion.

14. At the end of "A Wagner Matinee," the author writes, "For her, just outside the door of the concert hall, lay the black pond with the cattle-tracked bluffs, the tall, unpainted house, naked as a tower . . ." Does the author mean that Aunt Georgiana's home is located outside the concert hall? Write a brief essay to explain why you think the author ends the story this way.

Name ______________________________ Date ______________

"A Wagner Matinée" by Willa Cather

Selection Test B

Critical Reading *Identify the letter of the choice that best completes the statement or answers the question.*

____ 1. The description of Aunt Georgiana as having "an incessant twitching of the mouth and eyebrows . . . resulting from isolation and monotony, and from frequent physical suffering" reveals her character through
A. a dialogue with another character.
B. the narrator's observations of her physical appearance.
C. her own thoughts and comments.
D. Mrs. Springer's reactions.

____ 2. The selection says that Aunt Georgiana and her husband "took a homestead in Red Willow County."[6] The "6" tells us we can find out more about Red Willow County
A. in footnote number six.
B. in the sixth definition under *County* in a dictionary.
C. in the sixth map at the end of the book.
D. by reading six paragraphs ahead.

____ 3. As a young boy, Clark appears to have been
A. oblivious and lazy.
B. tough and quick-witted.
C. studious and dull.
D. diligent and sensitive.

____ 4. We learn in the first paragraph that the letter announcing Aunt Georgiana's arrival comes from Nebraska. Therefore, we assume she lives in Nebraska. We can find out Aunt Georgiana lives on a small homestead in Red Willow County by
A. using an atlas.
B. reading a footnote.
C. reviewing past sentences.
D. reading ahead.

____ 5. Which of the following aspects of Aunt Georgiana's life does the author appear to value most highly?
A. piety
B. poverty
C. modesty
D. devotion

____ 6. The description of the Nebraska farm creates an atmosphere of
A. adventure and tension.
B. desolation and hardship.
C. boredom and apathy.
D. productivity and vitality.

Name ______________________________ Date ______________

___ 7. Which of the following factors probably contributed most to Aunt Georgiana's general bewilderment during her visit?
A. the long and difficult journey to Boston
B. her age, which had brought about a certain forgetfulness
C. the contrast in settings between Boston and the Nebraska farm
D. the suddenness of her departure from Nebraska

___ 8. What is the central idea of "A Wagner Matinée"?
A. the oppression of women by men
B. the high price of foolish young love
C. the pain of realizing what you have lost
D. the hardships of frontier

___ 9. What can the reader infer about Aunt Georgiana's character from the following passage?

She questioned me absently about various changes in the city, but she was chiefly concerned that she had forgotten to leave instructions about feeding half-skimmed milk to a certain weakling calf.

A. She tended to be absent-minded in her daily chores.
B. She found it difficult to rely on others.
C. She focused more on her responsibilities than on what gives her pleasure.
D. She disliked the city and longed to be back on the farm.

___ 10. Why does Clark come to live with Aunt Georgiana as a boy?
A. He was orphaned when he was a young boy.
B. His parents sent him there while they traveled in Europe.
C. He was an apprentice farmer for his Uncle Howard.
D. The selection does not explain.

___ 11. Which is a reading strategy for clarifying?
A. knowing how other characters feel about the main character
B. knowing what tense the sentence is written in
C. memorizing sections of texts
D. rereading a previous passage to refresh your memory

___ 12. The tone of "A Wagner Matinée" can best be described as
A. sympathetic.
B. distant.
C. accusatory.
D. apologetic.

___ 13. Which of the following passages is an example of characterization?
A. "There they measured off their eighty acres by driving across the prairie in a wagon. . . . "
B. "When the musicians came out and took their places, she gave a little stir of anticipation. . . . "
C. "The world there is the flat world of the ancients. . . . "
D. ". . . the people filed out of the hall chattering and laughing, glad to relax and find the living level again. . . . "

Name ____ Date ____________________

Vocabulary and Grammar

____ **14.** Which word is closest to the italicized word in the following excerpt?

"Well, we have come to better things than the old *Trovatore* at any rate, Aunt Georgie?" I queried, with well-meant *jocularity*.

A. love
B. shyness
C. caution
D. humor

____ **15.** Clark uses the word *reverential* to describe his feelings for his aunt, meaning he

A. fears her.
B. respects her.
C. ignores her.
D. dislikes her.

____ **16.** The selection tells us that, before the concert, Aunt Georgiana seems *semi-somnambulant* and *inert*. The two words that best describe her state of being are

A. *timid* and *respectful*.
B. *sleepy* and *motionless*.
C. *restless* and *cheerful*.
D. *still* and *fearful*.

____ **17.** Which sentence includes an intensive pronoun?

A. The isolation built upon itself to create a lonely prison.
B. The ladies looked among themselves to see who appeared to be the finest.
C. We ourselves enjoyed the Wagner concert very much.
D. He silently congratulated himself for making the correct decision.

Essay

18. There are several indications that Aunt Georgiana retained her love of music throughout her time in Nebraska. In an essay, describe which details in the selection indicate that music remained alive in Aunt Georgiana's heart, even years after she left the conservatory.

19. At the end of the story, Aunt Georgiana pleads with Clark that she does not want to leave the concert. Write an essay in which you interpret the deeper meaning of her response to the end of the concert. What does leaving the concert hall symbolize for Aunt Georgiana? Support your explanation with details from the story.

20. In first-person narration, the reader learns only as much about the narrator as the narrator chooses to reveal. A person reading "A Wagner Matinée" learns a great deal more about Aunt Georgiana than about her nephew Clark. Write a descriptive essay about Clark, the narrator, based on information in the story. Although nothing is said about Clark's appearance, you can infer his personality from his thoughts, statements, and actions. Be as specific as possible, and support your observations with examples from the text.

Name ______________________________ Date ______________

Writing About Literature—Unit 4

Compare and Contrast Literary Themes

Prewriting: Reviewing the Material

Answer the questions in the chart below to explore your impressions about each writer's attitude toward the enemy.

Questions	Selection 1	Selection 2	Selection 3
Does each writer seem sure of the rightness of his or her cause?			
Does each writer seem eager for armed conflict?			
Does any writer express fear that the enemy might be victorious?			
Does any writer express sympathy for or understanding of the enemy?			
Does any writer seem to lack strong feeling toward the enemy?			

Drafting: Organizing Examples

Use the graphic organizers below to help you decide which organizational strategy to use before you begin to write.

Grouping Ideas

Similarities between selections:

↓

Differences between selections:

Grouping Selections

Points about Selection 1:

↓

Points about Selection 2:

↓

Points about Selection 2:

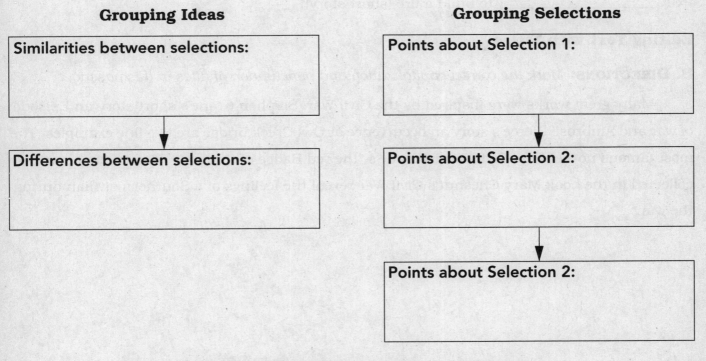

Name ______________________________ Date ______________

Comparing and Contractin Literary Themes: Integrating Grammar Skills

Review your draft to make sure you have correctly formatted and capitalized the titles of the literary works you cite. Underline or italicize the titles of full-length books. Enclose the titles of shorter works—such as poems, short stories, speeches, and songs—in quotation marks. Use the following rules when capitalizing titles:

- Capitalize the first word and all other key words.
- DO NOT capitalize the articles *a, an,* and *the*—unless they are the first word of the title.
- DO NOT capitalize conjunctions and prepositions—unless they are the first or last word of the title or unless they contain four letters or more.
- Always capitalize verbs, no matter how short.

EXAMPLES: "The Fall of the House of Usher" (short story)
"Go Down, Moses" (song)
<u>The Adventures of Huckleberry Finn</u> (book)

Punctuating and Capitalizing Titles

A. Directions: *Rewrite the following titles, adding capital letters, quotation marks, and underlining where they are needed.*

1. ____________________ the outcasts of poker flat (short story)
2. ____________________ life on the mississippi (book)
3. ____________________ to build a fire (short story)

Editing Text with Titles

B. Directions: *Mark the correct capitalization and punctuation of titles in this passage.*

Many great works were inspired by the Civil War. Stephen Crane's short story an Episode of war and Ambrose Bierce's story an occurrence at Owl Creek bridge are two fine examples. The most famous novel of the Civil War is Crane's "the red Badge of Courage." The journal entries collected in the book Mary Chesnut's Civil War reveal the feelings of a Southern civilian during the war.

Name ______________________ Date ______________

Writing Workshop—Unit 4

Research: Research Paper

Prewriting: Choosing Your Topic

Answer the questions in the chart below to choose a topic of interest for your research.

What broad subjects like the environment, politics, sports, technology, or literature interest you?	
What specific categories of that subject do you find appealing?	
What people in history or current events would you like to understand better?	

Drafting: Using a Formal Outline

Complete the outline below to organize your ideas and supporting information before writing.

I. Introduction
  A. Interesting Opening
  B. Thesis Statement
II. Body Paragraph 1
  A. Topic Sentence
  B. Supporting Evidence
  C. Supporting Evidence
III. Body Paragraph 2
  A. Topic Sentence
  B. Supporting Evidence
  C. Supporting Evidence
IV. Body Paragraph 3
  A. Topic Sentence
  B. Supporting Evidence
  C. Supporting Evidence
V. Body Paragraph 4
  A. Topic Sentence
  B. Supporting Evidence
  C. Supporting Evidence
VI. Conclusion
  A. Restatement of Thesis
  B. Memorable Closing

Name ______________________________ Date ______________

Writing Workshop—Unit 4

Research Report: Integrating Grammar Skills

Revising Your Paragraphs

As you introduce blocks of information in your report, help the reader follow your train of thought from one paragraph to another. When you revise, **add transitions to improve the flow of ideas.** Transitional words and phrases show the relationships between ideas and clarify the connections you want readers to make. The following chart shows common transitions used to show different kinds of relationships:

chronological order	first, next, recently, later, finally
comparison-and-contrast	both, like, unlike, however, on the other hand
cause-and-effect	as a result, therefore, because
details that support a main idea	in addition, furthermore, for instance, for example

Adding Transitions

DIRECTIONS: *Copy the following paragraphs from a research report. Then revise the paragraphs by adding transitions where they are needed to show the relationships between ideas.*

Two early American writers who promoted a spirit of individualism were Ralph Waldo Emerson and Henry David Thoreau, who were neighbors in Concord, Massachusetts. Fourteen years older than Thoreau, Emerson was a major influence on his younger friend. Emerson's essay, called "Self-Reliance," inspired Thoreau to trust his own instincts about right and wrong.

Thoreau believed in self-reliance. He put his ideas to the test in more extreme ways. He lived by himself in a cabin at Walden Pond for two years, where he observed nature and wrote his best-known work, *Walden*. He once spent a night in jail, rather than pay a tax that might help support a war he did not believe in. This experience led to his famous essay "Civil Disobedience," which has inspired generations of social activists, including Martin Luther King, Jr.

Name ____ Date ____________________

Spelling—Unit 4

Proofreading Practice

DIRECTIONS: *Proofread the following passage, looking for 22 misspelled words. Cross out each misspelled word, and write it correctly in the space above.*

There were many quarrels between the North and the South that led to the catastrofee of the Civil War. Writers on both sides debaited the issues of slavery and the rights of individual states. They engajed in speculation on the potenchial of these issues to divide the Union.

Northerners regarded slaves as oppresed people and insisted that slavery could not spread into new western territorys. Southerners clamed their dependance on the slave system as an essential part of their economy. They said that their cotton plantations rekwired slave labor.

The Republican Party pledged itself to stoping the spread of slavery. When its candidate, Abraham Lincoln, was elected in 1860, South Carolina seceded, or resined, from the Union. This action precipitaited six other Southern states to follow suit and align with South Carolina to form the Confederate States of America.

As the first shots of the war were fired by Confederate and Union armys at Fort Sumter in 1861, no one could foresee the tragedies that lay ahead. The North was a region of industrial progres and possesed great wealth. However, Union leaders could not predict the persistance with which Southern troops would fight to redress their grievances, despite great loss of life and economic distres.

When President Lincoln gave his Gettysburg Addres in 1863, he was honoring the soldiers that lay buryed in a Pennsylvania battlefield after the bloodiest battle of the war, a Union victory that was a major turning point. His speech was part of a dedicashen ceremony for the cemetery there. Although the event could have been a celebrateion of a Northern victory, Lincoln instead payed tribute to the dead. He asked Americans to make sure that the soldiers had not died in vane. He pledged that "government of the people, by the people, for the people, shall not perish from the earth."

Name ______________________________ Date ______________

Communications Workshop—Unit 4

Critique Persuasive Arguments

While listening to the persuasive speech, fill out the following chart to help you critique the speaker's argument.

Topic of presentation: ______________________________

What is the speaker's position?
What facts support the generalizations he or she makes?
Does the speaker use circular reasoning? Explain.
Does the speaker persuade by using the bandwagon effect? Explain.
What faulty or misleading information is given?
What makes the speaker's position convincing or not convincing?

Name ______________________________ Date ______________

Suggestions For Further Reading—Unit 4

DIRECTIONS: *Think about the books suggested for this Unit that you have read. Then, on a separate sheet of paper, answer the discussion questions and take notes for your literature circle.*

The Adventures of Huckleberry Finn by Mark Twain

Discussion In a small group, discuss the character of Jim by answering these questions:

- What character traits does Jim possess and what is his role in the book?
- Given the time in which the book was written, would you consider Jim a progressive, sympathetic character or a stereotypical, unsympathetic character?
- What point does Twain make about race relations by including Jim as a major character in the book?

Connections—Literature Circle Some critics have criticized the ending of *The Adventures of Huckleberry Finn.* Discuss whether you thought the ending was realistic, whether it was satisfying, and whether it enhanced or detracted from the major themes of the book.

My Ántonia by Willa Cather

Discussion Some critics have characterized the book as "a series of departures." In a small group, discuss how the book can be seen as a series of departures and the effect that this has on the mood of the work.

Connections—Literature Circle Discuss the following questions in a small group: How do barriers of language and country of origin isolate people from one another in the book? How do these differences contribute to the experience of life on the frontier?

The Sea Wolf and Selected Stories by Jack London

Discussion In a small group, debate whether you think *The Sea Wolf* is best described as an adventure novel, a love story, a novel about maturing to adulthood, or a novel about competing ideas of life.

Connections—Literature Circle Discuss whether Larsen's punishment fits the crime. Explain your answer using your knowledge of what he has done.

Narrative of the Life of Frederick Douglass by Frederick Douglass

Discussion In a small group, discuss the following question: What were Douglass's most powerful arguments against the institution of slavery?

Connections—Literature Circle President Lincoln and Frederick Douglass admired each other and met several times during Lincoln's presidency. Why do you think that these two men admired each other?

Spoon River Anthology by Edgar Lee Masters

Discussion In "Silas Dement—Caroline Branson," how do the realizations of the three characters confirm or contradict their lives?

Connections—Literature Circle Based on these writings, what does Master seem to value most and least in life?

ANSWERS

Diagnostic Test 5, p. 2

MULTIPLE CHOICE

1. ANS: C
2. ANS: A
3. ANS: D
4. ANS: C
5. ANS: B
6. ANS: C
7. ANS: B
8. ANS: A
9. ANS: C
10. ANS: A
11. ANS: D
12. ANS: D
13. ANS: B
14. ANS: B
15. ANS: B

Unit 4 Introduction

Names and Terms to Know, p. 5

A. 1. I; 2. D; 3. A; 4. J; 5. B; 6. C; 7. E; 8. F; 9. G; 10. H

B. Sample Answers

1. The Fugitive Slave Act contributed greatly to growing hostility between the North and South, because while the South thought the law was reasonable and fair, the North viewed it with fury.
2. The Civil War had been brewing for many years, but the election of Abraham Lincoln was like holding a match to a stick of dynamite. Because Lincoln was part of the antislavery Republican party, his election forced the South to look to itself for a new government, the Confederacy.
3. The Second Industrial Revolution presented challenges as well as inventiveness. As skyscrapers, mass transit, and department stores emerged in cities, so did noise, crowds, and pollution.
4. Frederick Douglass's most famous work was *Narrative of the Life of Frederick Douglass*, an autobiography that powerfully described his rise from humble beginnings as a slave to a great writer and orator. It also laid out details for readers that documented the evils of slavery.

Focus Questions, p. 6

Sample Answers

1. The economy of the North was varied, while the economy of the South depended greatly upon the institution of slavery. In addition, as people learned about some of the horrors of slavery, more fuel was added to the arguments against it. As the nation expanded, the decision about whether new states should be slave states or free states contributed to disagreements about which region would become more powerful.
2. Following the Civil War, there was an increase in industrialization and urbanization. Much of it was uncontrolled, creating an atmosphere that greatly needed reform. Farmers and immigrants moved to the cities for work, but the surplus of available labor created conditions of poverty.
3. As the nation grew, Americans were by and large optimistic. However, the Civil War stole their idealism as they realized that the new nation had great challenges. Realistic writers such as Ambrose Bierce and Stephen Crane spoke of the horrors of wartime. Willa Cather wrote about adapting to the loneliness of prairie life, and Edith Wharton described conflicts in Eastern society. Mark Twain was a realist who wrote about the life he knew, adopting a natural dialect and style that readers could identify with. Naturalists such as Jack London portrayed reality as a conflict between the individual and outside forces, focusing on how nature or fate affected people.

"An Episode of War" by Stephen Crane
"Willie Has Gone to the War," words by George Cooper, music by Stephen Foster

Vocabulary Warm-up Exercises, p. 8

A.
1. comrades
2. bugler
3. sympathetically
4. lieutenant
5. infantry
6. roaming
7. stragglers
8. spectators

B. Sample Answers

1. On the beach, we saw an aggregation of hundreds of seagulls.
2. Ollie appropriated Mike's bicycle, and Mike couldn't ride it for the rest of the day.
3. We were very surprised at the astoundingly large number of concertgoers.
4. Berating me soundly, Dad harshly criticized me for my unkindness to my brother.
5. The game was a catastrophe for our football team, which lost by a score of 35-0.
6. That school was very well endowed, with exceptionally fine facilities for athletics.
7. Away at camp, Manuel felt unhappy and homesick and would pine for home every day.
8. The art exhibit was singular, resembling no other show that had been held before.

Reading Warm-up A, p. 9

Sample Answers

1. haunting melody; The army bugler wore a splendid full-dress uniform.
2. (officer in charge of a regiment); The lieutenant was respected by those both within and outside of the military.
3. (soldiers on foot); on land
4. late; at the end
5. (at liberty); *wandering*
6. (fondly); *sympathy, sympathize, sympathetic*
7. those in the group; After the championship win, Tom celebrated with his comrades on the lacrosse team.
8. in attendance; *audience*

Reading Warm-up B, p. 10

Sample Answers

1. school kids and local music fans; *group*
2. (had no money for equipment); Paul appropriated Ira's soccer ball because he needed it for the game.
3. shouting criticisms; The opposite of *berating* is *praising* or *complimenting.*
4. (disastrously); A hurricane can cause considerable damage to homes and businesses.
5. (surprisingly); *predictably*
6. (gift); Preston was endowed with speed and agility, and he was a nimble player on the basketball court.
7. No one had ever heard anything like them; *remarkable, unique*
8. sighing and calling his name; *A person might pine for a homemade meal or a familiar neighborhood.*

Literary Analysis: Realism and Naturalism, p. 11

Sample Responses

1. Naturalism: The event of being shot is a force beyond the lieutenant's control.
2. Naturalism: This passage emphasizes the lieutenant's and the women's reactions to an event outside their control; Realism: The reaction reflects realistic responses to the lieutenant's injury.

Reading Strategy: Recognize Historical Details, p. 12

1. **War tactics:** Most battles were hand-to-hand combat, making injury likely. When Willie goes off to war, his lover grieves because of the high chance that he will be injured or killed.
2. **Medicine:** Medicine was less advanced and wartime hospitals were short on staff and supplies, increasing the chances that an injury would become life threatening. The lieutenant's injury turns into an amputation, whether necessary or not.
3. **Communication:** Letters to families took a long time, particularly during wartime. When the lieutenant returns home, his family does not know about his amputation.
4. **Transportation:** Soldiers moved by horse or by foot. Injured men could not be rushed to an emergency room. The lieutenant has to bring himself to the field hospital, which probably made his condition worse.

Vocabulary Builder, p. 13

A. 1. gregarious; 2. egregious; 3. congregation; 4. aggregate

B. 1. B; 2. C; 3. B; 4. D

C. 1. A; 2. C; 3. B

Grammar and Style: Correct Use of *like* and *as,* p. 14

A.
1. as if
2. as if
3. as if
4. like
5. like

B. The student's response must be a one-paragraph description of an event. It must contain at least two prepositional phrases beginning with *like* and two subordinate clauses beginning with *as, as if,* or *as though.*

Enrichment: Photograph, p. 17

Suggested Responses

1. "Willie Has Gone to the War":
   And weep for my lov'd one, my own,
   My Willie has gone to the war!
2. "An Episode of War":
   He wore the look of one who knows he is the victim of terrible disease and understands his helplessness.
3. "An Episode of War":
   The low white tents of the hospital were grouped around an old schoolhouse.
4. "An Episode of War":
   An interminable crowd of bandaged men were coming and going. Great numbers sat under the trees nursing heads or arms or legs.
5. Suggested response: The soldiers look resigned to their fates, an expression that might reflect dignity or simply despair.

Selection Test A, p. 18

Critical Reading

1. ANS: D	DIF: Easy	OBJ: Reading Strategy
2. ANS: B	DIF: Easy	OBJ: Interpretation
3. ANS: D	DIF: Easy	OBJ: Reading Strategy
4. ANS: B	DIF: Easy	OBJ: Literary Analysis
5. ANS: B	DIF: Easy	OBJ: Reading Strategy
6. ANS: B	DIF: Easy	OBJ: Literary Analysis

7. **ANS:** C	**DIF:** Easy	**OBJ:** Comprehension
8. **ANS:** C	**DIF:** Easy	**OBJ:** Comprehension
9. **ANS:** B	**DIF:** Easy	**OBJ:** Comprehension
10. **ANS:** A	**DIF:** Easy	**OBJ:** Literary Analysis

Vocabulary and Grammar

11. **ANS:** B	**DIF:** Easy	**OBJ:** Vocabulary
12. **ANS:** A	**DIF:** Easy	**OBJ:** Grammar

Essay

13. Students' essays should reflect that the characters are involved in a war that they did not plan and probably did not want to fight. The main character has even less control over his fate because he is not engaged in battle when he is wounded by a stray bullet. Finally, he has no control over what happens to his arm as the result of his wound.

    Difficulty: *Easy*

    Objective: *Essay*

14. Students' essay may suggest that the song reflects the speaker's memory of the happy times she and her lover spent in the glade. Although she knows he is dead and not coming back, her song is a tribute to the happiness they once had.

    Difficulty: *Easy*

    Objective: *Essay*

Selection Test B, p. 21

Critical Reading

1. **ANS:** C	**DIF:** Easy	**OBJ:** Comprehension
2. **ANS:** B	**DIF:** Average	**OBJ:** Comprehension
3. **ANS:** B	**DIF:** Challenging	**OBJ:** Literary Analysis
4. **ANS:** D	**DIF:** Challenging	**OBJ:** Interpretation
5. **ANS:** A	**DIF:** Challenging	**OBJ:** Interpretation
6. **ANS:** B	**DIF:** Average	**OBJ:** Reading Strategy
7. **ANS:** B	**DIF:** Challenging	**OBJ:** Interpretation
8. **ANS:** C	**DIF:** Easy	**OBJ:** Reading Strategy
9. **ANS:** D	**DIF:** Average	**OBJ:** Literary Analysis
10. **ANS:** C	**DIF:** Average	**OBJ:** Literary Analysis
11. **ANS:** D	**DIF:** Challenging	**OBJ:** Interpretation
12. **ANS:** B	**DIF:** Average	**OBJ:** Reading Strategy

Vocabulary and Grammar

13. **ANS:** A	**DIF:** Average	**OBJ:** Vocabulary
14. **ANS:** A	**DIF:** Easy	**OBJ:** Vocabulary
15. **ANS:** B	**DIF:** Average	**OBJ:** Grammar
16. **ANS:** B	**DIF:** Challenging	**OBJ:** Grammar
17. **ANS:** C	**DIF:** Average	**OBJ:** Grammar

Essay

18. Students who address "Willie Has Gone to the War" will likely cite the heroine's universal feelings of loss, loneliness, hope, and longing. Students who address "An Episode of War" may note that the lieutenant's injury at the story's beginning makes him a sympathetic character. Accept any essay that contains a well-reasoned argument in support of the writer's opinion.

    Difficulty: *Easy*

    Objective: *Essay*

19. Students may focus on the song's hope, noting that the glade is untouched by war and will bloom again in spring; its despair, pointing out that the speaker is weeping for her loved one and that "The leaves of the forest will fade"; or on other sentiments, such as love and longing. Accept any conclusion that is well supported with lyrics from the song.

    Difficulty: *Average*

    Objective: *Essay*

20. Students should define Realism as a literary movement whose advocates sought to depict real life as faithfully and accurately as possible by focusing on ordinary people faced with the harsh realities of everyday life. They may point out how the lieutenant was wounded while occupied with mundane duties and trace his journey through the harsh realities of the battle zone. They should also mention how Crane's use of vivid and historically accurate details heightens the story's realism.

    Difficulty: *Challenging*

    Objective: *Essay*

"Swing Low, Sweet Chariot" and "Go Down, Moses" Spirituals

Vocabulary Warm-up Exercises, p. 25

A.
1. spiritual
2. band
3. fugitives
4. captivity
5. legal
6. banned
7. rebellions
8. deprived

B. Sample Answers
1. F; Activists are often involved in issues and causes.
2. T; A chariot was typically owned by upper-class people in ancient times.
3. F; *Enacted* means "put into effect."
4. T; *Eventually* means "after a certain passage of time."
5. T; A network is a group that is linked or associated.
6. F; *Oppressed* means "harshly put down," so oppressed people probably would feel unhappy.
7. F; A pharaoh was the Egyptian king in ancient times.
8. F; *Smite* means "to strike forcefully."

Reading Warm-up A, p. 26

Sample Answers

1. (song); "Swing Low, Sweet Chariot" is a famous spiritual that probably dates from the 1800s.
2. taken away; It would die.
3. hostages without freedom; *freedom*
4. (against the system); *revolts*
5. (forbidden); The opposite of *banned* is *permitted.*
6. lawful; *unlawful, illegal*
7. (group); Out in the desert, a band of robbers attacked the caravan of travelers.
8. running from the law; Several prisoners escaped, but the police succeeded in recapturing the fugitives.

Reading Warm-up B, p. 27

Sample Answers

1. ordering; The legislature recently enacted a law that raises the driving age in our state to twenty-one.
2. (in the ruler's house); in ancient Egypt
3. privileged to ride; a fancy car
4. after some time; The opposite of *eventually* is *immediately.*
5. (shocked and saddened); The opposite of *oppressed* is *liberated.*
6. like-minded groups; Aaron called on a network of friends to help publicize the event.
7. intent on the cause; recycling; hybrid cars
8. (hitting hard); In karate class, I had to smite the wood block twice to break it in half.

Literary Analysis: Refrain, p. 28

Sample Responses

1. "Swing low, sweet chariot,/Coming for to carry me home" or "Coming for to carry me home"
2. Yes. They are repeated regularly through out the song.
3. No. The line occurs only once in the song.
4. Their repetition increases the intensity and the urgency of the spiritual's message.
5. The refrains in both spirituals refer to the desire for freedom. In "Swing Low, Sweet Chariot" the refrains refers to a release—that of death and going to Heaven. In "Go Down, Moses" the refrains are couched as a demand for freedom during life. The refrains in "Go Down, Moses" are much more militant than those of "Swing Low, Sweet Chariot."

Reading Strategy: Listen, p. 29

Sample Responses

"Swing Low, Sweet Chariot"

Cell 1. In second verse *see* and *me* rhyme

Cell 2. "Swing low, sweet chariot" and "Coming for to carry me home"

Cell 3. yearning or longing

Cell 4. Encourages patience and faith in eventual freedom from hardship

"Go Down, Moses"

Cell 1. "Pharaoh" and "go;" "land" and "stand;" "said" and "dead"

Cell 2. "Go down, Moses" "Way down in Egypt land" "Tell old Pharaoh" "To let my people go"

Cell 3. persistence and determination

Cell 4. Eventually the powerless will triumph over the powerful.

Vocabulary Builder, p. 30

A. 1. suppress
2. express
3. pressurize
4. press
5. impression
6. depression

B. 1. B; 2. A

C. 1. E; 2. C

Grammar and Style: Direct Address, p. 31

A. 1. Boys, you should sing only the refrain.
2. Listen carefully, Stephanie, and you'll hear the rhythm.
3. No direct address.
4. No direct address.
5. You can be the next soloist, Troy.
6. No direct address.
7. My dear child, you must not be nervous about singing.
8. Once again, Ms. Lipton, you've done an excellent job of preparing the chorus.

B. The name that appears at the beginning of the sentence must be followed by a comma, the name that appears in the middle of the sentence must be preceded and followed by commas, and the name that appears at the end of the sentence must be preceded by a comma.

Enrichment: Social Studies, p. 34

1. A pharaoh is a king and has a great amount of power over his subjects.
2. the owner of the plantation
3. They were kept down and oppressed.
4. They, too, were oppressed.
5. He told the pharaoh to let his people go.
6. The spiritual also demands freedom. The demand is directed toward the owners of the slaves.

Selection Test A, p. 35

Critical Reading

1. ANS: B	DIF: Easy	OBJ: Literary Analysis
2. ANS: D	DIF: Easy	OBJ: Interpretation
3. ANS: C	DIF: Easy	OBJ: Literary Analysis
4. ANS: C	DIF: Easy	OBJ: Reading Strategy

5. ANS: B	DIF: Easy	OBJ: Comprehension
6. ANS: A	DIF: Easy	OBJ: Reading Strategy
7. ANS: A	DIF: Easy	OBJ: Literary Analysis
8. ANS: D	DIF: Easy	OBJ: Interpretation
9. ANS: B	DIF: Easy	OBJ: Interpretation
10. ANS: B	DIF: Easy	OBJ: Reading Strategy

Vocabulary and Grammar

11. ANS: A	DIF: Easy	OBJ: Vocabulary
12. ANS: B	DIF: Easy	OBJ: Grammar

Essay

13. Students' essays might suggest that "Swing Low, Sweet Chariot" is a lyrical and hopeful wish for freedom, while "Go down, Moses" is a demand for that same freedom. The first is a polite plea, while the second is a direct command.

    Difficulty: *Easy*

    Objective: *Essay*

14. Students' essays might explain any of the following codes: *chariot*—travel or a route on the Underground Railroad; *home*—a state without slavery; *Jordan*—the Ohio River, or a border between slave and free territories; *band of angels*—"conductors" on the Underground Railroad; safe houses; *get there*—reach freedom; *tell my friends*—tell those who have already escaped.

    Difficulty: *Easy*

    Objective: *Essay*

Selection Test B, p. 38

Critical Reading

1. ANS: C	DIF: Easy	OBJ: Comprehension
2. ANS: A	DIF: Average	OBJ: Literary Analysis
3. ANS: D	DIF: Challenging	OBJ: Reading Strategy
4. ANS: C	DIF: Average	OBJ: Comprehension
5. ANS: D	DIF: Easy	OBJ: Literary Analysis
6. ANS: C	DIF: Average	OBJ: Literary Analysis
7. ANS: A	DIF: Average	OBJ: Reading Strategy
8. ANS: D	DIF: Easy	OBJ: Interpretation
9. ANS: D	DIF: Average	OBJ: Interpretation
10. ANS: A	DIF: Average	OBJ: Literary Analysis
11. ANS: C	DIF: Challenging	OBJ: Comprehension
12. ANS: B	DIF: Average	OBJ: Interpretation
13. ANS: C	DIF: Average	OBJ: Reading Strategy
14. ANS: B	DIF: Challenging	OBJ: Literary Analysis

Vocabulary and Grammar

15. ANS: A	DIF: Challenging	OBJ: Grammar
16. ANS: B	DIF: Easy	OBJ: Grammar
17. ANS: D	DIF: Challenging	OBJ: Vocabulary

Essay

18. Students should recognize that, in a veiled way, "Go Down, Moses" is about escaping slavery during life, whereas "Swing Low, Sweet Chariot" is about death's deliverance from hardship. The recurring refrain of "Let my people go" would have been more disturbing and worrisome to a slave owner than the references to Heaven and angels in "Swing Low, Sweet Chariot." Students may also cite the mention of violence (smiting the first-born) in "Go Down, Moses" as part of the spiritual's undercurrent of rebellion.

    Difficulty: *Easy*

    Objective: *Essay*

19. For "Swing Low, Sweet Chariot," students should indicate that the release from hardship is not expected until after death. "Swing Low, Sweet Chariot" does not, therefore, have a "rebellious" feel to it. Students may say that faith in God and Heaven are an important part of the mood of the spiritual. For "Go Down, Moses," students should recognize that the spiritual speaks of the possibility of freedom during life by its recounting the story of Moses and the enslaved Israelites' escape from slavery. The mood of "Go Down, Moses," therefore, has elements of rebellion, bravery, and determination.

    Difficulty: *Average*

    Objective: *Essay*

20. Students may cite the fact that Tubman was called the Moses of her people. The repeated refrain, "Go down, Moses" could refer to Tubman's repeated trips from the North back *down* to the South to guide more people to freedom. Students may also mention that Tubman's repeated risking of her own life during her journeys paralleled the risk Moses took in standing up to the Egyptian pharaoh.

    Difficulty: *Challenging*

    Objective: *Essay*

from *My Bondage* and *My Freedom*
by Frederick Douglass

Vocabulary Warm-up Exercises, p. 42

A.
1. consternation
2. incompatible
3. congenial
4. domestic
5. apt
6. variable
7. overthrow
8. victorious

B. Sample Answers

1. The T-shirt label chafed the back of my neck and made my skin feel uncomfortable.
2. Consenting to our proposal, Rose gave us permission to begin the plan's first phase.
3. Ken was so destitute that he had to make do with a very small house and no automobile.
4. When she heard that comment, Yolanda expressed her mirth with a smile and a chuckle.

Reading Warm-up A, p. 43

Sample Answers

1. tried to hide the comic book . . . as if she might be angry; To my *consternation*, the boss called me in for a thorough review of my job performance.
2. (the family meals, the after-dinner TV sessions)
3. trying to make friends; The opposite of *congenial* is *aloof* or *unfriendly*.
4. Nate was surely old enough to know how to read . . . the fact that he couldn't seemed . . . with the intelligence she could see in his eyes; *compatible, reconcilable*
5. (sometimes he understood, sometimes he didn't); *changeable, fluctuating*
6. eventually grasping everything she explained to him; The opposite of *apt* is *inept* or *incapable*.
7. (a gang of villains . . . the government and rule the country); *subvert, overturn*
8. having conquered his first book; *conquering, triumphant*

Reading Warm-up B, p. 44

Sample Answers

1. many people supported . . . there was some . . . to the idea, however; *resistance*
2. (against the preconceived notions); *wore away, rubbed against*
3. even with amusement or; The comedian's hysterical jokes were greeted with *mirth* in the audience.
4. passed two acts . . . to the enlistment of African Americans; *disagreeing*
5. (was cautiously delayed); Dad urged me to drive with *prudence* during the heavy storm.
6. (runaways from the moral . . . of slavery); *evil, corruption*
7. far from being . . . of courage and skill; The opposite of *destitute* is *rich*.
8. . . . the attention of all Americans with their heroic deeds; *fastened*

Literary Analysis: Autobiography, p. 45

Sample Responses

1. The effects are strength and self-knowledge. Writing this as an autobiography makes the writer seem more real and the passage more convincing.
2. In this passage, the perceptions and effects are pain and despair. Describing images such as a "dragon ready to pounce" from a first-hand viewpoint draw the reader into Douglass's horror at being enslaved.
3. The effects of this passage are anger and sorrow. By using the first person, Douglass demonstrates anger, rather than merely reporting it.

Reading Strategy: Establish a Purpose, p. 46

Possible Responses

Thoughts: Frederick's recognition of his future as a slave

Feelings: Frederick's affection for his mistress

Events: Frederick's reading in snatches whenever alone

Vocabulary Builder, p. 47

A. 1. beneficiary; 2. benign; 3. beneficent; 4. beneficial

B. 1. C; 2. A; 3. D; 4. E; 5. F; 6. B

Grammar and Style: Correlative Conjunctions, p. 48

A.
1. no only . . . but . . . also
2. whether . . . or
3. Neither . . . nor
4. none
5. none

B. Sample Responses

1. so children must obey their parents.
2. nor the captain had slept for days.
3. or go to the museum.
4. but they also burned farms and houses.
5. or ford the river.

Enrichment: Career as a Teacher, p. 51

Suggested Responses

1. **Passage:** In teaching me the alphabet . . . my mistress had given me the "inch," and now, no ordinary precaution could prevent me from taking the "ell." **Lesson:** By learning the fundamentals, interested students will be motivated to learn more.
2. **Passage:** I used to carry . . . a copy of Webster's spelling book in my pocket; and, when sent on errands, or when play time was allowed me, I would step . . . aside, and take a lesson in spelling. I usually paid my tuition fee . . . with bread. . . . **Lesson:** As a child, Douglass learned to spell by paying boys to teach him on his free time. This anecdote could be used as inspiration for those who don't completely understand the value of reading.
3. **Passage:** When I was about thirteen years old, and had succeeded in learning to read, every increase of knowledge, especially respecting the free states, added something to the almost intolerable burden of the thought—"I am a slave for life." **Lesson:** For Douglass, reading freed his mind and made him knowledgeable about his condition of slavery. This story could be used to encourage others to learn to read.

Selection Test A, p. 52

Critical Reading

1. ANS: B	DIF: Easy	OBJ: Comprehension
2. ANS: C	DIF: Easy	OBJ: Comprehension
3. ANS: C	DIF: Easy	OBJ: Literary Analysis
4. ANS: B	DIF: Easy	OBJ: Literary Analysis
5. ANS: C	DIF: Easy	OBJ: Reading Strategy
6. ANS: B	DIF: Easy	OBJ: Literary Analysis
7. ANS: B	DIF: Easy	OBJ: Interpretation
8. ANS: C	DIF: Easy	OBJ: Reading Strategy
9. ANS: C	DIF: Easy	OBJ: Interpretation
10. ANS: D	DIF: Easy	OBJ: Interpretation

Vocabulary and Grammar

11. ANS: A	DIF: Easy	OBJ: Vocabulary
12. ANS: C	DIF: Easy	OBJ: Grammar

Essay

13. Students may say that they would have been less patient than Douglass in waiting for opportunities they knew they deserved. They may also say that they would have been able to wait, knowing that better times were ahead.

    Difficulty: *???*

    Objective: *???*

14. Students should mention that without education, people are limited in their activities and the ability to think about a variety of subjects. In Douglass's case, the book he bought led him to think about freedom and how he wanted to live his life.

    Difficulty: *???*

    Objective: *???*

Selection Test B, p. 55

Critical Reading

1. ANS: D	DIF: Average	OBJ: Interpretation
2. ANS: D	DIF: Average	OBJ: Comprehension
3. ANS: A	DIF: Challenging	OBJ: Interpretation
4. ANS: D	DIF: Average	OBJ: Comprehension
5. ANS: B	DIF: Challenging	OBJ: Literary Analysis
6. ANS: D	DIF: Challenging	OBJ: Reading Strategy
7. ANS: C	DIF: Challenging	OBJ: Interpretation
8. ANS: A	DIF: Average	OBJ: Interpretation
9. ANS: C	DIF: Average	OBJ: Reading Strategy
10. ANS: B	DIF: Average	OBJ: Literary Analysis
11. ANS: D	DIF: Average	OBJ: Literary Analysis
12. ANS: C	DIF: Easy	OBJ: Reading Strategy

Vocabulary and Grammar

13. ANS: B	DIF: Easy	OBJ: Vocabulary
14. ANS: B	DIF: Average	OBJ: Vocabulary
15. ANS: A	DIF: Easy	OBJ: Grammar
16. ANS: B	DIF: Easy	OBJ: Vocabulary
17. ANS: C	DIF: Challenging	OBJ: Grammar

Essay

18. Students should provide details that show that Mrs. Auld was a benevolent and congenial woman at the outset who, after having been persuaded not to teach Frederick to read or write, became angry and harsh in her behavior towards him whenever she suspected him of attempting to read. One example of her changed behavior is the incident of her rushing at him with fury to snatch away a book or newspaper.

    Difficulty: *Easy*

    Objective: *Essay*

19. Students will probably argue in favor of this statement, since this is the position Douglass persuasively supports with incidents and examples throughout his account. Students may support their position with the example of the young white boys who, not yet trained as slaveholders, are naturally sympathetic to Douglass. Accept any answer that is well-supported with examples from the text.

    Difficulty: *Average*

    Objective: *Essay*

20. Some students will support this statement, noting that Mrs. Auld could not incorporate her husband's attitude without undergoing a complete transformation from benevolent to harsh, angry, and domineering. Others may explain her behavior as a twisted sort of benevolence, arguing that Mrs. Auld hoped to spare young Frederick the recognition of his horrid situation that learning might bring.

    Difficulty: *Challenging*

    Objective: *Essay*

"An Occurrence at Owl Creek Bridge"
by Ambrose Bierce

Vocabulary Warm-up Exercises, p. 59

A. 1. assented
2. rustic
3. audibly
4. intervals
5. keen
6. assassin
7. convulsively
8. matchless

B. Sample Answers

1. T; The *congestion* of heavy traffic on the highway might delay travelers.
2. F; *Etiquette* stresses politeness and good manners.
3. T; *Ineffable* means "difficult or impossible to express."
4. F; A *luminous* theory would, by definition, shed light on a problem.
5. T; A *perilous* mission might be expected to hold dangers.
6. T; Since a *sentinel* functions as a guard or watchman, it would not be suitable for him or her to fall asleep.
7. F; *Summarily* connotes rapid action.
8. F; *Velocity* refers to speed, not weight.

Reading Warm-up A, p. 60

Sample Answers

1. ruthless as the attitude; *killer, murderer*
2. (sometimes loudly); *silently, inaudibly*
3. strongly; *sharp*
4. then gasp spasmodically for breath); *in a twitching manner*
5. vigorously disagree; True cynics would never agree with that idea.
6. (each day at dawn and midday)
7. (overcomes all others); *incomparable, peerless, unequaled, unsurpassed*
8. "simple . . . even when they did not live in the country"

Reading Warm-up B, p. 61

Sample Answers

1. must be greeted politely according to a formal code; *Etiquette* requires you to use certain forms of address when you attend a meeting with the head of state.
2. (was leisurely indulging in a favorite pastime); *promptly*
3. to destroy the Owl Creek bridge; *safe, secure*
4. slows down . . . of a fast-paced plot; *swiftness, speed*
5. (vivid . . . he sheds light on Farquhar's inner state of consciousness); The opposite of *luminous* is *obscure* or *shadowy*.
6. the overcrowding . . . of thoughts in Farquhar's mind give way to a single goal; *crowdedness*
7. (standing watchfully); All night long, a *sentinel* patrolled the perimeter of the armed camp, keeping watch.
8. he cannot translate his emotions into words; *able to be expressed*

Literary Analysis: Point of View, p. 62

Sample Responses

1. I am thirty-five years of age and have come to the end of my life. I am a southern planter of fine background and am about to be hanged for the crime of patriotism.
2. As the man fell through the bridge, the watching soldiers swayed back slightly, as if they had all inhaled simultaneously and might hold their breath until he died. He did not die immediately; as he dangled in the air he seemed to come to life, if only for a short time.

Reading Strategy: Identify Chronological Order, p. 63

Sample Responses

1. The "preternatural" sensory experience suggests the heightened sensations some people believe occur just before death.
2. The whirling Farquhar does here might suggest the turning of a body at the end of a rope.
3. The scene is not natural. The large road seems untraveled, and there is no sign of life anywhere.

Vocabulary Builder, p. 64

A. 1. the highest good; 2. with highest praise

B.
1. summarily
2. effaced
3. imperious
4. etiquette
5. malign
6. oscillation
7. deference
8. apprised

Grammar and Style: Semicolons in Compound Sentences, p. 65

A.
1. It did not appear to be the duty of these two men to know what was occurring at the center of the bridge; they merely blockaded the two ends of the foot planking that traversed it.
2. He wore a mustache and pointed beard, but no whiskers; his eyes were large and dark gray, and had a kindly expression which one would hardly have expected in one whose neck was in the hemp.
3. The intervals of silence grew progressively longer; the delays became maddening.

B. Sample Responses

1. Peyton Farquhar thinks he is escaping from his enemies, but actually he is dying.
2. Peyton Farquhar thinks he is escaping from his enemies; actually he is dying.

Enrichment: The Legal System, p. 68

Students will choose different aspects to cover in a defense trial. Suggested responses:

1. Peyton Farquhar performed an act in defense of his "country." (Use to minimize sentencing.)
2. Peyton Farquhar performed an act to provide for the safety of his wife and children. (Use to invite emphathy from judge and jury.)

3. Peyton Farquhar did not perform an act that would hurt or kill someone; the act involved property damage only. (Use to minimize the seriousness of the crime.)
4. Peyton Farquhar knowingly committed an illegal act with full knowledge of the punishment. (Acknowledge, but use defenses 1–3 in response.)
5. Peyton Farquhar had probably committed such acts before, although no solid evidence is provided. (Object to this statement as unproven.)
6. Peyton Farquhar acted in a time of war. (Use to justify Farquhar's actions or request reduced sentencing.)
7. Peyton Farquhar was somewhat "tricked" into this act by a federal scout. (Use to suggest Farquhar's inherent innocence.)
8. The punishment seems too severe for the crime. (Use to minimize sentencing.)

Selection Test A, p. 69

Critical Reading

1. **ANS:** B	**DIF:** Easy	**OBJ:** Comprehension
2. **ANS:** C	**DIF:** Easy	**OBJ:** Reading Strategy
3. **ANS:** D	**DIF:** Easy	**OBJ:** Reading Strategy
4. **ANS:** C	**DIF:** Easy	**OBJ:** Comprehension
5. **ANS:** D	**DIF:** Easy	**OBJ:** Literary Analysis
6. **ANS:** B	**DIF:** Easy	**OBJ:** Interpretation
7. **ANS:** C	**DIF:** Easy	**OBJ:** Interpretation
8. **ANS:** B	**DIF:** Easy	**OBJ:** Literary Analysis
9. **ANS:** D	**DIF:** Easy	**OBJ:** Reading Strategy
10. **ANS:** B	**DIF:** Easy	**OBJ:** Reading Strategy

Vocabulary and Grammar

11. **ANS:** B	**DIF:** Easy	**OBJ:** Vocabulary
12. **ANS:** C	**DIF:** Easy	**OBJ:** Grammar

Essay

13. Students' essays should reflect that the setup of the story is pessimistic. Readers are led to believe that Farquhar will escape the noose and be reunited with his wife. In fact, all of this "action" occurs only in Farquhar's imagination as he is dying.
Difficulty: *Easy*
Objective: *Essay*
14. Students' essays should reflect that the story shows war as a hopeless experience: War breaks up families; it leads men to betray one another; it leads to the deaths of many soldiers and others; it causes much grief and suffering.
Difficulty: *Easy*
Objective: *Essay*

Selection Test B, p. 72

Critical Reading

1. **ANS:** A	**DIF:** Average	**OBJ:** Literary Analysis
2. **ANS:** A	**DIF:** Average	**OBJ:** Comprehension
3. **ANS:** C	**DIF:** Challenging	**OBJ:** Reading Strategy
4. **ANS:** B	**DIF:** Challenging	**OBJ:** Interpretation
5. **ANS:** C	**DIF:** Easy	**OBJ:** Interpretation
6. **ANS:** B	**DIF:** Average	**OBJ:** Literary Analysis
7. **ANS:** D	**DIF:** Easy	**OBJ:** Reading Strategy
8. **ANS:** D	**DIF:** Average	**OBJ:** Comprehension
9. **ANS:** B	**DIF:** Average	**OBJ:** Reading Strategy
10. **ANS:** B	**DIF:** Challenging	**OBJ:** Comprehension
11. **ANS:** A	**DIF:** Average	**OBJ:** Interpretation
12. **ANS:** C	**DIF:** Average	**OBJ:** Literary Analysis

Vocabulary and Grammar

13. **ANS:** D	**DIF:** Challenging	**OBJ:** Vocabulary
14. **ANS:** B	**DIF:** Average	**OBJ:** Vocabulary
15. **ANS:** B	**DIF:** Easy	**OBJ:** Vocabulary
16. **ANS:** C	**DIF:** Easy	**OBJ:** Grammar
17. **ANS:** A	**DIF:** Average	**OBJ:** Grammar

Essay

18. Students will probably feel that Bierce does *not* agree. His view of war is so grim that he clearly feels all things people do in war are neither fair nor justified.
Difficulty: *Easy*
Objective: *Essay*
19. Students should realize that the meeting is critical to the story: the Union army would not have captured Farquhar had he not been entrapped by the Federal scout. Students can infer from its core of deception that the rest of the story contains a key deception: Farquhar thinks that he has escaped and returned home when he has actually been hanged.
Difficulty: *Average*
Objective: *Essay*
20. Some students may prefer a true sequence of events and an objective point of view, perhaps because continuity could help the reader follow the story better and make it more straightforward. Other students may prefer to keep the story as written, perhaps because the changing point of view and sequence of events help make the story interesting.
Difficulty: *Challenging*
Objective: *Essay*

"The Gettysburg Address" and "Second Inaugural Address" by Abraham Lincoln
"Letter to His Son" by Robert E. Lee

Vocabulary Warm-up Exercises, p. 76

A. 1. arrayed
2. pursued
3. restrict
4. strive
5. duration
6. virtuous
7. establishment
8. prosperity

B. Sample Answers
1. F; People usually *avert* their eyes when they are lying to someone.
2. T; Seeing someone you like after such a long absence might be fun to *anticipate*.
3. T; Young children are too young for such responsibilities and must be cared for by adults.
4. T; Remaining objective means not agreeing with any information until all sides have been heard.
5. F; Typically, the southern areas of the county are hotter because they are closer to the equator.
6. F; *Strife* is a negative quality that most people don't want, particularly family and friends.
7. T; Personalities vary based on all of the individual qualities that a person exhibits.
8. T; Most people would agree to argue or fight for a belief that they held dear.

Reading Warm-up A, p. 77

Sample Answers

1. In war, one of the goals is to capture the enemy, therefore they must be sought out; The police *pursued* the subject on foot rather than in their cars because the robber ran into the woods.
2. It wouldn't be able to be done for as long because it requires a lot of energy; Answers will vary.
3. still referred to today; Once he and his officers had finished the *establishment* of their priorities, they were able to begin their tasks.
4. long, neat lines of cannons, troops standing shoulder to shoulder, mounted generals; Books on shelves might be *arrayed* alphabetically.
5. The soldiers they commanded; George Washington is considered *virtuous* because he was a successful general and the first President of the United States.
6. Deer are fast and jumpy and therefore hard to catch; Water polo is a sport in which a goal is to keep the ball within a certain area.
7. Yelling as loudly as possible; Everyday the football team would strive to improve their performance.
8. It meant that you lived closer to your neighbors, therefore it wasn't necessary to climb hilltops and shout; *Prosperity* signifies a good thing and sometimes even signifies substantial wealth.

Reading Warm-up B, p. 78

Sample Answers

1. Such conflict is tragic, especially when it is between fellow countrymen; Organized crime in the early 1900s brought about a lot of corruption.
2. If someone is not prepared for major changes, it could cause a hardship; His *strife* was obvious, as he labored up the numerous stairs on crutches.
3. not giving in; If the soldiers could resist the speculation of battle, they were able to spend their time relaxing or being social.
4. In general, they made it negative; poor weather and boredom.
5. enemy soldiers; She didn't want to *contend* with her best friend for the prize, so she let her win.
6. Because they had no way of knowing what the weather was going to be; by watching television or checking it on the Internet.
7. on activities that provided entertainment; To *avert* the traffic jam, the bus took an alternative route.
8. each having their specific place; for organizational purposes

Literary Analysis: Diction, p. 79

1. B; 2. A; 3. A; 4. A; 5. A; 6. A; 7. A; 8. B

Reading Strategy: Use Background Knowledge, p. 80

Sample Responses

1. Lee admired Washington and his policies, and had a great love for his country.
2. Lee's earlier freeing of his slaves demonstrated his willingness to act on principles, regardless of their popularity.
3. Lee was a patriot who had served the United States in its army for a long time.

Vocabulary Builder, p. 81

A. 1. C; 2. A; 3. B; 4. D

B. 1. bless
2. honor
3. condemned
4. recognize
5. affliction
6. spite
7. chaos
8. atonement

Grammar and Style: Parallel Structure, p. 82

A. 1. that nation, any nation, so conceived, so dedicated
2. that (from these . . .), that (we here . . .), that (this nation), that (government)
3. (of) the people, (by) the people, (for) the people

B. Responses should include at least two examples of parallel structure. Two possible examples are rewriting the reasons for the war using parallel structure (The northern states were states of trade, states of industry, and states with large cities) and emphasizing the split loyalties (It was a war that forced Americans to fight against each other—brother against brother, friend against friend).

Enrichment: Music, p. 85

Suggested Response

"Imagine" by John Lennon. *Lyrics:* ". . . Imagine there's no countries, / It isn't hard to do, / nothing to kill or die for, / No religion too, / Imagine all the people / living life in peace . . ." *Comparison*: The song describes a world without the political tensions leading to war, a world in which people are united by love. Its themes are similar to Lee's hatred of war and Lincoln's belief in equality for all, but contrast with Lincoln's passion about defending freedom to the death.

Selection Test A, p. 86

Critical Reading

1. ANS: B	DIF: Easy	OBJ: Comprehension
2. ANS: D	DIF: Easy	OBJ: Literary Analysis
3. ANS: C	DIF: Easy	OBJ: Reading Strategy
4. ANS: B	DIF: Easy	OBJ: Literary Analysis
5. ANS: B	DIF: Easy	OBJ: Reading Strategy
6. ANS: B	DIF: Easy	OBJ: Comprehension
7. ANS: C	DIF: Easy	OBJ: Interpretation
8. ANS: C	DIF: Easy	OBJ: Reading Strategy
9. ANS: A	DIF: Easy	OBJ: Interpretation
10. ANS: B	DIF: Easy	OBJ: Comprehension

Vocabulary and Grammar

11. ANS: C	DIF: Easy	OBJ: Vocabulary
12. ANS: B	DIF: Easy	OBJ: Grammar

Essay

13. Students' essays may reflect that Lincoln means to suggest that the Union soldiers who died at Gettysburg died so that the Union could continue and not be split into two countries. He is asking for support.

Difficulty: *Easy*

Objective: *Essay*

14. Students' essays should reflect that Lee agreed with his son that the North had acted aggressively toward the South. He also said he would sacrifice everything to keep the Union intact except honor. Students may suggest that the actions of the North were such that Lee finally felt he was honor bound to defend the Confederacy.

Difficulty: *Easy*

Objective: *Essay*

Selection Test B, p. 89

Critical Reading

1. ANS: C	DIF: Average	OBJ: Comprehension
2. ANS: B	DIF: Easy	OBJ: Interpretation
3. ANS: B	DIF: Average	OBJ: Interpretation
4. ANS: C	DIF: Challenging	OBJ: Literary Analysis
5. ANS: A	DIF: Average	OBJ: Comprehension
6. ANS: B	DIF: Easy	OBJ: Comprehension
7. ANS: D	DIF: Average	OBJ: Reading Strategy
8. ANS: A	DIF: Easy	OBJ: Reading Strategy
9. ANS: D	DIF: Average	OBJ: Literary Analysis
10. ANS: B	DIF: Easy	OBJ: Literary Analysis
11. ANS: A	DIF: Challenging	OBJ: Reading Strategy
12. ANS: B	DIF: Challenging	OBJ: Reading Strategy
13. ANS: D	DIF: Challenging	OBJ: Interpretation

Vocabulary and Grammar

14. ANS: C	DIF: Easy	OBJ: Vocabulary
15. ANS: A	DIF: Challenging	OBJ: Vocabulary
16. ANS: C	DIF: Easy	OBJ: Grammar
17. ANS: C	DIF: Average	OBJ: Vocabulary

Essay

18. Students should provide details to show that Lincoln and Lee both wished to preserve the Union at all costs. For example, they might include Lee's statement ". . . I can anticipate no greater calamity for the country than a dissolution of the Union" or Lincoln's attempt at Gettysburg to inspire new devotion to the Union.

Difficulty: *Easy*

Objective: *Essay*

19. Most students will cite as Lincoln's purpose that he is trying to reunite the North and South and "bind up the nation's wounds." Supporting details might include Lincoln's listing of the many commonalities between North and South, such as the experience of the war itself. The parallel structure Lincoln uses further emphasizes the link he has drawn between these common features.

Difficulty: *Average*

Objective: *Essay*

20. Lincoln will likely be described as a humble, idealistic, God-fearing man. Lee will likely be described as a passionate, emotional, and extremely loyal man. However, accept any characterization that is well-supported with details from the text.

Difficulty: *Challenging*

Objective: *Essay*

From the Scholar's Desk

Nell Irvin Painter Introduces "An Account of an Experience with Discrimination" by Sojourner Truth, p. 92

1. Sojourner Truth served with a volunteer group of anti-slavery women who helped poor people from the battle-fields of Virginia and from slaveholding Maryland.
2. She told how one streetcar conductor had not stopped for her and how another conductor had tried to push her from the platform of the car.
3. The first American history is that of Washington, D.C., a southern city. The second American history is that of discrimination against African Americans throughout the United States.
4. It was national in scope because racial discrimination was national.
5. Frederick Douglass: traded blows with conductors who tried to push him out of his seat. Harriet Tubman: suffered shoulder injuries when she was dragged out of her seat and thrown into the baggage car. Frances Ellen Watkins Harper: experienced humiliating conflicts on streetcars and railroads.
6. Sample questions: What kinds of source material do you find most useful? What areas of research would you recommend to a young historian today?

Nell Irvin Painter

Listening and Viewing, p. 93

Sample answers and guidelines for evaluation:

Segment 1: Nell Irvin Painter's interest in history developed while she studied abroad in France and Africa and began to ask herself questions about her own country's history. Students may answer that historians write about significant events and people of the past. Their writings are important to society because they explain, clarify, and analyze past events for a modern-day audience.

Segment 2: Sojourner Truth was a preacher, abolitionist, and feminist who became an important national symbol during the Civil War. Nell Irvin Painter wants her audience to know that Truth was born and raised in New York, which was then a slave state. She also did not say "Aren't I a woman?" at a convention, as she has been famously quoted for over a century.

Segment 3: Primary sources are documents which are intimate to an event and the people directly involved in the event; they are often more personal, emotional, and detailed than sources written by people many years later. These sources are important to Nell Irvin Painter's work because the information in her book must be as accurate as possible.

Segment 4: Nell Irvin Painter believes that it is important for students not to take the first thing they are told as fact but instead to look at it critically, realizing that there are many layers and that history is much more complicated. Students may answer that they can learn more about a historical event or era and get a more personal, intimate account of history from a different perspective.

from *Civil War Diaries, Journals, and Letters*

Vocabulary Warm-up Exercises, p. 95

A.
1. tatters
2. extinguished
3. discrimination
4. demonstration
5. witty
6. recruits
7. proclamation
8. suffrage

B. Sample Answers
1. T; Most happenings occur when court is in session.
2. F; *Communicative* people like to talk.
3. T; First something occurs, the action, and then the *consequence* follows.
4. T; When something is *intercepted*, its course has been taken over by someone or something else.
5. T; When the sky is clear at night, often times there are many stars visible to the eye.
6. T; Car accidents can be very serious, so receiving minor injuries could be seen as fortunate.
7. F; *Strenuous* exercise actually increases the heart rate because more blood is required.
8. F; *Valor* means courage and bravery, therefore, all heroes have it.

Reading Warm-up A, p. 96

Sample Answers
1. because of a common belief; announcement
2. It is not a good thing because someone is being oppressed; The *suffrage* movement was always trying to promote its cause in hopes for a change.
3. the slaves; No, because someone is at a disadvantage.
4. *Recruit* means newcomer; answers will vary.
5. growing numbers of people, assembled; All of the noise was coming from the *demonstration* in front of the jailhouse.
6. comedians, actors/actresses, talk show hosts; yes, because it is basically a talent for communicating
7. (put out); cigarettes, thirst
8. because the employer would think the person was sloppy, disrespectful, dirty; shredded

Reading Warm-up B, p. 97

Sample Answers
1. to know the person was still alive; being with family
2. to share information and learn news; Yes, we are social beings and like to express ourselves.
3. (taken); a football, a phone message

4. in the case of war, death; Yes, if the cause or result is a positive consequence.
5. significant; There was a *multitude* of her favorite candies in the dish for her birthday.
6. because people would write for hours; exercise, babysitting
7. (hero); courage
8. because the war was finally over; Court was *adjourned* at 4:00 P.M., just like the judge said.

Literary Analysis: Diaries, Journals, and Letters, p. 98

Sample Responses

1. When Mary Chesnut tells that she does not usually listen to what the men are saying, she tells personal information that is usually restricted to a diary or journal.
2. It is a personal anecdote, typical of personal writings such as diaries or journals.
3. We learn that Goss, when about to undertake something unusual or desperate (like fighting or courting), concentrates on personal details.
4. Goss was nervous about enlisting.
5. Goss was probably a pleasant, witty person who had much self-confidence and believed that his opinion was important.
6. Since a diary or journal is written by one person about events he or she has experienced, McKim would only know what he had personally seen and done.
7. Since Jackson is writing a letter to his wife, he assumes she remembers the coat. Jackson probably would not have included the information. He obviously meant this information to be only for his wife.

Reading Strategy: Distinguish Fact from Opinion, p. 99

Possible Responses

1. Fact: John Manning was on Beauregard's staff. Opinion: John Manning was pleased as a boy.
2. Fact: Anderson went into Fort Sumter. Opinion: Anderson is a "green goose."
3. Fact: The woman's dress is on fire. Opinion: She is a foolish woman.
4. Fact: The shirt was flannel. Opinion: The flannel shirt was coarse and unpleasant, too large at the neck, too short elsewhere.
5. Fact: The little brigade swept on. Opinion: The little brigade was gallant.
6. Fact: Order was restored by everyone's efforts. Opinion: The efforts were strenuous.

Vocabulary Builder, p. 100

A. 1. E; 2. F; 3. D; 4. C; 5. A

B. 1. surrender
2. daringly
3. presentiment
4. stubborn
5. calmness

C. 1. B; 2. C

Grammar and Style: Capitalization of Proper Nouns, p. 101

A. 1. Emancipation Proclamation
2. Battle of Gettysburg
3. none
4. Fort Sumter
5. Ulysses S. Grant

B. Sample Responses
1. the Civil War
2. Richmond
3. the Morning Herald
4. President Lincoln
5. Behind the Enemy Lines

Enrichment: Journals, p. 104

Suggested Responses

Three possible responses: "An Account of the Battle of Bull Run"—the fact that Stonewall Jackson was slightly injured at the Battle of Bull Run and he felt the battle was the hardest he had been in; "An Account of an Experience With Discrimination"—the details surrounding Sojourner Truth's experience with discrimination; from *Mary Chesnut's Civil War*—the Southern opinions expressed by Mary Chestnut about the attack on Fort Sumter.

Selection Test A, p. 105

Critical Reading

1. ANS: B	DIF: Easy	OBJ: Comprehension
2. ANS: C	DIF: Easy	OBJ: Reading Strategy
3. ANS: D	DIF: Easy	OBJ: Literary Analysis
4. ANS: B	DIF: Easy	OBJ: Comprehension
5. ANS: B	DIF: Easy	OBJ: Comprehension
6. ANS: D	DIF: Easy	OBJ: Reading Strategy
7. ANS: B	DIF: Easy	OBJ: Literary Analysis
8. ANS: C	DIF: Easy	OBJ: Interpretation
9. ANS: B	DIF: Easy	OBJ: Reading Strategy
10. ANS: B	DIF: Easy	OBJ: Literary Analysis

Vocabulary and Grammar

11. ANS: B	DIF: Easy	OBJ: Vocabulary
12. ANS: B	DIF: Easy	OBJ: Grammar

Essay

13. Students' essays should reflect that Goss joins the army to gain chances for travel and promotion. This desire

suggests that his civilian life has not been exciting. However, he soon finds that military life has its own boredom, and he cannot express his opinions.

Difficulty: *Easy*

Objective: *Essay*

14. Students' statements should reflect that McKim is questioning why his brigade had no support from other brigades in its attack. A more direct statement might be: "When we attacked the enemy, we got no backup support. Daniels may or may not have been obeying orders, but if he was, who was stupid enough to give such orders?"

Difficulty: *Easy*

Objective: *Essay*

Selection Test B, p. 108

Critical Reading

1. **ANS:** B	**DIF:** Challenging	**OBJ:** Comprehension
2. **ANS:** A	**DIF:** Average	**OBJ:** Reading Strategy
3. **ANS:** C	**DIF:** Easy	**OBJ:** Comprehension
4. **ANS:** C	**DIF:** Easy	**OBJ:** Reading Strategy
5. **ANS:** A	**DIF:** Easy	**OBJ:** Comprehension
6. **ANS:** B	**DIF:** Average	**OBJ:** Literary Analysis
7. **ANS:** A	**DIF:** Challenging	**OBJ:** Literary Analysis
8. **ANS:** C	**DIF:** Average	**OBJ:** Reading Strategy
9. **ANS:** A	**DIF:** Average	**OBJ:** Interpretation
10. **ANS:** D	**DIF:** Easy	**OBJ:** Reading Strategy
11. **ANS:** C	**DIF:** Average	**OBJ:** Interpretation
12. **ANS:** A	**DIF:** Challenging	**OBJ:** Interpretation
13. **ANS:** B	**DIF:** Easy	**OBJ:** Literary Analysis

Vocabulary and Grammar

14. **ANS:** B	**DIF:** Average	**OBJ:** Vocabulary
15. **ANS:** B	**DIF:** Average	**OBJ:** Vocabulary
16. **ANS:** B	**DIF:** Easy	**OBJ:** Grammar
17. **ANS:** A	**DIF:** Challenging	**OBJ:** Vocabulary

Essay

18. Mary Chesnut: The conflicts are between the Union and the Confederate at Fort Sumter and between Mary Chesnut's love of the Confederacy and her dislike of war; Warren Lee Goss: Goss is caught between his prewar civilian life and his new role as an enlisted man; Randolph McKim: The conflict is the Battle of Gettysburg; Stonewall Jackson: The conflicts are the Battle of Bull Run and the underlying conflict between Jackson's pride in his troops and his modesty; Reverend Henry M. Turner: The conflict is between slavery and freedom; Sojourner Truth: The conflict is between Truth and those who seek to deprive her of her rights.

Difficulty: *Easy*

Objective: *Essay*

19. Students' essays should indicate that Goss's writing is very personal and familiar, whereas McKim's account is factual and to the point. The explanation should be supported by appropriate details from the two works.

Difficulty: *Average*

Objective: *Essay*

20. Students' essays should accurately identify and describe the characters. Comparison and contrast would be structured around parallel features or characteristics and should be well supported with details from the selections.

Difficulty: *Challenging*

Objective: *Essay*

Benchmark Test 5, p. 111

MULTIPLE CHOICE

1. **ANS:** A
2. **ANS:** A
3. **ANS:** C
4. **ANS:** D
5. **ANS:** A
6. **ANS:** A
7. **ANS:** B
8. **ANS:** D
9. **ANS:** D
10. **ANS:** B
11. **ANS:** B
12. **ANS:** D
13. **ANS:** B
14. **ANS:** C
15. **ANS:** A
16. **ANS:** A
17. **ANS:** B
18. **ANS:** D
19. **ANS:** A
20. **ANS:** B
21. **ANS:** C
22. **ANS:** B
23. **ANS:** D
24. **ANS:** D
25. **ANS:** A
26. **ANS:** D
27. **ANS:** C
28. **ANS:** B
29. **ANS:** A
30. **ANS:** B
31. **ANS:** D
32. **ANS:** B

33. ANS: A

ESSAY

34. Field reports should be detailed, factual, and based on observation.
35. Essays should describe the impact and importance of the writers' significant life experiences.
36. Students should answer the question specifically. Reasons for the commencement and termination of the autobiography should be clear and tied to the original statement.
37. Essays should state writers' opinions and support them with examples and quotations.
38. Historical events should be identifiable, and diary entries should describe their importance from an ordinary person's point of view.

Diagnostic Test 6, p. 117

MULTIPLE CHOICE

1. ANS: B
2. ANS: C
3. ANS: D
4. ANS: A
5. ANS: B
6. ANS: C
7. ANS: B
8. ANS: D
9. ANS: C
10. ANS: A
11. ANS: D
12. ANS: D
13. ANS: A
14. ANS: D
15. ANS: D

"The Boys' Ambition" from *Life on the Mississippi* and "The Notorious Jumping Frog of Calaveras County" by Mark Twain

Vocabulary Warm-up Exercises, p. 121

A.
1. narrative
2. sociable
3. humbly
4. withstand
5. compliance
6. monotonous
7. deliberate
8. contribution

B. Sample Answers

1. A shy person or someone who really wanted to fit in would hate to be *conspicuous*.
2. I would rather have comfort than *grandeur,* because I have to live there all the time.
3. Loud thunder makes a storm *impressive,* and so does lightning and a lot of wind and rain.
4. No, because I would get bored if I was *indifferent* about football.
5. Kids *loathe* bedtime because they don't want to miss any fun.
6. I don't think so, because why would they want to help hungry people if they were *ruthless*?
7. The phone ringing all the time makes life less *tranquil,* although it might make me feel more *tranquil* to know people could call me if they wanted to.
8. Exchange students are more *transient,* because they go back home after not too long.

Reading Warm-up A, p. 122

Sample Answers

1. (books); A poem or short story could also be a *contribution* to literature.
2. (slow); The opposite of *deliberate* speaking might be "babbling" or "chattering."
3. (outgoing); Yes, because celebrities need to be *sociable* to deal with fans and reporters.
4. endless round of dinners and events; "Exciting" or "fun" could be the opposite of *monotonous.*
5. (fame); *Humbly* means "not in a conceited way".
6. tried to behave "properly"; A teacher or police officer might require *compliance.*
7. (whole last paragraph); Yes, because a *narrative,* or story, can be true or made-up.
8. her pleading; They might not be able to *withstand* peer pressure.

Reading Warm-up B, p. 123

Sample Answers

1. (awe, admiring); *Grandeur* means "magnificence."
2. recognize every landmark for twelve hundred miles, by day or by night; It's *impressive* because twelve hundred miles is a huge distance, and landmarks are hard to see at night.
3. (tree); A large snow bank, for instance, would be *transient.*
4. actually filled with hidden hazards; A person who is relaxing might be *tranquil.*
5. a "faint dimple" on the water's surface; A grizzly bear would be *conspicuous* in a classroom.
6. being awoken in the middle of the night to take over at the helm; "Love" or "adore" would be the opposite of *loathe.*
7. (mockery); If the pilot were not *ruthless,* he might be kind to Clemens instead of insulting him.
8. the scenic beauty of the Mississippi; *Indifferent* means "not caring much one way or another."

Literary Analysis: Humor, p. 124

1. dialect
2. dialect and exaggeration
3. dialect
4. dialect and colorful simile or metaphor

Reading Strategy: Understand Regional Dialect, p. 125

Sample Responses

1. He was so strange about betting that he would bet on anything. He would even bet the opposite of his original bet if he couldn't persuade anyone else to.
2. Smiley had a mare. Others called the mare the fifteen-minute nag, but only to tease. They called her that because naturally she was faster than that. Smiley used to win money by betting on that horse, eventhough she was slow and always seemed to have something wrong with her.
3. The dog didn't look like he was worth much. You wouldn't expect the dog to do much except lie around, look mean, and wait for a chance to steal something. But as soon as someone bet money on that dog, he seemed to become another dog entirely. His jaw would stick out like the front of a steamboat does, and his teeth would suddenly show and shine like the steam-boat's burning furnaces.
4. Suddenly he would grab the other dog by the joint of its hind leg. He would freeze his jaw on that leg, not biting or chewing on it, but just gripping and hanging on. He would hang on until people stopped him, even if it took a year.

Vocabulary Builder, p. 126

A. 1. monolingual; 2. monoplegia; 3. monosyllable; 4. monosomic

B. 1. D; 2. H; 3. A; 4. E; 5. G; 6. C; 7. B; 8. F

Grammar and Style: Double Negatives, p. 127

A.
1. There couldn't be anything mentioned.
2. He didn't try any more to win the fight.
3. He had no opportunities to speak of.
4. He did nothing for three months.
5. I have no frog.

B.
1. She cannot have a dog.
2. correct
3. They had no business there, either.
4. He wouldn't take a bribe from the lawyer.
5. correct

Enrichment: Jargon, p. 130

Suggested Response

Students should choose a job either that they have done themselves or with which they are very familiar (a parent's job that they've visited, for example). Students should choose several different words to fill out the chart and be able to give each word a specific definition.

Selection Test A, p. 131

Critical Reading

1. ANS: A	DIF: Easy	OBJ: Comprehension
2. ANS: C	DIF: Easy	OBJ: Interpretation
3. ANS: B	DIF: Easy	OBJ: Literary Analysis
4. ANS: D	DIF: Easy	OBJ: Comprehension
5. ANS: B	DIF: Easy	OBJ: Literary Analysis
6. ANS: B	DIF: Easy	OBJ: Reading Strategy
7. ANS: A	DIF: Easy	OBJ: Interpretation
8. ANS: C	DIF: Easy	OBJ: Reading Strategy
9. ANS: A	DIF: Easy	OBJ: Interpretation
10. ANS: B	DIF: Easy	OBJ: Reading Strategy

Vocabulary and Grammar

11. ANS: B	DIF: Easy	OBJ: Vocabulary
12. ANS: C	DIF: Easy	OBJ: Grammar

Essay

13. Students' essays might reflect that for boys living in a small town along a large river, being a steamboatman would have been an exciting life. It would have taken them to distant places and given them the opportunity to meet many new people and have new experiences.
    Difficulty: *Easy*
    Objective: *Essay*
14. Students' essays may reflect that each of the animals may have had a skill of some kind, but that none of them could do what Wheeler says they could do. For example, the dog probably was a tough fighter, but it is doubtful that it lay down and died when it lost a fight. Writers use exaggeration to provide humor and make a story more interesting to the reader.
    Difficulty: *Easy*
    Objective: *Essay*

Selection Test B, p. 134

Critical Reading

1. ANS: C	DIF: Easy	OBJ: Comprehension
2. ANS: B	DIF: Challenging	OBJ: Comprehension
3. ANS: B	DIF: Challenging	OBJ: Interpretation
4. ANS: A	DIF: Average	OBJ: Reading Strategy
5. ANS: D	DIF: Average	OBJ: Interpretation
6. ANS: C	DIF: Challenging	OBJ: Interpretation
7. ANS: D	DIF: Challenging	OBJ: Literary Analysis
8. ANS: D	DIF: Average	OBJ: Literary Analysis
9. ANS: B	DIF: Easy	OBJ: Reading Strategy

10. ANS: A	**DIF:** Average	**OBJ:** Interpretation
11. ANS: D	**DIF:** Average	**OBJ:** Reading Strategy
12. ANS: C	**DIF:** Challenging	**OBJ:** Interpretation
13. ANS: A	**DIF:** Average	**OBJ:** Literary Analysis

Vocabulary and Grammar

14. ANS: B	**DIF:** Average	**OBJ:** Vocabulary
15. ANS: B	**DIF:** Average	**OBJ:** Vocabulary
16. ANS: D	**DIF:** Average	**OBJ:** Grammar
17. ANS: A	**DIF:** Average	**OBJ:** Vocabulary

Essay

18. Students should state that Simon Wheeler is the main character, as he tells the story from his unique point of view. Students should define the main character as the character around whom the story revolves or on whom it focuses. Though he is not the subject of his own narrative, he drives the action of the short story, and his interpretation and telling of the events give the story its distinctive humorous tone. Students should support their response with examples from the story, including how Wheeler's storytelling is humorous, and how the very premise of the story is derived from Wheeler's actions.

Difficulty: *Easy*

Objective: *Essay*

19. Students should give examples of all three techniques. Examples of exaggeration include the desire to kill the apprentice engineer in "The Boys' Ambition" and Simon Wheelers's tale in "The Notorious Jumping Frog of Calaveras County." Examples of embellishment include the apprentice engineer's escape from the steamboat accident as well as several statements made by Simon Wheeler. Many examples of regional dialect can be found in the dialogue from either story.

Difficulty: *Average*

Objective: *Essay*

20. Students' essays should explain why the unknown has a much greater appeal than the familiar, and give one or more of these examples from "The Boys' Ambition": instances of the boys' dreaming of different careers as the "perfect" career; and the idea that life on the Mississippi River in a steamboat would be idyllic.

Difficulty: *Challenging*

Objective: *Essay*

"The Outcasts of Poker Flat" by Bret Harte

Vocabulary Warm-up Exercises, p. 138

A.
1. associate
2. frailer
3. commiseration
4. provisions
5. significantly
6. indications
7. pallid
8. worldly

B. Sample Answers
1. I want to lose weight, and *consequently*, I avoid ice cream and cake.
2. David lives on the *outskirts* of town, far from the center.
3. The *wily* mouse hid where it could not be easily caught.
4. Because he always *retained* his wit and charm, people enjoyed his company.
5. The bookstore owner is *notorious* for her bad temper.
6. Falling down and skinning her knee *provoked* the child to burst out crying.
7. If you want straight As, it is *advisable* to study hard.
8. The hotel's *seclusion* made it difficult for Ivan to visit tourist sites.

Reading Warm-up A, p. 139

Sample Answers
1. <u>"Lucky" Jack Lewis</u>; An *associate* in school is a classmate.
2. (very); Two or three inches would make me feel *significantly* taller.
3. (dark); No, watermelon with plenty of color usually tastes sweeter than *pallid* watermelon.
4. (boy); If a friend looked *frailer,* I might suggest fresh air and exercise, or going to the doctor.
5. <u>a long, hard journey</u>; Shivering and teeth chattering are *indications* that someone is feeling cold.
6. <u>No money either, by the look of him, and no tools or provisions</u>; If he didn't feel *commiseration,* he might say, "Tough luck, kid! Get lost."
7. (claim), (money), (tools); I would pack sandwiches, fruit, and snacks as *provisions* for a picnic.
8. The *worldly* wealth they are after is gold.

Reading Warm-up B, p. 140

Sample Answers
1. <u>where the open prairie began</u>; On the *outskirts* of my town you would find a commercial strip with lots of chain stores.
2. (loneliness); *Seclusion* means being alone, away from crowds.
3. Other words for *consequently* might be "because of this" or "for this reason."
4. <u>packed a great deal more</u>; It would be *advisable* to pack a tent, food and water, a flashlight, and a sleeping bag.
5. (drinking water); I have *retained* a mug that was a birthday gift years ago.
6. <u>they could die of thirst</u>; I probably would not want to go to a place that was *notorious,* because it means it is known for a bad reason.

7. brought barrels of water east from California, charging as much as $100 for a single glass; No, because someone who was *wily* might cheat you or take advantage of you.
8. write to a friend back East, "STAY AT HOME."; The urge for adventure, or the hope of finding gold, might have *provoked* the friend to head West anyway.

Literary Analysis: Regionalism, p. 141

1. Poker Flat is not usually a moral town
2. the surrounding land of Poker Flat
3. the surrounding land of Poker Flat
4. Mr. Oakhurst in particular and professional gamblers in general

Reading Strategy: Question the Text, p. 142

Sample Responses

1. The town of Poker Flat decided to get rid of "all improper persons."
2. It allows the generosity of Mr. Oakhurst to be established.
3. It causes the outcasts to camp and eventually get snowed in.
4. To compare and contrast "innocent" characters with the "outcast" characters of the story.

Vocabulary Builder, p. 143

A. 1. antebellum
2. antebellum
3. postbellum

B. 1. vituperative
2. bellicose
3. expatriated
4. querulous
5. recumbent
6. anathema
7. vociferation
8. equanimity

Grammar and Style: Coordinating Conjunctions in Compound Sentences, p. 144

A. 1. *or*—indicates a choice or possibility between two adjectives; *and*—links two verb phrases
2. *and*—links two independent clauses; *or*—indicates a choice or possibility between two verbs
3. *but*—shows a contrast between two independent clauses; *and*—links two independent clauses

Sample Responses

B. 1. John Oakhurst, two women, and a suspected thief were escorted to the outskirts of town.
2. When he awakens the next morning, Mr. Oakhurst discovers that it has snowed during the night and that Uncle Billy has stolen the mules and horses but not the provisions.

Enrichment: Social Studies, p. 147

Suggested Response

Students should be able to name each character as an outcast or an innocent, then complete the chart for each character with specific examples from the selection.

Mr. Oakhurst

Outcast

He is a professional gambler and has won money from local residents.

He returned Tom Simson's money to him, and shows kindness and consideration upon his exile.

The Duchess

Outcast

She is unrefined.

She shows an "innocent" quality when outside of Poker Flat and shows a general affection for Piney Woods.

Mother Shipton

Outcast

She is crude and vulgar.

Upon banishment, she starves herself to save others, particularly Piney Woods.

Uncle Billy

Outcast

He is a drunkard and possible thief.

He does not really show any unstereotypical behaviors.

Tom Simson

Innocent

He sees good and assumes innocence in all the outcasts and sees adventure in the hardship.

He does not really show any stereotypical behaviors.

Piney Woods

Innocent

She sees good and assumes innocence in all the outcasts and sees adventure in the hardship.

She admits to the Duchess that she does not know how to pray.

Selection Test A, p. 148

Critical Reading

1. ANS: B	DIF: Easy	OBJ: Literary Analysis
2. ANS: C	DIF: Easy	OBJ: Comprehension
3. ANS: D	DIF: Easy	OBJ: Reading Strategy
4. ANS: C	DIF: Easy	OBJ: Reading Strategy
5. ANS: C	DIF: Easy	OBJ: Literary Analysis
6. ANS: A	DIF: Easy	OBJ: Interpretation
7. ANS: A	DIF: Easy	OBJ: Comprehension
8. ANS: C	DIF: Easy	OBJ: Interpretation
9. ANS: D	DIF: Easy	OBJ: Interpretation
10. ANS: C	DIF: Easy	OBJ: Literary Analysis

Vocabulary and Grammar

11. ANS: A	DIF: Easy	OBJ: Vocabulary
12. ANS: B	DIF: Easy	OBJ: Grammar

Essay

13. Students' essays should reflect that Mr. Oakhurst, as a gambler, thinks a lot about luck. He tries to see the outcasts' situation in terms of lucky and unlucky events. Students may point out that the outcasts do not get the luck they deserve, since only Tom escapes with his life.
    Difficulty: *Easy*
    Objective: *Essay*
14. Students' essays may suggest that Mr. Oakhurst's suicide does make sense. He is a gambler and believes that people have runs of good luck and bad luck. Other students may suggest that his suicide does not make sense because a gambler is always waiting for his luck to change.
    Difficulty: *Easy*
    Objective: *Essay*

Selection Test B, p. 151

Critical Reading

1. ANS: C	DIF: Easy	OBJ: Literary Analysis
2. ANS: B	DIF: Easy	OBJ: Comprehension
3. ANS: A	DIF: Average	OBJ: Reading Strategy
4. ANS: D	DIF: Challenging	OBJ: Interpretation
5. ANS: D	DIF: Challenging	OBJ: Reading Strategy
6. ANS: A	DIF: Average	OBJ: Interpretation
7. ANS: A	DIF: Average	OBJ: Interpretation
8. ANS: D	DIF: Average	OBJ: Literary Analysis
9. ANS: C	DIF: Easy	OBJ: Interpretation
10. ANS: A	DIF: Average	OBJ: Comprehension
11. ANS: C	DIF: Average	OBJ: Reading Strategy
12. ANS: B	DIF: Challenging	OBJ: Literary Analysis
13. ANS: C	DIF: Average	OBJ: Literary Analysis

Vocabulary and Grammar

14. ANS: A	DIF: Easy	OBJ: Vocabulary
15. ANS: C	DIF: Easy	OBJ: Grammar
16. ANS: B	DIF: Challenging	OBJ: Vocabulary
17. ANS: B	DIF: Average	OBJ: Vocabulary

Essay

18. Students should explain that Mr. Oakhurst was a gambler and that he loved poker. He saw being snowed in as a streak of bad luck that eventually led to a losing game. Therefore, it makes sense that he would use the lowest ranked card to represent himself, signifying that he knew he would lose this "hand" in the card game of life.
    Difficulty: *Easy*
    Objective: *Essay*
19. Students' answers will vary, depending on the position they take. Either position can be correct, provided it is clearly articulated and supported with examples from the selection and details about the character of Mr. Oakhurst.
    Difficulty: *Average*
    Objective: *Essay*
20. Students' answers will vary, depending on the position they take. Students should be graded on their clarity and support of their positions. They should use details from the selection, including the leadership Mr. Oakhurst shows the party after they are left, as examples of strength, and his suicide as an example of weakness.
    Difficulty: *Challenging*
    Objective: *Essay*

"Heading West" by Miriam Davis Colt
"I Will Fight No More Forever" by Chief Joseph

Vocabulary Warm-up Exercises, p. 155

A.
1. severity
2. fulfilled
3. consequence
4. pedestrian
5. shrewd
6. implements
7. ravine
8. dingy

B. Sample Answers
1. We will both be in Chicago during the same week in July, so our visits there will <u>coincide</u>.
2. Groups of <u>emigrants</u> leave their native countries for many different reasons.
3. The newspaper editors highlighted their <u>foremost</u> reason for endorsing the governor's plan.
4. He was so <u>genial</u> that most people wanted him for a friend.
5. Stan was <u>nonplused</u> when he heard the news, remarking that it was astonishing.

Reading Warm-up A, p. 156

Sample Answers

1. <u>or tools</u>; Pam brought salad forks, serving spoons, and other *implements* for the picnic.
2. (clever); *cunning*
3. <u>demand for fur hats and coats was high . . . a busy trader might make a handsome profit</u>; *result*
4. (would walk beside his horses)
5. (going up or down a steep); *gully, gulch, gorge*
6. <u>must have been difficult and challenging</u>; *gentleness, mildness*

7. (the hardships they encountered . . . sometimes even nonexistent); Half the shops on the *dingy*, poorly maintained street were boarded up.
8. its mission as a mobile container; *satisfied, achieved*

Reading Warm-up B, p. 157

Sample Answers

1. and the same year would . . . with the discovery of gold there; We planned our visit to New Orleans so that it would *coincide* with Mardi Gras.
2. (almost immediately became the . . . destination in the west); *prime, most important*
3. . . . attracted not only Americans . . . from all over the world . . . poured into California; Substantial numbers of people born in that Caribbean country have become *emigrants*, leaving their native shores.
4. . . . of new arrivals numbered 100,000 in 1849 alone; *abundance, multitude*
5. (life in the mining camps was seldom friendly or . . . greed and jealousy often erupted into violence); The opposite of *genial* is *unfriendly* or *hostile*.
6. the very same tools that a miner . . . could . . . be used as dangerous weapons; *handles*
7. in his astonishment; a surprising or astonishing event
8. (sitting down to a lavish . . . in one of the neighborhood's fine restaurants); *fine meal*

Literary Analysis: Tone, p. 158

A. 1. B; 2. D

B. Students should identify the adjective they choose. The entry should reflect the tone through descriptive words and details.

Reading Strategy: Respond, p. 159

Possible Response

Students may mention that "freezing to death" and "find them dead" evoke powerful images, which help them understand the motivation of Chief Joseph's speech.

Vocabulary Builder, p. 160

A. Sample Responses

1. The archaeologist dug up many bowls and pots made of terra cotta.
2. The astronaut jumped up and down happily on terra firma after climbing out of the space shuttle.
3. To the Nez Percé, who came from farther west, Oklahoma was terra incognita.

B.
1. emigrants
2. profusion
3. genial
4. pervading
5. terra firma

Grammar and Style: Sentence Fragments, p. 161

A. Sample Responses

1. correct
2. We go up, up, up, and upstairs to our lodging rooms.
3. We are traveling on board the steamer "Cataract," bound for Kansas City.

B. Sample Responses

1. We found ourselves in this miserable hotel before we knew it. The fare is miserable. It consists of herring boiled with cabbage. The beds are miserable and dirty, and an odor pervades the house that is not at all agreeable. The mistress is gone.
2. We are one mile from the city, and Dr. Thorn has broke his wagon tongue; it must be sent back to Kansas City to be mended. Fires are kindled; the women begin cooking; we eat supper sitting around on logs, stones, and wagon tongues.

Enrichment: Social Studies, p. 164

Suggested Responses

Students should respond to the questions with detailed descriptions of circumstances, emotions, and feelings. They should use the selections as a guide; for example, they may draw on the experience of the Nez Percé to show why their group had to leave Earth. Students' diary entries should put all of their answers to use, to one degree or another, and expand on their responses. They should not be afraid to use their imaginations, and should be ready to read their entries to the class and respond to questions.

Selection Test A, p. 165

Critical Reading

1. ANS: C	DIF: Easy	OBJ: Comprehension
2. ANS: B	DIF: Easy	OBJ: Interpretation
3. ANS: C	DIF: Easy	OBJ: Literary Analysis
4. ANS: D	DIF: Easy	OBJ: Reading Strategy
5. ANS: A	DIF: Easy	OBJ: Literary Analysis
6. ANS: C	DIF: Easy	OBJ: Reading Strategy
7. ANS: D	DIF: Easy	OBJ: Comprehension
8. ANS: A	DIF: Easy	OBJ: Literary Analysis
9. ANS: C	DIF: Easy	OBJ: Interpretation
10. ANS: D	DIF: Easy	OBJ: Interpretation

Vocabulary and Grammar

11. ANS: C	DIF: Easy	OBJ: Vocabulary
12. ANS: D	DIF: Easy	OBJ: Grammar

Essay

13. Students' essays may mention the dangers of paying money to unknown people; eating poor food and drinking bad water; dangerous situations with the transportation; bad weather; unpleasant and/or dangerous

traveling companions; and so on. Students may say the risks made the journey seem more exciting, especially for children, who generally like adventure. Others may say that the dangers made the journey unwise.

Difficulty: *Easy*

Objective: *Essay*

14. Students' responses should express the sadness of Chief Joseph and his concern for the future of his people. Students may add that Chief Joseph is able to see that a change in his people's history is about to take place and that he is unable to prevent it.

Difficulty: *Easy*

Objective: *Essay*

Selection Test B, p. 168

Critical Reading

1. ANS: B	**DIF:** Average	**OBJ:** Literary Analysis
2. ANS: A	**DIF:** Average	**OBJ:** Comprehension
3. ANS: A	**DIF:** Challenging	**OBJ:** Comprehension
4. ANS: C	**DIF:** Challenging	**OBJ:** Literary Analysis
5. ANS: C	**DIF:** Challenging	**OBJ:** Reading Strategy
6. ANS: A	**DIF:** Average	**OBJ:** Reading Strategy
7. ANS: D	**DIF:** Average	**OBJ:** Literary Analysis
8. ANS: D	**DIF:** Average	**OBJ:** Interpretation
9. ANS: C	**DIF:** Easy	**OBJ:** Literary Analysis
10. ANS: A	**DIF:** Average	**OBJ:** Interpretation
11. ANS: C	**DIF:** Average	**OBJ:** Reading Strategy
12. ANS: D	**DIF:** Easy	**OBJ:** Interpretation
13. ANS: B	**DIF:** Easy	**OBJ:** Reading Strategy

Vocabulary and Grammar

14. ANS: C	**DIF:** Average	**OBJ:** Vocabulary
15. ANS: D	**DIF:** Average	**OBJ:** Vocabulary
16. ANS: C	**DIF:** Easy	**OBJ:** Vocabulary
17. ANS: A	**DIF:** Easy	**OBJ:** Grammar

Essay

18. Students can describe how people may have been impressed by the simple humanity of the Chief's words, as well as the sufferings of his people. Students should discuss how people may have also been moved by pity for the defeated; by the caring of a leader for his family and people; by the realization that these "enemies" were humans too; and by guilt over the government's actions.

Difficulty: *Easy*

Objective: *Essay*

19. Students should include among the costs to the Colts such things as selling their farm; sending their money to the Vegetarian Company; separation from old friends and relatives, some of whom they will never see again; the labor of starting all over again; and the lack of services and amenities on the frontier. Dangers include disease, accidents, depredations of others, the loss of their investment, and the fear of the unknown.

Difficulty: *Average*

Objective: *Essay*

20. Students should identify Chief Joseph's decision to surrender as coming from his realization that further fighting cannot help his people. He risks appearing less heroic in order to save what is left of his people. The stark repetition of *dead* conveys his feelings of loss, and the images of his people freezing convey his sorrow. His desire for time to look for his children conveys his caring attitude. His weariness with war grows from his love of his people.

Difficulty: *Challenging*

Objective: *Essay*

"To Build a Fire" by Jack London

Vocabulary Warm-up Exercises, p. 172

A.
1. methodically
2. aggressively
3. circulation
4. imperative
5. likewise
6. panicky
7. floundered
8. undesirable

B. Sample Answers
1. T; Three flat tires would cause *agitation* because that is a lot of bad luck and trouble for one week.
2. T; If you are a fly, *entanglement* in a spider's web is the first step in becoming the spider's dinner.
3. F; July in Texas is really hot, which is just the opposite of *arctic*.
4. F; Getting a *penalty* is bad news for the team.
5. F; Shakespeare's plays are the reason for his lasting fame, or *immortality*.
6. T; If I had always *yearned* to travel, I would like the chance to take a trip.
7. F; *Capsizing* the life boat could cause the passengers to drown.
8. T; She *asserted* her right to have a seat on the bus just like anyone else.

Reading Warm-up A, p. 173

Sample Answers

1. being lost alone in the wilderness, hungry, cold, and unprepared; Another *undesirable* situation would be arriving at a party in a costume and finding out that it is not a costume party.
2. Sit down, take a deep breath, and think methodically; The opposite of *panicky* would be "calm" or "relaxed."

3. (carefully); I could use a pencil and paper to make a list of everything I have with me or what I need to do, which would be thinking *methodically*.
4. Instead of *likewise*, you could say "similarly" or "also."
5. that you keep your body temperature up; Before riding a bicycle downhill, it is *imperative* that you know how to brake.
6. you can lose forty percent of your heat through your head; "Moving around" means the same thing as *circulation*.
7. getting even more lost; No, because *floundered* suggests aimlessness and clumsiness.
8. (wave); A soccer player might charge down the field *aggressively*.

Reading Warm-up B, p. 174

Sample Answers

1. barking madly; Babies usually show their *agitation* by crying.
2. (frozen); *Arctic* terrain would be dangerous because you could freeze to death.
3. No woman had ever won the Iditarod; Abraham Lincoln earned *immortality* by writing the Emancipation Proclamation.
4. they dragged her through the brush; *Capsizing* the sled would be bad because she might fall off and get hurt, and the sled might be damaged.
5. struggled to keep the lines clear; A dolphin in a fishing net would be an example of an *entanglement*.
6. Riddles might have *asserted* authority by calling out commands or pulling the dogs up short.
7. The "ultimate *penalty*" would have been dying in the blizzard.
8. became the first woman to win the "Last Great Race on Earth"; Someone might *yearn* to be elected the President of the United States.

Literary Analysis: Understanding Conflict, p. 175

1. external; person against nature
2. external; person against nature
3. internal; person against himself
4. external; person against another character
5. external; person against nature
6. external; person against nature
7. internal; person against himself
8. external; person against fate

Reading Strategy: Predict, p. 176

Students should cite specific clues, predictions based on those clues, and the actual outcomes from the text. For example, Clue: . . . [the dog] experienced a vague but menacing apprehension that subdued it and made it slink along at the man's heels . . .; Prediction: the man may not realize how dangerous the cold really is; Outcome: the dog's instincts were correct.

Vocabulary Builder, p. 177

A. Sample Answers

1. Ejecting means to be thrown out. The pilot threw himself out of the plane.
2. To object is to throw your opinion against something. We were sure the coach would be against our missing practice.
3. When you are sad or disappointed, your spirits cold be described as thrown down. Jillian's spirits were down when she failed the test.

B. 1. C; 2. D; 3. D; 4. D

Grammar and Style, p. 178

A.

1. If he fell down tells *under what circumstances* it would shatter itself.
2. none
3. So long as he walked four miles an hour tells *to what extent* he pumped blood to the surface.
4. for he would be forced to stop and build a fire tells *why* it meant delay.
5. where the ice jams of the freeze-up had formed tells *where* it was all pure white.

B. Sample Answers

1. The man tried to avoid walking where spring water lay hidden under the snow.
2. Because the man built a fire right under a snow-laden tree, the snow fell and extinguished the flame.

Enrichment: Films About Survival, p. 181

Suggested Responses

As students watch films that deal with survival under challenging conditions, they should keep the character traits and fate of the man in "To Build a Fire" in mind. For example, in a scene at the beginning of *Return of the Jedi*, Han Solo and Luke Skywalker are caught outside the shelter at night, where conditions are very cold and harsh. Solo finds Luke, who had been injured, and covers him in the entrails of a deceased mount until he has the chance to erect a shelter. Unlike the man in "To Build a Fire," they stay sheltered in one area until help arrives the next day. Han Solo's intelligence and cunning allow him and Luke to survive.

Suggested Responses

In their profiles for adaptable characters, students will probably include traits such as intelligence, forethought, and an ability to size up and react to new situations. They should support their points by citing events from "To Build a Fire" and the films. For example, they might include as a trait the willingness to listen to others. The man in "To Build a Fire" did not listen to the advice of an old-timer who insisted that "no man must travel alone in the Klondike after fifty below."

Selection Test A, p. 182

Critical Reading

1. ANS: B   DIF: Easy   OBJ: Literary Analysis

2. **ANS:** C	**DIF:** Easy	**OBJ:** Reading Strategy
3. **ANS:** B	**DIF:** Easy	**OBJ:** Comprehension
4. **ANS:** B	**DIF:** Easy	**OBJ:** Reading Strategy
5. **ANS:** B	**DIF:** Easy	**OBJ:** Interpretation
6. **ANS:** D	**DIF:** Easy	**OBJ:** Literary Analysis
7. **ANS:** A	**DIF:** Easy	**OBJ:** Interpretation
8. **ANS:** D	**DIF:** Easy	**OBJ:** Interpretation
9. **ANS:** B	**DIF:** Easy	**OBJ:** Comprehension
10. **ANS:** A	**DIF:** Easy	**OBJ:** Literary Analysis

Vocabulary and Grammar

11. **ANS:** B	**DIF:** Easy	**OBJ:** Vocabulary
12. **ANS:** B	**DIF:** Easy	**OBJ:** Grammar

Essay

13. Students may suggest that without names, both the man and the dog can represent all humans and all animals. The writer is suggesting that human beings who confront nature without knowledge do not survive. The dog represents all animals, whose instincts give them much more chance of surviving in the natural world than humans.

Difficulty: *Easy*

Objective: *Essay*

14. Students' essay should reflect that the man is skilled at building and lighting a fire, but he has not taken into account that he builds the second fire under a tree laden with snow. He cannot imagine the outcome: the killing of the fire by falling snow.

Difficulty: *Easy*

Objective: *Essay*

Selection Test B, p. 185

Critical Reading

1. **ANS:** C	**DIF:** Average	**OBJ:** Literary Analysis
2. **ANS:** C	**DIF:** Average	**OBJ:** Comprehension
3. **ANS:** A	**DIF:** Average	**OBJ:** Literary Analysis
4. **ANS:** C	**DIF:** Challenging	**OBJ:** Interpretation
5. **ANS:** D	**DIF:** Easy	**OBJ:** Interpretation
6. **ANS:** D	**DIF:** Average	**OBJ:** Reading Strategy
7. **ANS:** B	**DIF:** Challenging	**OBJ:** Literary Analysis
8. **ANS:** A	**DIF:** Challenging	**OBJ:** Interpretation
9. **ANS:** B	**DIF:** Average	**OBJ:** Literary Analysis
10. **ANS:** B	**DIF:** Average	**OBJ:** Interpretation
11. **ANS:** C	**DIF:** Average	**OBJ:** Reading Strategy
12. **ANS:** C	**DIF:** Easy	**OBJ:** Reading Strategy

Vocabulary and Grammar

13. **ANS:** C	**DIF:** Average	**OBJ:** Vocabulary
14. **ANS:** B	**DIF:** Average	**OBJ:** Grammar
15. **ANS:** D	**DIF:** Challenging	**OBJ:** Grammar
16. **ANS:** A	**DIF:** Challenging	**OBJ:** Vocabulary
17. **ANS:** C	**DIF:** Easy	**OBJ:** Vocabulary

Essay

18. Students should describe their challenge in as much detail as possible. They should also mention the experience of the man, showing why respect for the power of what they are challenging is also important. They might mention learning about their challenge, welcoming advice from people who have experienced similar challenges, being careful and observant, and working at keeping—and using—their heads.

Difficulty: *Easy*

Objective: *Essay*

19. Students should mention that the man has no more respect for the cold than he does for the dog; he feels he can subdue them both simply by asserting his human power. His attitude toward taking extra precautions is that doing so would be a sign of weakness; he does not confront nature with the imagination or intelligence that successful humans muster in place of instinct. The dog, of course, follows instincts, which are more reliable than the thoughts of the man. The dog has no "ego"; he uses experience as a guide.

Difficulty: *Average*

Objective: *Essay*

20. Students who were uncertain for most of the story may mention details such as the man's generally cheerful state of mind, his powers of keen observation, his ability to make a fire at lunch time, etc. In opposition to these, they should mention the man's ignorance of the nature of the cold, his lack of imagination, his increasingly dangerous and stupid errors, and the instincts of the dog. Students who knew the outcome early in their reading should cite what provided clues. They should also mention if they knew how the end would come, and which clues helped.

Difficulty: *Challenging*

Objective: *Essay*

"The Story of an Hour" by Kate Chopin

Vocabulary Warm-up Exercises, p. 189

A. 1. intention
2. absolutely
3. powerful
4. revealed
5. significance
6. paralyzed
7. countless
8. perception

B. Sample Answers

1. T; A dictionary provides *illumination* because it explains the meaning of words.
2. F; That much salt would give the food a very strong taste, not a *subtle* one.
3. T; The *inability* to tell colors apart is known as color blindness.
4. T; Trying again in the face of failure shows *persistence*.
5. F; A house's *eaves* are the overhanging parts of its roof.
6. F; Begging and pleading are the same thing as *imploring*.
7. F; *Trivial* problems are not important, and would not upset an easygoing person.
8. T; Reading self-help books can be a sign that someone is *striving* to change.

Reading Warm-up A, p. 190

Sample Answers

1. (many); "Few" could be the opposite of *countless*.
2. (definition); To find out the *significance* of a word, I might look in a dictionary or ask someone.
3. Her tone of voice; If my *intention* was to spend a lot of money, I would start by taking a long trip around the world.
4. run out and buy *that*; No, when people are *absolutely* full they do not have room for dessert.
5. (motionless); No, because if I were *paralyzed* I could not move.
6. You see things differently; If the person started acting differently, or you learned something new about the person, that could change your *perception*.
7. (showed); I feel annoyed when a movie's ending is *revealed* to me before I see it, because that can ruin the movie for me.
8. (strong); The smell of a perfume could be described as *powerful*.

Reading Warm-up B, p. 191

Sample Answers

1. (important); No, I do not think taking a pet for a checkup is *trivial*, because it is important to be sure your pet is healthy.
2. by the porch, resting in the shade under the eaves; An igloo or a teepee would not have *eaves*.
3. he dropped it at my feet, then pushed at me with his nose; I showed *persistence* when I finished reading a book that I thought was hard.
4. No, symptoms such as sneezing and a runny nose are obvious rather than *subtle*.
5. Blue may be seriously ill; The opposite of *striving* might be achieving something without effort, or it might be not trying at all.
6. (pet him); Begging or pleading are other words for *imploring*.
7. He showed his *inability* to take a hint by trying to get Kevin to throw the ball even after Kevin said, "Not now."
8. (entire next-to-last paragraph); I might look for *illumination* in a book on pet care, or ask someone who has a lot of experience caring for pets.

Literary Analysis: Irony, p. 192

1. Situational irony: Students should choose a passage that illustrates how the outcome of an action or situation is different from what the reader expects.
2. Dramatic irony: Students should choose a passage that illustrates how the readers are aware of something that a character in the story does not know.

Reading Strategy: Recognize Ironic Details, p. 193

Sample Responses

Students should cite ironic details from the text, explain what they expected to happen, and then what actually happened. Two examples follow.

Ironic detail: Knowing that Mrs. Mallard was afflicted with heart trouble, great care was taken to break to her as gently as possible the news of her husband's death; **What you expected:** Mrs. Mallard to be upset by the news of the death; **What actually happened:** Mrs. Mallard begins to look forward to a long life without her husband.

Ironic Detail: drinking in the elixir of life; breathed a quick prayer that life might be long; **What you expected:** Mrs. Mallard to lead a long and happy life; **What actually happened:** Mrs. Mallard dies unexpectedly.

Vocabulary Builder, p. 194

A. 1. C; 2. E; 3. D; 4. F; 5. B; 6. A

B.
1. repression
2. importunities
3. tumultuously
4. forestall
5. elusive

Grammar and Style: Appositives and Appositive Phrases, p. 195

A.
1. A breeze, the delicious breath of rain, swept through the house.
2. The well-known author Kate Chopin gave the opening address at the meeting.
3. Louise Mallard felt trapped by marriage, a repressive institution.
4. The announcement of Mallard's death was a mistake, a serious error with dire consequences.
5. One Victorian author, Kate Chopin, had strong opinions about the place of women in society.

B.
1. Mrs. Mallard found herself whispering a single word over and over—"free."
2. An oak barrier, the bedroom door, kept Josephine from seeing what her sister was doing.

3. A soaring eagle, she felt unfettered by the restraints of time.

Enrichment: Social Studies, p. 198

Suggested Responses

Pre-discussion questions:

1. Students should recognize the differences between husband-and-wife relationships in the era of the story and today. For example, is the idea that a woman could feel imprisoned in a marriage still valid, and if so, is it valid for the same reasons?
2. Students should recognize the similarities in custom between the era of the story and today—for example, the way bad news is broken and the conduct of family and friends.
3. Students should recognize the differences in the roles of men and women and how, if the roles were reversed, a man might not have to hide his true feelings. A man might also not feel as trapped in the marriage as a woman because of the gender roles of the time.

Post-discussion questions:

1. Students should arrive at a group answer for each question, and record each answer on a sheet of paper.
2. Students should recognize the differences between their own answers and the group answers, and that the differences stem from students' different experiences and opinions. They should also recognize how the answers differ due to gender, age, or family background.
3. Students should be aware of gender differences in the answers, and what they say about how each gender views marriage. Students should also be aware of how each group views the appropriateness of Mrs. Mallard's actions.
4. Students should share their views on marriage and what it takes to make a marriage work. They should also comment on the Mallards' marriage and from the reaction of Mrs. Mallard, draw conclusions about how it worked.

Selection Test A, p. 199

Critical Reading

1. **ANS:** B	**DIF:** Easy	**OBJ:** Comprehension
2. **ANS:** A	**DIF:** Easy	**OBJ:** Reading Strategy
3. **ANS:** D	**DIF:** Easy	**OBJ:** Reading Strategy
4. **ANS:** C	**DIF:** Easy	**OBJ:** Literary Analysis
5. **ANS:** C	**DIF:** Easy	**OBJ:** Literary Analysis
6. **ANS:** A	**DIF:** Easy	**OBJ:** Interpretation
7. **ANS:** D	**DIF:** Easy	**OBJ:** Comprehension
8. **ANS:** D	**DIF:** Easy	**OBJ:** Literary Analysis
9. **ANS:** B	**DIF:** Easy	**OBJ:** Comprehension
10. **ANS:** D	**DIF:** Easy	**OBJ:** Reading Strategy
11. **ANS:** A	**DIF:** Easy	**OBJ:** Interpretation

Vocabulary and Grammar

12. **ANS:** B	**DIF:** Easy	**OBJ:** Vocabulary
13. **ANS:** C	**DIF:** Easy	**OBJ:** Grammar

Essay

14. Students' essays should reflect that the words are ironic because the doctors think Mrs. Mallard died of the shock of joy, not the horror, of seeing her husband still alive. Some students may also suggest that the cause of death being called "heart disease" is ironic because Mrs. Mallard's feelings might seem heartless.
    Difficulty: *Easy*
    Objective: *Essay*
15. Students' essays should reflect that Chopin, in this story, suggests that marriage signals the end of personal freedom for one or both of the parties. The fact that the parties in question are kind, rather than cruel, makes no difference to her.
    Difficulty: *Easy*
    Objective: *Essay*

Selection Test B, p. 202

Critical Reading

1. **ANS:** A	**DIF:** Easy	**OBJ:** Interpretation
2. **ANS:** C	**DIF:** Average	**OBJ:** Reading Strategy
3. **ANS:** B	**DIF:** Average	**OBJ:** Reading Strategy
4. **ANS:** C	**DIF:** Easy	**OBJ:** Comprehension
5. **ANS:** B	**DIF:** Average	**OBJ:** Comprehension
6. **ANS:** C	**DIF:** Average	**OBJ:** Interpretation
7. **ANS:** B	**DIF:** Easy	**OBJ:** Literary Analysis
8. **ANS:** D	**DIF:** Average	**OBJ:** Interpretation
9. **ANS:** A	**DIF:** Challenging	**OBJ:** Interpretation
10. **ANS:** D	**DIF:** Challenging	**OBJ:** Reading Strategy
11. **ANS:** A	**DIF:** Easy	**OBJ:** Literary Analysis
12. **ANS:** C	**DIF:** Challenging	**OBJ:** Literary Analysis
13. **ANS:** C	**DIF:** Challenging	**OBJ:** Literary Analysis

Vocabulary and Grammar

14. **ANS:** D	**DIF:** Average	**OBJ:** Grammar
15. **ANS:** B	**DIF:** Average	**OBJ:** Vocabulary
16. **ANS:** C	**DIF:** Easy	**OBJ:** Vocabulary
17. **ANS:** D	**DIF:** Average	**OBJ:** Vocabulary

Essay

18. Students who admire Mrs. Mallard should mention that she felt trapped in her marriage, that in accepting her feelings she is throwing off hypocrisy, and that her desire to face the world alone reflects strength of character. Those who condemn her should stress that her joy is selfish, that her thoughts about weeping as she

sees her husband's body seem hypocritical, that her freedom has come from the death of another human being, one she supposedly loved.

Difficulty: *Easy*

Objective: *Essay*

19. Students should back their conclusions using details from the story and their own knowledge of prevailing Victorian attitudes. Whether they argue that Josephine would support her sister or think her wicked, they should realize that Josephine would be deeply shocked at first. Students should conclude that Richards would probably be totally uncomprehending of and scandalized by Mrs. Mallard's feelings and cite one or more of the following reasons: He is a close friend of the husband; he has the Victorian attitude that women need men to shelter them from the shocks of life; and he may believe that women don't want freedom from marriage.

Difficulty: *Average*

Objective: *Essay*

20. Students who agree that Mrs. Mallard is a victim should mention the irony that her only escape from the strictures of Victorian marriage is the death of her husband. Freedom for a married woman is simply not a choice. Those who disagree may mention that the reason she feels joy so soon after her husband's presumed death is that she did not let herself be completely victimized by marriage. In her heart, she did not buy into the prevailing attitudes. As a widow, she will probably be stronger and live a more enjoyable life than others in her position, who are true victims.

Difficulty: *Challenging*

Objective: *Essay*

"Douglass" and "We Wear the Mask" by Paul Laurence Dunbar

Vocabulary Warm-up Exercises, p. 206

A.
1. devious
2. tortured
3. grins
4. mask
5. passionate
6. swarm
7. tempest
8. harsh

B. Sample Answers

1. T; A *bark* is a boat or ship, so it would typically be located on the water.
2. T; *Dissension* connotes conflict.
3. F; *Ebb* refers to a withdrawing tide, not an advancing one.
4. F; *Guile* would normally suggest that a person wouldn't be trustworthy.
5. F; *Myriad* connotes large numbers.
6. T; A *salient* argument is prominent.
7. F; By definition, *subtleties* are often hard to identify.
8. T; People who are *vile* should probably be avoided.

Reading Warm-up A, p. 207

Sample Answers

1. happily; *smiles*
2. (wearing the . . . brave cheerfulness); figuratively
3. rages a . . . painful emotions; *storm*
4. (scolds); gentle, *soft*
5. (filled the air) (angry bees); Locusts are insects that *swarm.*
6. punishing; "You look *pained*, Karen. You have to stop punishing yourself."
7. try to trick; We have to be devious when we are planning a surprise party.
8. (truly love); uninterested; *passive*

Reading Warm-up B, p. 208

Sample Answers

1. probably beyond counting; The hive contained *myriad* bees, and their droning hum was clearly audible.
2. (one of the most important . . . features); The opposite of *salient* is *minor* or *insignificant.*
3. hideous; *beautiful, lovable*
4. warships . . . terrifying mask was fixed to the prow of the . . . to frighten opponents
5. (and to reduce conflict, or . . .); The opposite of *dissension* is *agreement, harmony,* or *concord.*
6. elaborate, complex; We found it difficult to follow the *subtleties* of the philosopher's argument.
7. or cunning, and naughty pranks
8. (and flow); figuratively

Literary Analysis: Rhyme, p. 209

1. true rhyme, end rhyme
2. true rhyme, end rhyme
3. true rhyme, end rhyme
4. true rhyme, end rhyme
5. slant rhyme, internal rhyme
6. true rhyme, internal rhyme
7. true rhyme, end rhyme
8. true rhyme, end rhyme

Reading Strategy: Interpret, p. 210

Samples of students' responses:

1. The "we" stands for African Americans. Some students may think it stands for all honorable people who value freedom.
2. Students will probably answer that it is the public sentiment on African Americans' position in society.
3. The shivering bark is the African American people as a group.

4. The "lonely dark" is the hard times the African Americans are living in.
5. He addresses it to Douglass because Douglass was known as a fighter for freedom for all African Americans.
6. The mask is hiding the true feelings of African Americans.
7. The cheeks and eyes must be hidden so that no one can see the true emotions of African Americans.

Vocabulary Builder, p. 211

A. 1. *beguiled* (to have been misled by deceit or craftiness)
2. *guileless* (innocent or naive, not exposed to guile)
3. *beguiler* (one who misleads by deceit or craftiness)
4. *beguiling* (misleading by deceit or craftiness)

B. 1. A; 2. D; 3. A; 4. B; 5. C

Grammar and Style: Punctuation of Interjections, p. 212

A. 1. Ah, Douglass! we have fall'n on evil days,
2. Nay! Let them only see us,
3. Now! When the waves of swift dissension swarm . . .
4. Oh! For thy voice high-sounding o'er the storm . . .

B. Sample Responses
1. No, I didn't like the movie.
2. Ah, why not?
3. Yes, we met the new neighbor.
4. No! The sky is blue!
5. Yes, he enjoys playing baseball.
6. Oh! She cut her hair very short!
7. Hey, I've been to Mexico.
8. Well, I want to go to dinner.

Enrichment: Art, p. 215

Suggested Responses

Students should describe the image or emotion, outline characteristics of their masks that portray the desired image or emotion, and then complete a drawing of their masks. Students should share their masks with classmates and describe the different features of the mask (eyes, nose, mouth) and how they convey the image or emotion.

Extension activity: Have students build their designed masks out of papier-maché and other suitable materials. They may then act out skits with their masks, or put them together with other students' masks for a classroom display.

Selection Test A, p. 216

Critical Reading

1. **ANS:** B	**DIF:** Easy	**OBJ:** Interpretation
2. **ANS:** D	**DIF:** Easy	**OBJ:** Literary Analysis
3. **ANS:** A	**DIF:** Easy	**OBJ:** Literary Analysis
4. **ANS:** A	**DIF:** Easy	**OBJ:** Reading Strategy
5. **ANS:** C	**DIF:** Easy	**OBJ:** Reading Strategy
6. **ANS:** D	**DIF:** Easy	**OBJ:** Literary Analysis
7. **ANS:** B	**DIF:** Easy	**OBJ:** Comprehension
8. **ANS:** C	**DIF:** Easy	**OBJ:** Comprehension
9. **ANS:** B	**DIF:** Easy	**OBJ:** Reading Strategy
10. **ANS:** D	**DIF:** Easy	**OBJ:** Interpretation

Vocabulary and Grammar

11. **ANS:** B	**DIF:** Easy	**OBJ:** Vocabulary
12. **ANS:** D	**DIF:** Easy	**OBJ:** Grammar

Essay

13. Students' essays may reflect that when one group of people have power and another group do not have power, the powerless must be careful not to show anger. Otherwise, the powerful will get angry in return and make the lives of the powerless much harder.

Difficulty: *Easy*

Objective: *Essay*

14. Students' essays should reflect that the poet imagines Douglass as the captain of a boat of African American passengers, caught in a storm—the strife caused by racial inequality. This scene imagines a captain guiding his ship safely through the dangers of a life of injustice.

Difficulty: *Easy*

Objective: *Essay*

Selection Test B, p. 219

Critical Reading

1. **ANS:** B	**DIF:** Average	**OBJ:** Comprehension
2. **ANS:** B	**DIF:** Average	**OBJ:** Reading Strategy
3. **ANS:** D	**DIF:** Challenging	**OBJ:** Reading Strategy
4. **ANS:** D	**DIF:** Easy	**OBJ:** Interpretation
5. **ANS:** D	**DIF:** Average	**OBJ:** Interpretation
6. **ANS:** B	**DIF:** Easy	**OBJ:** Literary Analysis
7. **ANS:** C	**DIF:** Average	**OBJ:** Literary Analysis
8. **ANS:** C	**DIF:** Easy	**OBJ:** Comprehension
9. **ANS:** D	**DIF:** Challenging	**OBJ:** Reading Strategy
10. **ANS:** C	**DIF:** Average	**OBJ:** Interpretation
11. **ANS:** B	**DIF:** Challenging	**OBJ:** Reading Strategy
12. **ANS:** A	**DIF:** Challenging	**OBJ:** Interpretation
13. **ANS:** A	**DIF:** Average	**OBJ:** Literary Analysis

Vocabulary

14. **ANS:** A	**DIF:** Challenging	**OBJ:** Vocabulary
15. **ANS:** C	**DIF:** Average	**OBJ:** Vocabulary
16. **ANS:** B	**DIF:** Average	**OBJ:** Vocabulary
17. **ANS:** C	**DIF:** Average	**OBJ:** Vocabulary

Essay

18. Students should indicate that the poem expresses the needs of African Americans who are pretending to be happy with their position instead of showing their true feelings. Students should use details from the poem to support their position, including how they wear masks that "hide" their eyes and cheeks and present a smile instead, and how the world does not see the tears and sighs of the people.

    Difficulty: *Easy*

    Objective: *Essay*

19. Students' answers will vary but should indicate that Dunbar was keenly aware that despite emancipation and victory in the Civil War, the struggles of the African American community went on and, in some ways, got worse. Details from the selections that support this include his plea to Douglass for his leadership, his statement in "Douglass" that the community is still awash in a tempest, and that they have to hide their true feelings in "We Wear the Mask."

    Difficulty: *Average*

    Objective: *Essay*

20. Students' answers will depend on the position they choose, but they should defend their positions with citations from one or both of the selections and any other knowledge they have of Dunbar's life and other works. Most students will probably feel the poem is about concealed racial fire, although the poem may be applied more universally to any group of people who face discrimination. Supporting examples include the bitter tone of "We Wear the Mask," the use of the word *guile* and the statement that African Americans are in "debt," and the line "but let the world dream otherwise," which suggests the foolishness of the outside world.

    Difficulty: *Challenging*

    Objective: *Essay*

Benchmark Test 6, p. 222

MULTIPLE CHOICE

1. ANS: A
2. ANS: B
3. ANS: D
4. ANS: B
5. ANS: B
6. ANS: D
7. ANS: C
8. ANS: C
9. ANS: B
10. ANS: A
11. ANS: D
12. ANS: A
13. ANS: D
14. ANS: A
15. ANS: B
16. ANS: C
17. ANS: A
18. ANS: D
19. ANS: B
20. ANS: C
21. ANS: B
22. ANS: A
23. ANS: D
24. ANS: C
25. ANS: B
26. ANS: D
27. ANS: A
28. ANS: D
29. ANS: B
30. ANS: A
31. ANS: C
32. ANS: C
33. ANS: C

ESSAY

34. Students should demonstrate an ability to describe a person and that person's influence in their life. They should use specific examples and details to show rather than tell about this person.
35. Students should demonstrate the position they support and the reasons for their position. They should include facts and specific details, use transitions to make their argument progress smoothly, and conclude persuasively.
36. Students' opinions should be clearly stated in an introductory paragraph. The remainder of the review should focus on a specific literary element. Opinions should be supported by examples from the text.

Diagnostic Test 7, p. 228

MULTIPLE CHOICE

1. ANS: B
2. ANS: D
3. ANS: D
4. ANS: B
5. ANS: C
6. ANS: D
7. ANS: A
8. ANS: B
9. ANS: C
10. ANS: D
11. ANS: A
12. ANS: C

13. ANS: B
14. ANS: C
15. ANS: B

"Luke Havergal" and **"Richard Cory"**
by Edwin Arlington Robinson
"Lucinda Matlock" and **"Richard Bone"**
by Edgar Lee Masters

Vocabulary Warm-up Exercises, p. 232

A. 1. memorable
2. rambled
3. medicinal
4. discontent
5. weariness
6. chiseled
7. schooled
8. repose

B. Sample Answers

1. No, someone who walked *imperially* would probably be proud or even arrogant.
2. I would give him the red one, because *crimson* is red.
3. Water would *quench* a fire, while gasoline would make it burn higher.
4. The hero behaves more *admirably*; the villain does evil things.
5. No, grades of *A* and *B* are more *consistent* with college plans.
6. No, someone who is *pessimistic* makes you feel bad about the future.
7. If she was *arrayed* in her best clothes, I would think she was going to a party.
8. Yes, if somebody has very little money he or she would be strongly *influenced* by price.

Reading Warm-up A, p. 233

Sample Answers

1. strong, brown, weather-beaten hands; The most *memorable* thing about my seventh-grade English teacher was her pointy high-heeled shoes.
2. (stray); Instead of *rambled*, you could say "wandered" or "moseyed."
3. the idea that a boy with a few minutes of free time was a boy looking for trouble; Someone might be *schooled* in the belief that kids need free time to develop their imaginations.
4. (exhaustion); Taking a nap is a good cure for *weariness*.
5. hospital room; Cough syrup is *medicinal*.
6. He rested on his back, eyes closed, his hands folded across his chest; No, he dislikes *repose* and would rather be doing things all the time.
7. (unhappy); Frowning and complaining are typical signs of *discontent*.
8. wooden cow; You could say "carved" instead of *chiseled*.

Reading Warm-up B, p. 234

Sample Answers

1. Her parents probably *influenced* her, and also her director and other actors she worked with or admired; *affected*
2. (toga); *Arrayed* means "dressed."
3. *Crimson* might be a school's team color.
4. (strode); A school principal might behave *imperially*.
5. (taught) (acted); An Olympic skater would skate *admirably*.
6. the memory of Ms. Graham; *Consistent* means "all the time, not just sometimes."
7. She might have felt *pessimistic* because the competition for movie roles is fierce, and lots of actors do not succeed even if they have talent.
8. If I wanted to do the opposite of *quench* a fire, I would light one, or feed one that was already going.

Literary Analysis: Speaker, p. 235

Sample Responses

1. The speaker must be a ghost, because he or she speaks "out of a grave."
2. It is likely that the woman is dead, since messages about her are brought by one who speaks from the grave, and because she can only be reached through leaves that whisper or by listening to the wind.
3. The speaker seems to be providing advice about a supernatural journey, one which would make it possible to contact a woman who cannot be contacted in the physical world. The meeting or contact Havergal seeks is likely to be supernatural, because the woman will call him "if [he] trusts her." The leaves cannot physically whisper to Havergal, and a kiss cannot be literally flaming on his forehead. In addition, the speaker is a ghost, and would seem to be more qualified to speak about the supernatural than the natural.
4. No, the speaker advises Havergal that "there is not a dawn in eastern skies/To rift the fiery night that's in your eyes," and that "the dark will end the dark, if anything," suggesting that there is no hope for Havergal, and that the only route he can take is a "bitter" one.
5. Something terrible must have happened to Luke Havergal, leaving him with a "fiery night" in his eyes. The speaker advises Havergal on how to contact or reunite with the woman he seeks or misses, so perhaps Havergal was separated from the woman, possibly by her death. It's possible that Havergal may have done something terrible, such as contributing to the woman's death, because the speaker seems to feel that there is no hope for him. The speaker may be suggesting that Havergal meet his death willingly.

Reading Strategy: Recognize Attitudes, p. 236

Suggested Responses

Students should identify the speaker in each poem, cite clues to the speaker's attitude, and write adjectives that describe the attitude. For example, in "Richard Cory" the speaker is one of the townspeople. Clues to the speaker's attitude include "he was a gentleman / always quietly arranged / admirably schooled." The attitude suggested by the clues is one of respect and admiration.

Vocabulary Builder, p. 237

A. 1. to separate into parts
2. to calm
3. to take a position (as an opinion)
4. to change the order of

B. degenerate; imperially; repose; epitaph

Grammar and Style: Noun Clauses, p. 238

A. 1. object of a preposition
2. direct object
3. object of a preposition

B. Sample Responses
1. Gorillas are what they are.
2. What you see is what you get.
3. I do not know why I must go.
4. Please give whoever wants one a sample of the new product.
5. I asked him about what he did during the weekend.

Enrichment: Dance, p. 241

Suggested Responses

Luke Havergal

Body movements: looking around, head often bowed, wandering aimlessly, wobbling while walking, slumped posture; **sounds:** howling winds, thunderstorm.

Richard Cory

Body movements: head held high, walking stiffly and in a definite direction, hands held behind back while walking, stopping to shake hands or nod at people; **sounds:** silence except for the sound of Richard Cory's heels as he walks briskly across a hard surface, like a floor or sidewalk.

Lucinda Matlock

Body movements: formal dances such as square dancing, stooping to garden or attend to a sick person, cleaning house (i.e., sweeping, making beds, washing dishes), sitting and sewing; **sounds:** lively, fast folk music.

Richard Bone

Body movements: lifting, carrying, chiseling, standing and listening, looking; **sounds:** mournful, funeral music, possibly bagpipes.

Selection Test A, p. 242

Critical Reading

1. **ANS:** B	**DIF:** Easy	**OBJ:** Comprehension
2. **ANS:** A	**DIF:** Easy	**OBJ:** Interpretation
3. **ANS:** C	**DIF:** Easy	**OBJ:** Literary Analysis
4. **ANS:** C	**DIF:** Easy	**OBJ:** Literary Analysis
5. **ANS:** B	**DIF:** Easy	**OBJ:** Interpretation
6. **ANS:** B	**DIF:** Easy	**OBJ:** Reading Strategy
7. **ANS:** C	**DIF:** Easy	**OBJ:** Reading Strategy
8. **ANS:** D	**DIF:** Easy	**OBJ:** Interpretation
9. **ANS:** B	**DIF:** Easy	**OBJ:** Reading Strategy
10. **ANS:** B	**DIF:** Easy	**OBJ:** Comprehension
11. **ANS:** C	**DIF:** Easy	**OBJ:** Comprehension

Vocabulary and Grammar

12. **ANS:** C	**DIF:** Easy	**OBJ:** Vocabulary
13. **ANS:** C	**DIF:** Easy	**OBJ:** Grammar

Essay

14. Students' essays should reflect that when we only see someone in public, we really don't know him or her. The townspeople envy Cory's wealth, looks, grace, and an admired place in the town. They do not look underneath that image.

Difficulty: *Easy*

Objective: *Essay*

15. Students' essays should reflect that both carvers of epitaphs and historians give the birth and death dates of the people about whom they write. Students might also suggest that in both occupations, the writers might be tempted to portray the people as better or more accomplished than they actually were.

Difficulty: *Easy*

Objective: *Essay*

Selection Test B, p. 245

Critical Reading

1. **ANS:** B	**DIF:** Average	**OBJ:** Comprehension
2. **ANS:** D	**DIF:** Average	**OBJ:** Interpretation
3. **ANS:** A	**DIF:** Average	**OBJ:** Comprehension
4. **ANS:** C	**DIF:** Easy	**OBJ:** Literary Analysis
5. **ANS:** B	**DIF:** Easy	**OBJ:** Literary Analysis
6. **ANS:** A	**DIF:** Easy	**OBJ:** Interpretation
7. **ANS:** A	**DIF:** Average	**OBJ:** Reading Strategy
8. **ANS:** C	**DIF:** Average	**OBJ:** Comprehension
9. **ANS:** A	**DIF:** Average	**OBJ:** Interpretation
10. **ANS:** B	**DIF:** Average	**OBJ:** Reading Strategy
11. **ANS:** D	**DIF:** Challenging	**OBJ:** Reading Strategy
12. **ANS:** B	**DIF:** Challenging	**OBJ:** Reading Strategy

Vocabulary and Grammar

13. **ANS:** A	**DIF:** Challenging	**OBJ:** Grammar
14. **ANS:** B	**DIF:** Average	**OBJ:** Vocabulary
15. **ANS:** D	**DIF:** Easy	**OBJ:** Vocabulary
16. **ANS:** A	**DIF:** Average	**OBJ:** Grammar
17. **ANS:** D	**DIF:** Challenging	**OBJ:** Grammar

Essay

18. Students should choose one of the four title characters and write a biographical essay on him or her. They can imagine details not mentioned in the poem, but they should support their imaginings with details from the poem. They should also draw biographical information from the tone of the poem; for example, from the tone of the portrait painted of him in the poem, Luke Havergal can be said to lead a sad and mournful life.

    Difficulty: *Easy*

    Objective: *Essay*

19. Students should recognize that Lucinda Matlock's tone is not bitter or angry, but in fact lovingly chiding of the younger generation. Students can support this statement with such details from the poem as her gentle tone, her life-loving attitude despite terrible tragedy, and her open and friendly demeanor, as portrayed by Masters.

    Difficulty: *Average*

    Objective: *Essay*

20. As it is unclear exactly what the speaker wants Luke Havergal to do, many interpretations are possible, provided they are supported by the text. The speaker tells Luke to go to the western gate, which might be a real gate, or a symbolic one. The speaker may want Luke to accept the death of the woman and the sadness that goes with it, or the speaker may be suggesting that Luke will have to die in order to be with the woman. The speaker seems to want Luke to take action without expecting that any happiness will come from it.

    Difficulty: *Challenging*

    Objective: *Essay*

"A Wagner Matinée" by Willa Cather

Vocabulary Warm-up Exercises, p. 249

A.
1. conjuror
2. alight
3. vainly
4. comprehend
5. eluding
6. pitiless
7. haggard
8. legacy

B. Sample Answers
1. F; *Absurdities* are illogical and irrational, so they would not be taken seriously.
2. T; *Characteristically* describes generally predictable behavior.
3. T; A person in a state of *frenzy* might act wildly.
4. F; Nations willing to sign a peace treaty would expect peaceful or *harmonious* relations.
5. T; Paralysis is virtually synonymous with lack of motion, or *immobility*.
6. T; A *pathetic* situation would arouse a feeling of compassion or pity.
7. T; Statues and sculptures are often found on a base, or *pedestal*.
8. F; *Wholly* means "entirely," so the entire house would have been renovated.

Reading Warm-up A, p. 250

Sample Answers
1. streamed off ships from Europe to . . . on American soil; Mary wanted to *alight* on the platform as soon as the train had come to a stop.
2. (could help the new arrivals . . . the challenges of building a new life . . . they could assist with learning an unfamiliar language . . .); *understand*
3. scorching summers and freezing winters; *merciful*
4. (passed down to their descendants); *inheritance*
5. (was so harsh . . . worn out with fatigue); The opposite of *haggard* is *rested* or *flourishing.*
6. struggle . . . and are crushed by the obstacles they encounter; *successfully, productively*
7. (are luckier . . . disaster and disappointment); *Eluding* their pursuers, the robbers managed to escape.
8. magical abilities; A *conjuror* always captures people's imagination, appealing to the audience by suggesting that the impossible is possible.

Reading Warm-up B, p. 251

Sample Answers
1. in an ideal performance, all these elements exist in a . . . balanced combination; The opposite of *harmonious* is *unbalanced* or *discordant.*
2. (some critics mock . . . that no reasonable person can take seriously); illogical
3. *typically; uncharacteristically*
4. which depend on coincidence so much that they are . . . unbelievable; *entirely*
5. (wild emotions); The opposite of *frenzy* is *calm* or *tranquility.*
6. static; *motionlessness*
7. unduly glorifying opera; figuratively
8. (ranging from the triumphant to the . . .)

Literary Analysis: Characterization, p. 252

1. Clark thinks his Aunt Georgiana's appearance is unsightly.
2. Aunt Georgiana was not an outwardly beautiful woman.
3. Aunt Georgiana eloped with her husband and moved with him to the Nebraska frontier, thus avoiding local criticism of her for marrying him.
4. Aunt Georgiana looked out for Clark when he was a boy.
5. Aunt Georgiana had lost something (music) that she loved very much.
6. The concert was an emotional experience for Aunt Georgiana.
7. Aunt Georgiana's hands, that once played the piano so well, are now deformed because of hard work.
8. Aunt Georgiana does not want to leave the life she remembers in Boston for her life in Nebraska.

Reading Strategy: Clarify, p. 253

Sample Responses

1. A chilblain is a painful swelling or sore caused by exposure to cold.
2. The trip started in Red Willow County, Nebraska, and ended in Boston, Massachusetts.
3. The Green Mountains are in Vermont.
4. Aunt Georgiana was a music teacher at the Boston Conservatory years earlier.
5. Venusberg is a legendary mountain in Germany where Venus, the Roman goddess of love, held court.
6. It reminded her of a young man she knew who used to sing the song.

Vocabulary Builder, p. 254

A.
1. nonmusical
2. nonmusical
3. musical
4. musical

B.
1. overture; prelude
2. with a quivering voice; tremulously
3. unable to move; inert
4. partly sleepwalking; semi-somnambulant
5. light-hearted joking; jocularity
6. very respectful; reverential

Grammar and Style: Reflexive and Intensive Pronouns, p. 255

A.
1. myself; reflexive
2. ourselves; intensive
3. himself; intensive
4. themselves; reflexive
5. themselves; reflexive
6. ourselves; reflexive

B. Sample Responses
1. The boys did the work themselves.
2. Lakisha bought herself a new jacket.
3. Now that you have bought a present for your sister, what will you buy yourself?
4. We wanted to treat ourselves, so we went on a boat ride.
5. Sometimes I really like to be by myself.

Enrichment: Music, p. 258

Suggested Response

Students may choose any song they are familiar with, or write one of their own. Students should be able to justify their choices by citing lines from the songs they have chosen or written and linking them to their own personality or self-image.

Selection Test A, p. 259

Critical Reading

1. ANS: B	DIF: Easy	OBJ: Literary Analysis
2. ANS: D	DIF: Easy	OBJ: Reading Strategy
3. ANS: D	DIF: Easy	OBJ: Literary Analysis
4. ANS: C	DIF: Easy	OBJ: Comprehension
5. ANS: B	DIF: Easy	OBJ: Interpretation
6. ANS: A	DIF: Easy	OBJ: Comprehension
7. ANS: B	DIF: Easy	OBJ: Literary Analysis
8. ANS: C	DIF: Easy	OBJ: Reading Strategy
9. ANS: A	DIF: Easy	OBJ: Reading Strategy
10. ANS: B	DIF: Easy	OBJ: Interpretation

Vocabulary and Grammar

11. ANS: C	DIF: Easy	OBJ: Vocabulary
12. ANS: A	DIF: Easy	OBJ: Grammar

Essay

13. Students' essays should reflect that in her youth, Aunt Georgiana was a musician. When she let romance take her away from that life, she was left with a love of music but with no way to express it. She warns Clark against having the same thing happen to him.

    Difficulty: *Easy*

    Objective: *Essay*

14. Students' essays should reflect that Aunt Georgiana's home is not really just outside the concert hall, but it might as well be. For when she leaves the hall and leaves Boston, she has nothing to look forward to except her empty life in Nebraska.

    Difficulty: *Easy*

    Objective: *Essay*

Selection Test B, p. 262

Critical Reading

1. **ANS:** B	**DIF:** Average	**OBJ:** Literary Analysis
2. **ANS:** A	**DIF:** Average	**OBJ:** Reading Strategy
3. **ANS:** D	**DIF:** Easy	**OBJ:** Interpretation
4. **ANS:** D	**DIF:** Average	**OBJ:** Reading Strategy
5. **ANS:** D	**DIF:** Average	**OBJ:** Interpretation
6. **ANS:** B	**DIF:** Average	**OBJ:** Interpretation
7. **ANS:** C	**DIF:** Challenging	**OBJ:** Reading Strategy
8. **ANS:** C	**DIF:** Average	**OBJ:** Comprehension
9. **ANS:** C	**DIF:** Challenging	**OBJ:** Literary Analysis
10. **ANS:** D	**DIF:** Average	**OBJ:** Comprehension
11. **ANS:** D	**DIF:** Easy	**OBJ:** Reading Strategy
12. **ANS:** A	**DIF:** Easy	**OBJ:** Interpretation
13. **ANS:** B	**DIF:** Challenging	**OBJ:** Literary Analysis

Vocabulary and Grammar

14. **ANS:** D	**DIF:** Average	**OBJ:** Vocabulary
15. **ANS:** B	**DIF:** Easy	**OBJ:** Vocabulary
16. **ANS:** B	**DIF:** Challenging	**OBJ:** Vocabulary
17. **ANS:** C	**DIF:** Average	**OBJ:** Grammar

Essay

18. Students should give some or all of the following examples of Aunt Georgiana's retaining her love of music: helping young Clark learn music, worrying that Clark may also have to sacrifice music, keeping some music books, enjoying the music of the young cow puncher, and all of her reactions during the Wagner concert.

    Difficulty: *Easy*

    Objective: *Essay*

19. Students should recognize that Aunt Georgiana's reluctance to leave the concert is really a desire to cling to a time and place in her life when she was once happy: when she lived in the cultured city of Boston and taught at the Conservatory. Now that she has been reawakened to the beauty of the life and music she gave up so long ago, she is desperate not to return to her hard, bleak life in Nebraska.

    Difficulty: *Average*

    Objective: *Essay*

20. Students should describe Clark on the basis of the selection. They may at first feel he is shallow because he seems to be ashamed of his aunt, but they should also recognize his sensitivity; he loves his aunt and appreciates the tremendous sacrifices she has made. Students may observe that Clark callowly takes for granted that which his aunt misses so dearly and seems to want to prove his cultural superiority, but they should also realize that he comes to understand and regret the depth of the pain awakened in his aunt.

    Difficulty: *Challenging*

    Objective: *Essay*

Writing About Literature—Unit 4

Compare and Contrast Literary Themes: Integrating Grammar Skills, p. 266

A. 1. "The Outcasts of Poker Flat"

2. Life on the Mississippi

3. "To Build a Fire"

B. Many great works were inspired by the Civil War. Stephen Crane's short story "An Episode of War" and Ambrose Bierce's story "An Occurrence at Owl Creek Bridge" are two fine examples. The most famous novel of the Civil War is Crane's The Red Badge of Courage. The journal entries collected in the book Mary Chesnut's Civil War reveal the feelings of a Southern civilian during the war.

Writing Workshop—Unit 4

Research Report: Integrating Grammar Skills, p. 268

Sample Revision

Two early American writers who promoted a spirit of individualism were Ralph Waldo Emerson and Henry David Thoreau, who were neighbors in Concord, Massachusetts. Fourteen years older than Thoreau, Emerson was a major influence on his younger friend. ***For example,*** Emerson's essay called "Self-Reliance" inspired Thoreau to trust his own instincts about right and wrong.

Like Emerson, Thoreau believed in self-reliance. ***Unlike Emerson,*** he put his ideas to the test in more extreme ways. ***For instance,*** he lived by himself in a cabin at Walden Pond for two years, where he observed nature and wrote his best-known book, *Walden*. ***Furthermore,*** he once spent a night in jail, rather than pay a tax that might help support a war he did not believe in. This experience led to his famous essay "Civil Disobedience," which has inspired generations of social activists, including Martin Luther King, Jr.

Spelling—Unit 4

Proofreading Practice, p. 269

1. catastrophe; **2.** debated; **3.** engaged; **4.** potential; **5.** oppressed; **6.** territories; **7.** claimed; **8.** dependence; **9.** required; **10.** stopping; **11.** resigned; **12.** precipitated; **13.** armies; **14.** progress; **15.** possessed; **16.** persistence; **17.** distress; **18.** buried; **19.** dedication; **20.** celebration; **21.** paid; **22.** vain